IN THE
COMPANY
of
WOMEN

IN THE
COMPANY
of
WOMEN

CANADIAN WOMEN TALK ABOUT
WHAT IT TAKES TO START AND MANAGE
A SUCCESSFUL BUSINESS

KATHERINE GAY

HarperBusiness
HarperCollins*PublishersLtd*

Photo of Brenda Schiedel: Ross Breadner Photography
Photo of Elizabeth Stewart: Sarkis

First edition

Canadian Cataloguing in Publication Data

Gay, Katherine, 1955–
In the company of women

"A HarperBusiness book".
ISBN 0-00-255731-2

1. Women-owned business enterprises - Canada.   2. New business
enterprises - Canada.   3. Businesswomen - Canada.   I. Title.

HD6072.6.C2G38 1997   658.1'141'082   C97-931232-9

97 98 99 ❖ HC 10 9 8 7 6 5 4 3 2 1

Printed and bound in the United States

For Selina Maud Legon,
my grandmother

CONTENTS

INTRODUCTION

When I began writing this book, I ran a computerized search of existing periodicals using the key words *women, entrepreneurs,* and *Canada*. The computer spit out one article from a 1995 issue of *Canadian Business*: "When Jeff Became Joyce," the story of a male entrepreneur who had a sex change.

Oh no, I thought. Over the course of the next year and a half, I talked to women entrepreneurs across Canada, and one woman entrepreneur in the United States. All were born women. Some were born entrepreneurs. Others learned, and the rest are still learning.

The entrepreneurial dream, with its emblems of power and risk, is less familiar to women than the mainstream dreams of a good job, a loving spouse, and children. But women's lives are changing, and the possibility of being one's own boss looms larger, either out of choice or necessity.

It is fitting that a century packed with change for women — winning the right to own property, to vote, to decide their reproductive role, to be equal with men in the workplace — should close with a new and powerful statement of women's capability: entrepreneurship. The time is ripe for North American women who have the self-confidence to see and seize the opportunity.

Self-confidence grows when there are known reasons to be confident. This book is all about those reasons. It is about entering a dark hall and knowing that others have gone before you and successfully made their way.

Katherine Gay
Toronto

CHAPTER 1

BURYING THE WHITE KNIGHT

Girls are taught to be nice. They just don't know.

— Marnie Walker

When I was a teenager, most of my female classmates thought they'd marry and have two kids and everything would be wonderful. Now young women say they're going to be a neurosurgeon and marry and have two kids and everything will be wonderful.

— Elizabeth Stewart

Whenever I wanted anything, I would figure out what I could do to get it. Some women get stuck, thinking that they're going to find a guy who will provide for them. You'd think they would have figured it out by now.

— Marcella Abugov

When I walk by a park, I look for the archetypal woman. She's the one on the bench, gazing into the distance, while at her feet a child has managed to locate the only mud puddle in sight. This woman, I imagine, is enjoying one of those merciful, random daydreams that transport her from this hard park bench, this job, this life. And perhaps her dream of release is not about a holiday, or a job that pays down the mortgage faster, but a free fall, something breathtaking in its daring — perhaps even her own company.

While entrepreneurial dreams are as old as the human imagination, their realization has been only a recent possibility for women. Consider that if the time humankind has spent on earth to date equaled an hour, then women have had the right to own property and vote for a second.

In the last two decades, North Americans — both men and women — have been jostled, unnerved, and often injured by economic and social dislocations. The old attitude of entitlement, once fostered by work-for-life employment practices and free-spending governments, is dying. People cannot and no longer want to depend on employers and governments for their security; they've seen or experienced the consequences.

With self-reliance an increasingly common theme in our society, it's not surprising that more and more women have begun their entrepreneurial journey. They've brushed off the dissembling of some powerful social icons on the way: educators bent on directing them to nurturing jobs like teaching and nursing, impossible beauty standards that gnaw at their self-esteem, and the cultural myth of the white knight — a man dedicated to caring for them.

Mona Bandeen, director of the Entrepreneurship Unit at the Faculty of Management, University of Toronto, is shocked by the enduring, wholesale belief in the white knight by secondary school girls. And Elizabeth Stewart, the president of Elizabeth Stewart Associates, a Toronto-based company selling marketing support services, is saddened about the naive complacency of many younger women. "They don't think about their future, and then they're shocked when they come up against barriers that they assumed were all gone. The barriers aren't gone; the fence has simply been moved. So we have a little more room before we run smack up against it. And that's where the shock sets in. In some ways our daughters are more devastated than we are. We've always known the fence was there."

The entrepreneurial lesson is a useful one for any woman. It changes the way she looks at life and her place and potential in it. It suggests that there is more than one solution to a problem, that opportunities are not always visible at first glance, that risktaking is not a dance with death, that compliance does not ensure personal security, that autonomy is exhilarating rather than frightening. This lesson is not part of the school curriculum, and it is not learned by enough young women.

These attitudes and skills can be taught, says Andrina Lever, past-president of Women Entrepreneurs of Canada, but it has to start early. "You can teach it in the same way you teach musical appreciation or ballet or literature. Not all students will end up as concert pianists, but they'll have an appreciation for creative free thinking and independent risktaking in a responsible way."

Despite all the shifts in society in the late twentieth century, the white knight rides on, unchallenged, until somewhere between sixteen and sixty years, the woman watches, shocked, as he is ignominiously unsaddled in one or more painful yet predictable ways. Lovers leave, marriages end, jobs vanish, parents disappoint. There is no lover, parent, mentor, degree, job, or employer with the ability or, let's face it, the inclination to keep you safe from all the harms of the dark.

A now older and wiser woman, having lost or broken those rose-colored glasses, may take this opportunity to reexamine the truth about her life. She may note the persistent wage disparity between the sexes, or the fact that companies boasting women in 10 percent of their senior management positions are viewed as progressive. She may see more clearly that job security has disappeared. And she may conclude that the employment offer is really all about risk, impermanence, and an excellent chance that her talents will be overlooked.

If she considers all of these things, something happens. Her perception shifts and, suddenly, the uncertainty, loneliness, and hard work involved in running one's own company just aren't as frightening anymore.

In 1991, the Canadian Advisory Council on the Status of Women wrote in their study, *The Glass Box:* "If negative job experiences or more general dissatisfaction with salaried employment encourage men and women alike to start their own business, we should again expect the number of women entrepreneurs to multiply."

They were right. Between 1981 and 1994, the number of self-employed women in Canada almost doubled, rising from 323,000 to 639,000, an increase of 97.8 percent.[1] It is estimated that 25 percent of Canadian homes had home offices in 1996; this will double to 50 percent by the turn of the century. The year 2000 is also expected to see almost half of Canada's new companies owned by women.[2] Furthermore, the percentage of women who have expressed satisfaction with their decision to become entrepreneurs could grow to 85 percent or higher.[3]

A study sponsored by the Bank of Montreal[4] found that in 1996, there were more than 700,000 women-led firms in Canada, providing employment for 1.7 million Canadians; that women own and/or operate nearly a third of all firms in Canada; and that the number of women-led firms is increasing at twice the national average.

"Self-employed" and "entrepreneurs" are terms used to describe women in charge of an organization's destiny. By contrast, a CEO of a public company that became successful before she was born could not be described as an entrepreneur, although her company is "woman-led." Furthermore, self-employed women and entrepreneurs each have unique characteristics and should be carefully differentiated.

"One of the problems I have with talking about entrepreneurialism is the way society defines it as anyone who starts a business," says Monica Belcourt, the author of a number of studies of women entrepreneurs and a professor at York University. "There's a difference between Sam Steinberg who started with a corner grocery store and became Steinberg's, a grocery chain, and the grocer on the corner who is still there."

Entrepreneurs are pulled or compelled by a vision that is bigger than themselves. They have the passion to learn many skills quickly in their bid for growth. The self-employed are compelled to fend for themselves.

An accountant who leaves an accounting job and offers freelance accounting services is a self-employed person. Many self-employed people are pushed into their role through external circumstances, such as job loss or divorce or the desire to spend more time with their children. Typically, they sell a skill, and their daily routine is similar to an employee with comparable skills. They are specialists and their company's growth is limited by their individual output. They also represent the majority of women-owned businesses: female ownership is more prevalent in small businesses in the service sector and with companies having fewer than five employees.

Both the self-employed and entrepreneurs accept risk, however eagerly or reluctantly, to achieve their goals, and both are included in this book.

ISABEL'S STORY

Evidence so far seems to suggest that the entrepreneurial experience changes a person, in some cases, considerably ... It has the potential to change self-perceptions, attitudes about risk, levels of personal and business confidence, and belief in one's self. [5]

— Lois Stevenson

Entrepreneurs are lonely people, highly competitive with incredible perseverance. Whether they're loud, quiet, intellectual, instinctive, they're all killers — not in the mean sense of the word but in the sense that they won't allow themselves to be stopped by anything.

— Dan Sullivan

During its first six years, I. Hoffmann + associates was managed by a self-employed woman. Then Isabel Hoffmann changed, and became an entrepreneur.

Hoffmann's company develops and manufactures recreational and educational CD-ROM games and Internet games. It also trains people to use various computer-based technologies such as desktop publishing, graphic design, and the Internet. Her competitors are primarily larger companies in the United States like Disney, Microsoft, Activision, Viacom, and Warner Brothers, who are also active in Internet and CD-ROM entertainment. She competes on the basis of quality; her weakness is a less advanced infrastructure and distribution system.

In her first role as a self-employed person, Hoffmann worked because she had to. In 1986, her contract as a lecturer in mathematics and computer science at the University of Toronto was not renewed. Overqualified for jobs within her grasp, she turned to self-employment. Her sole proprietorship sold computer consulting services, and her only asset was herself. She didn't feel compelled to grow beyond her own capacity to produce, even in the face of opportunities to do so.

Today she is an entrepreneur. The transformation came in 1990, after she had given birth to a son. Hoffmann started thinking about focusing, growing, and hiring. But she questioned her capabilities: *Do I trust my forecasts? Do I trust my business skills? Do I have marketing skills? And I realized, actually, that I didn't.*

She enrolled in an executive MBA program, made it through the first year and then quit, along with several other people with entrepreneurial mindsets. In 1993, she incorporated her company, took out a small business loan for $15,000, and hired four people. Since incorporation, the company has doubled its revenue volumes virtually every year. In 1997, her company purchased the entertainment and educational CD-ROM business of Ottawa-based Corel for $22 million. Today, at age thirty-seven, Hoffmann has close to a hundred employees, sales of $7 million, and plans to undertake an IPO (initial public offering) by 1999.

"I almost don't have a life, but I love it," Hoffmann says. "When I'm in the middle of a deal, I have more energy than when I'm not." She works twelve hours a day and often eighteen hours, with no desire to stop. "I want to have more time with my husband and kid, absolutely, but I want quality time, not quantity time. Because I have much less time, I get much more out of it." Rather than feeling defensive about her lifestyle, she attacks the devotion of North American society to "hours of mindless entertainment." North America, she says bluntly, "is in big trouble."

In her business, a day just isn't complete without a setback, so a strong will and a healthy ego are critical to survival. Hoffmann has picked up the rhythm of going three steps back to go five steps forward. For example, she spent a full year negotiating a huge contract for CD-ROM games with a prospective customer. The deal looked imminent until it came time to sign the contract. The customer wanted ownership of all of Hoffmann's work, including Internet rights. By this time, she had invested hundreds of thousands of dollars in game development. She balked, expecting the other side to continue the negotiations. They didn't.

But she's learning, and her learning curve matches the company's growth. In her first dance with a bank, the bank led. When she returned to her bank in 1993 for a line of credit, she stipulated the conditions and the amount, threatened to end the relationship if she didn't get exactly what she wanted, and wrote a tough letter to the bank's higher-ups. "I played poker and won."

She's also learned to make big decisions by herself. Her company began as a service business, providing technology training and creative, technology-based services to businesses. It was very profitable, but it was not the kind of business Hoffmann wanted.

"It just didn't cut it for me. I wanted to be in product. But the decision took me a good year of pacing back and forth. After a year of talking and talking, I said, *To hell with it — why am I talking to others about it? This decision should come from me. It's what I want to do.*"

When she's not sure about something, she turns to her three key advisers. "Sometimes, if they're really opposed, I'll just get out of it. I'm not afraid of changing direction and taking calculated risks, and I'm not afraid to go in front of my group and say, *I was wrong about this and we're changing direction.*"

Her husband is one of those three key people. A visual artist, he works for the company as the executive producer, evaluating the graphics and text of games. She met him when she was lecturing at the University of Toronto. One of her students often mentioned a certain friend, frequently remarking on how similar his friend and Hoffmann were. Eventually, she asked to be introduced, and two months later they were married.

In addition to being the chief negotiator, problem solver, decision maker, and financial manager of her company, Hoffmann is the official "crap detector." The ability to detect lack of substance or a waste of time comes in handy, since she spends a lot of time dealing with various levels of the provincial and federal governments. "They like to come by the office and pick my brain and justify that they're liaising with the community. This is the kind of thing you don't want happening in your office. You want to know who they are and what they want before they show up. I'm very good at saying, *Cut the crap. Let's get to the point. What's your objective? If you don't have one, don't come into my office.*"

Hoffmann has also learned that the business world is short on saints, that three-quarters of businesses are unethical. The injustice currently plaguing her comes from a supplier who regularly recruits her employees. She maintains her equilibrium by having a short memory about injuries inflicted on her or her company. "If someone does something really nasty to me in my personal or business life, I forget it. I'm always able to go back and be friendly and not have any rancor. It allows me to move on.

"I'm not saying that some days I don't feel sick, and question why I'm doing this, but that's not often. The next day I'm okay. I decide to fight and win." Her son has the same iron will. The two of them can't play games together because neither is a good loser. "My husband has a hard time with the two of us," she says.

Although Hoffmann's father owned his own architectural firm in Portugal, she does not see him as an entrepreneur — because he put his ethics ahead of his business. "As a result, he was not able to go very far." Her father approved municipal projects and constantly received offers of bribes. Not only did he refuse them, he went one step further and chastised the bribers, trying to get them to see the error of their ways.

"My father did not have the capacity to turn these situations around in a way that was positive for him. He became a missionary, trying to change the world. That's not at all my intention. My intention is to act ethically, but I know I'm not going to change the world. I will change it to the extent that I can live with it and still benefit."

Many entrepreneurs have a profound distrust of authority, and Hoffmann is no exception. As a child in Portugal, she was labeled a poor student until she became seriously ill and had to convalesce at home. Her parents hired a tutor, and she went from being the worst student to the best. From then on, she questioned the authority of those in charge of labeling others, and believed only in herself.

Hoffmann's affinity for deal making developed early. She devised a way to get some of her sister's allowance by cutting her dolls' hair. "The plan was that I would give haircuts to her dolls, initially for free, but if she liked them, then for money. But my father found out, and I didn't get to phase two."

At one point, exasperated, her father told her not to speak to him unless the topic had nothing to do with a negotiation. He said, "You are not allowed to talk with me if all you want is to make deals: *I'll do this if you do that.* It's constant dealing. Talk to me about literature or music." She also argued with her father about the way he ran his business. "It's his fault, though," she says, laughing. "He raised us to have opinions."

When she was seventeen, she came to Canada to go to school. The culture shock was difficult in itself, but then her parents' assets were seized by the communist regime in Portugal. Almost overnight, Hoffmann was no longer a privileged child in a family accustomed to chauffeurs and maids. She worked at Howard Johnson's for three years to pay her tuition fees and support herself. Her parents followed her to Canada to wait out the communist regime in Portugal. Her father was nobody in Canada, and her mother found work at the Bay as a sales clerk.

Because of her family's history, Hoffmann is hesitant to conclude that she is a success. She says, "I can't help noticing that I'm under forty and I've done a hell of a lot. But I don't trust success. It's very short-lived. You have to change so much to keep it. Everything dies in life: my father was so successful, and then we saw everything collapse."

Hoffmann, who once initiated a prolonged sexual harassment suit and won, is thick-skinned about gender issues in the business world. "Women are rare in this industry, which makes me unique, and I don't mind that part of it. I'm a nonconformist, and I think people should always see themselves as unique and take a stand."

She doesn't use her gender to try to influence others, nor does her gender influence the way she runs her company. "I talk as if I'm male. Very rarely do I feel that I am being suckered. Sometimes I catch myself being too easy, and leaning on the emotional side, traits I associate with being female. But that's a stupid label."

It's stupid, she says, because men and women have been pushed by society to act in stereotypical ways. "My husband is so caring, so emotional, that many people would say he is woman-like. But for a long time men were not allowed to be emotional, so they closed it out."

Hoffmann's worst enemy is boredom, and her nirvana is an endless stream of different challenges. She's staved off boredom because she is doing something different every year. In 1993, she focused on CD-ROM production; in 1994 and 1995, the Internet consumed her. In 1996, she won the award for Entrepreneur of the Year in the Emerging Entrepreneur category, and today she is working on her goal of going public.

"I joke that the day I go public, the new board of directors will tell me, *You go too fast for us; you're too entrepreneurial*, and they'll kick

me out. I'll think about it for a few months, travel around the world —
because by that time I'll probably have quite a bit of money — and then
I'll start again."

Hoffmann is ferocious in her admonition that parents not kill the
imagination of their children. "We should be telling them that anything
is possible if you try hard enough," she says. "I believe that if you want
something very much, you can do it."

Nothing is exempt from this philosophy. One night when she was
putting her son to bed, he was mourning the fact that people were
unable to return to the past and expressing his wish to stay young
forever. Hoffmann said to him, "Okay, when you grow up, you're going
to invent a time machine. But now you have to go to sleep. And tomorrow, when you get up, you're going to learn your math, because if you're
going to invent a time machine, you need a lot of math."

HOW ARE WOMEN ENTREPRENEURS DIFFERENT?

*Some people are born entrepreneurs. They're the children with
the paper routes and they sell this, that, and the other, and
they often don't stay in education. They are the true entrepreneurs and in the past, they have usually been guys.*

— Dianna Rhodes

*Many entrepreneurs seem to be driven by a magnificent
obsession, some idea, concept, or theme that haunts them
and that eventually determines what kind of business they
choose to be in.*

— Manfred Kets de Vries

I remember years ago when I was president of the Canadian Association of Women Executives and Entrepreneurs. There was a corporate woman who became an entrepreneur. We all found that peculiar and fascinating. I remember going for a walk with her and saying, What's the difference? *And she said,* I still have to work with assholes, but now I get to choose them.

— Elizabeth Stewart

I've had a couple of people tell me that I approach my business like a man. I don't know what that means. Maybe that's a compliment.

— Melodie Stewart

Women have different lives

Some women entrepreneurs resent the suggestion that they are somehow different from their male counterparts. After all, they've played the same marketplace game, according to the same rules, and they're still on the board. The intimation that they were innately advantaged or disadvantaged irritates and at times, offends.

But women's lives are very different from men's. Their aspirations are still constrained by a limited range of job opportunities and limited access to senior management experience. Their obligation to family frequently interrupts and compromises careers. Their social networks often develop out of their children's schedules or relationships with other women, not their business activities. And while many men succeed in their careers by sharply separating them from their personal lives, many women can't or won't make that choice.

A full 17 percent of small and medium-sized enterprises are owned exclusively by females.[6]

Women entrepreneurs are different from their male counterparts because their lives and options are different. And in entrepreneurialism,

Female entrepreneurs tend to own small rather than large companies: 24 percent have companies with sales less than $250,000 or fewer than five employees.[7]

they have found a place in the world where, baby, it just doesn't get better than this. After all, their alternative is to work in a hierarchy determined by men and supported by women, with less freedom and authority and a smaller chance of reward. Given her nature and the nature of employment today, it is difficult for the entrepreneurial woman to thrive in any environment other than that of her own design.

An entrepreneurial career is a harbor from many of the external storms of being female. It offers the purest form of pay-for-performance possible, without the filters of bureaucracy and bias.

With all these advantages, why have women been so slow to take the entrepreneurial path?

Every man, no matter how entrenched his career as an employee, never completely forgets that there is another path. In the back of his mind, it's a card up his sleeve, to be played if his career goes awry or the right opportunity arises. The possibility of being your own boss, of setting your own limits to success, is as satisfying as a lottery ticket: wonderful if you win, and, at the least, a deeply gratifying daydream.

For most women, self-employment is a new and unfamiliar road, darkened by family obligations, absent business networks, a society reluctant to give its full endorsement, good old-fashioned fear, and few visible examples to follow.

Yet thousands of women, without fanfare, have built and operated successful businesses. Their anonymity may be because, during the start-up years, most of their waking hours are poured into the company, with any time left over offered apologetically to family members.

Female entrepreneurs tend to run sole proprietorships, own smaller businesses, operate in the service sector, and have younger companies than their male counterparts.[8]

Later, when the company has matured and there is a little more breathing space, these women recommit to important personal relationships that

> **Female business owners are younger and report significantly lower personal net worth than their male business counterparts. They have less business and managerial experience.[9]**

have suffered during the start-up years, or they find new ones. Because work and family are the top two time consumers, it is not surprising that the local boards of trade, chambers of commerce, and media know little about the female successes in their midst.

Stereotypes have also worked to diminish the recognition of women entrepreneurs' success. Words like "hobby," "shop," and "boutique" are most often associated with women's businesses, suggesting smallness and safety, discretion rather than obligation, and puttering rather than power. Women who push outside this narrow stereotype are depicted as superwomen, whom others may revere but never hope to follow.

Women are developing their self-confidence

No one can make you feel inferior without your consent.

— Eleanor Roosevelt

A 1989 study that set out to determine whether women and men entrepreneurs are different concluded: "It would seem that females are motivated by the same need for money, the wish to be independent, and the identification of business opportunities as their male counterparts."[10] In fact, the study found no significant differences between a male and a female entrepreneur's persistence, aggression, independence, nonconformity, need to achieve, and leadership.

But there was one difference, according to the study. "Only on one important factor do males and females appear to differ significantly: self-confidence." Women apparently have less of it than men.

But self-confidence is crucial for success, suggests another study by

Lois Stevenson.[11] Stevenson identified the following key success factors for women entrepreneurs:

1. Self-confidence and faith in one's ability
2. Sound pre-start plans and goals based on thorough research of the market, product, consumer
3. Dedication, determination, and persistence
4. Adequate financial backing
5. Other people for support and encouragement
6. A great deal of fortitude

Marina Heidman, a career transition consultant with KPMG, suggests the reason that women hold on longer to marginal businesses than men[12] may be tenacity — developed to compensate for their lack of self-esteem.

The fear of failure lives in a lot of women's closets. In a 1990 Quebec-based study of women owner-managers,[13] 57 percent of women starting their own business reported fears of bankruptcy, loss of their financial investment, market limitations, conflicts with employees and associates, failure, and inability to adapt.

But men surely have these fears as well. Perhaps the real difference lies in how the two sexes put a voice to their personal confidence-busters.

"I'm not big on universal differences between the sexes, but there are a few worth making," says Helen Sinclair, president of BankWorks Trading Inc., a company she started in June of 1995 to sell Canadian banking products, services, and technology abroad. "I think women are hellishly more honest than men about their lack of self-confidence, and they're prepared to let it all hang out. Men don't believe that's a virtue. Men believe that you paper it over and if somebody says, *How's business?* you say, *Fabulous.* But it's actually a mark of self-confidence to say, *I had a bad month, and I'm really pissed off.*"

David Pearce backs up Sinclair's observation. His company, Acuity Psychometrics, a Toronto-based firm, tests individuals for entrepreneurial and other attributes. He concludes that the temperament and motivations between entrepreneurial men and women are no different. But there are other factors that can make men and women *appear* to be different.

Pearce is the father of three daughters, and this experience has convinced him that girls are raised differently from boys. "Girls learn to get along and to share in groups, whereas boys tend to fight. A female's personality, which communicates her ego, aggressiveness, and dominance in a different way than a male's personality, can shield the hard edges associated with entrepreneurial traits. A male entrepreneur may be much more confrontational and make much blunter use of his ego than a woman would. In the woman, it ends up being more productively used because it's not a hammer that is always out there."

Giselle Briden, president of the Magellan Group, an Ottawa-based promoter of special events and business and personal development seminars, echoes Pearce's observation. "In our culture, the male ego — not confidence — has become incredibly large. I don't see that in women. Women in a competitive or threatening situation, instead of acting out of ego, act strategically. They take into account how to use the human element to their advantage."

Andrina Lever believes that low self-confidence is a big issue for women, but that few women will honestly admit to it. Financing is a huge issue for women entrepreneurs, she says, in large part because many women don't have the confidence to march into the bank and ask for it.

"Even in fundraising, women will go in and ask for $5,000, while men will go and ask for $100,000," she says. "I think women have to think like men. I often ask myself how a man would handle this situation, and then make my decision accordingly. I've worked with men my whole career, so I try to learn from that."

Ego is notably absent in entrepreneurial award winners, says Mona Bandeen, who helps manage the Canadian Woman Entrepreneur of the Year Awards. Upon receiving their awards, they may be asked when they knew they had created a great company. These women will often retort, dazed, *two minutes ago.*

Society has long credited self-confidence to the male side of the character ledger, balanced by modesty for women. But entrepreneurialism is clearly all about self-confidence. When a female vice president at a Canadian bank remarked that "entrepreneurs are so egotistical," Paula Jubinville replied, "They have to be. They're all alone. What else is going to shore them up when times get tough? They're the person with the last line of responsibility." Learning to acquire the self-confidence to survive and succeed is tougher for women, she says, since they are only now starting to see strong female role models.

Women are redefining their rightful place in society

That women have more of some attributes than men and vice versa is generally viewed as fact. Women are nurturing, men less so. Women are consensus builders, men less so. But if the truth is that women simply express the same aggression and ego that men do but in a different way, then traditional society's decree of separate working destinies for men and women no longer applies. Just because a woman is nurturing, why destine her to giving sponge baths to sick people for the rest of her life?

Our view of entrepreneurship as requiring the attributes of a chest-thumping male may be for no reason other than long, wrong assumptions. "A lot of the skills needed in an entrepreneurial career parallel the natural skills that women have learned over centuries in their role as females: coordinating, problem solving, delegating, the spirit of stick-to-it-iveness," says Marina Heidman.

Babs Sullivan and her husband own the Strategic Coach, a company that helps men and women entrepreneurs manage their lives and businesses better. Sullivan is struck by the entrepreneurial women she meets in her company's workshops. "They seem to be more flexible with themselves. Their personality is ... I wouldn't call it softer than men's — it's a different kind of energy, more flexible. It's the way they relate to themselves."

Her explanation for this difference is that women with children have a greater pull from home. "Many men have wives who do everything for them. They don't have to organize that part of their lives; it's handled. Even if a man is really into his kids, it's not the same."

When a workshop does not have a woman in it, Sullivan finds that the mood of the group is different. "I have an informal belief that men are more honest with themselves when women are in the room. Women have a better bullshit monitor: men sense that it's not going to fly with women in the room, so they don't even try."

Based on her experiences watching senior women executives leave corporate life to build successful entrepreneurial careers, Heidman believes that many attributes of a successful entrepreneur can emerge over time. "On their own, without the limits placed on them as employees, they can create their own environment, which may unleash potential they didn't know they had — confidence and a sense of autonomy and independence, power and control over their life," she says. "And a broader life too."

CHAPTER 2

HAVING WHAT IT TAKES

You have to want to do it so badly and be stubborn enough to just keep going until you get to where you want to be. And you have to have a lot of common sense.

— Angela de Martigny

I'm unemployable now, because I couldn't handle someone else telling me what to do.

— Roz Usheroff

If you can't eat lunch alone, you can't be an entrepreneur. You don't have a peer group. You're alone.

— Marnie Walker

To succeed as an entrepreneur, you have to have three things going for you. You have to be *the right kind of person*, someone who will flourish in an entrepreneurial environment. You have to have *the right skills* to manage and grow your business. And you have to have *the right idea*, which will generate revenues above your costs.

Do You Have What It Takes To Be An Entrepreneur?

- Do you want to be the one who makes the decisions and takes the risks?
- Are any members of your immediate family entrepreneurs?
- Can you walk up to a total stranger and talk about your company?
- Growing up, did you ever initiate an entrepreneurial venture to make money that lasted more than a few months?
- Do you think of yourself as someone who always has a hundred ideas on the go?
- Are you adept at managing several tasks simultaneously?
- Can you step back from the detail and see the big picture?
- Do you have a clear vision of where you want to go with your idea or company?

THE RIGHT KIND OF PERSON

I would recommend being an entrepreneur to my daughter. When you're an employee, it's almost as if you're living in a box with a lid. When you're an entrepreneur, you're solely responsible for everything you do, so you can just fly with it if you want. You can decide whatever direction you take. Yes, you take all the responsibility for the losses if it doesn't work out, but the important thing is that you can do what you want to do.

— Shelley Fisher

Bonnie Bickel invented the retail concept of off-the-shelf interior design with her chain of financially quixotic stores, B. B. Bargoons. Wanda

Dorosz elbowed the Bay Street boys to one side when she created a venture capital firm out of thin air. Sarah Band owns a kitchen store. Marnie Walker built a bussing company with sales of $2 million a year.

These women are all entrepreneurs, which the *Random House Dictionary* describes as someone who organizes and manages a business with considerable initiative and risk.

Monica Belcourt, a professor at York University, proposes that female entrepreneurs typically have these characteristics in common:

- They have entrepreneurial attributes like the need to achieve and the need for independence and assertiveness.
- They have role models.
- There has been a critical event in their lives that has motivated them to avoid dealing with authority figures in their careers.

To some extent, entrepreneurs are born, not made, in that some personality traits are very important for success. One has to be outgoing and assertive, not submissive. One has to want to win, so much in fact that long hours, a marginalized existence — hopefully temporary — and a relentless foreboding of imminent doom seem to be reasonable prices to pay for it. And one has to be independent, not dependent, and capable of withstanding the isolation of running a company.

"I don't think just anyone could be an entrepreneur," says Dianna Rhodes, head of Dianna Accessories and past-president of the Canadian Association of Women Executives and Entrepreneurs. "Some people are more comfortable taking direction from others. If you give them a clean piece of paper, they can't do it. It's not a weakness — those are the people who prop up the likes of me. It's just that their strengths are different from mine."

Rhodes prefers giving direction, not taking it. She is troubled that many people who have lost their positions as employees view self-employment as a seamless next step. "A lot of them have been damaged by downsizing, and now they are going to be damaged as entrepreneurs. Some of them simply won't make it."

Successful entrepreneurs have a very clear vision of where they're going and how they're going to get there. "I'm not sure you can teach that to somebody," says Andrina Lever. "A lot of people think they have that vision, but they also need tenacity, creative thinking, and an ability to get from A to B."

Entrepreneurial men and women tend to be highly assertive and confident, with a take-charge nature, says Acuity president Dave Pearce. "They are usually impatient people, which we describe as having a *sense of urgency,*" he says. "They're proactive and bottom-line oriented, which means they're not so much concerned with process as they are with the end result. They're deadline oriented quite naturally."

Entrepreneurs typically have a great deal of nervous energy and thrive in a fast-paced working environment that requires juggling a lot of balls and having many things on the go. They also have an independent nature — a need to work without set guidelines, rules, and procedures. "They're comfortable with risk, which typically means that failure's okay," says Pearce. "They're certainly trying to succeed, but they're not afraid to fail."

Are you an entrepreneur? Researchers are generally agreed that if you are, you have the following characteristics:[1]

A high need for achievement

You dislike routine tasks, welcome responsibility for your own decisions, and prefer work that tests your skills and abilities. You need feedback about your success or failure. Money is an important measure of your success, but sheer pleasure in your success is at least as important as money.

A belief that you are in control of your destiny

If you believe that you are in control of your destiny and that your efforts will define your life, you are said to have an internal locus of control. You are self-confident. People who believe in horoscopes and luck are said to have an external locus of control; they do not make good entrepreneurs.

A comfort with calculated risktaking

Low-risk activities bore you because there is no challenge. But you are not a gambler. You will try to avoid high risks because you want to win. Although entrepreneurs are generally viewed by the rest of society as being eager to take big risks, in fact they accept risks only after careful planning, thinking, and weighing the risks against the returns.

An ability to live with ambiguity and risk

Will your company survive the next recession? Will customers stop calling you tomorrow? How will you feed your family next month? Ambiguity, or the uncertainty of the future, may make you anxious, but not crazy with fear. Rather, you see it as a challenge that you can win because, after all, you are in control of your destiny.

Type A behavior pattern

"Pigheadedness is important," says Elizabeth Stewart. "You have to be the kind of person who can bash your head against a brick wall and open your eyes even though the blood is running down. In the corporate world, that's not a very attractive characteristic." You compete with yourself and constantly push yourself to achieve more in less time. You have the traits of a Type A personality, which include a sense of urgency, impatience, ambition, and competitiveness.

A need for control and autonomy

You don't want to depend on anyone else for your welfare, or act as a subordinate to someone else. You want to control your own destiny and don't need the endorsement of others to accomplish your goals.

Creativity and innovation

You like the freedom to experiment and can respond quickly and creatively to changes in your environment. You are constantly thinking of new ways to excel and improve.

Realism

Bob Wilson, a coordinator of the federal government's Self-Employment Assistance program, uses the following criteria to screen applicants:

Motivation. Do you have a realistic view of what self-employment will do for you? People love the idea of being their own boss, but that idea is more fantasy than fact: entrepreneurs are accountable to banks, suppliers, customers, and family. "So we look to see if the motivation is realistic, or whether it's a pipe dream," says Wilson. "Self-employment won't solve your problems in life."

Commitment. Do you have the discipline to persevere? Are there factors that might compromise commitment, such as health, family problems, or the lack of a supportive network?

Positive Attitude. Do you feel that you can face and deal with the roadblocks that are inevitable with starting and growing a business? Do you have the positive attitude that is necessary to win the trust of customers, suppliers, and banks and other investors?

ANOTHER PERSPECTIVE: THE KOLBE INDEX

How you actually go about achieving your goals is also an important measure of your potential success as an entrepreneur. According to Kathy Kolbe, Phoenix-based creator of the Kolbe Conative Index, the human mind is composed of three parts:

1. The *cognitive* part, which includes intelligence, education, and skills sets.
2. The *affective* part, which is where emotions, motivations, and beliefs reside.
3. The *conative* part, which has to do with striving, desire, and volition.

The Kolbe Index measures the conative aspects of a person's personality. It is used by the Strategic Coach in Toronto to help entrepreneurs understand how they behave to reach a goal. This striving instinct is classified into four categories: Quick Start, Fact Finder, Follow Through, and Implementer. Within each of these four categories are three operating zones that indicate level of intensity: resistant, accommodating, and insistent.

Many successful entrepreneurs have the quality called Quick Start, which includes a willingness to take risks and even exhilaration from risk-taking. In fact, the typical entrepreneurial profile is Insistent Quick Start and Accommodating Fact Finder. An Insistent Quick Start naturally generates change. "They want to find a better way to do it. They want to deal with it *now*, come up with new ideas, and go for it," Sullivan says. Unless this person has a support group to execute her ideas, disaster is almost guaranteed. The Fact Finder category describes the instinct to probe, to research how things were done before. They may not choose to do it the way it's been done before, but they do the research and then make their decisions based on the facts rather than intuition.

"Not all entrepreneurs are Quick Starts," says Sullivan. "We have a high predominance of Insistent Quick Starts in our program, but we also have a number of people who are high in other action modes, and they're successful too. It's just that how they accomplish things is different." For example, one of Sullivan's clients is a lawyer in Calgary, and the top litigator in her firm. She is an Insistent Fact Finder and Insistent Follow Through. "She is the lowest Quick Start I've ever seen, and yet she blows her competition away," remarks Sullivan. "She hardly ever goes to court because she kills them in the preparation, and she knows it."

Sullivan finds that delegation is hardest for people who are high in Fact Finder and Follow Through because they're so good at details and so committed to getting it perfect. The Implementer category, which is usually seen in people who use their hands to build or operate physical things, is rarely seen in entrepreneurs, Sullivan finds.

The Strategic Coach uses this index to help entrepreneurs identify what they are good at and what they are bad at, and then encourages them to delegate tasks in their weak areas to others. "If someone's an Insistent Quick Start, a Resistant Follow Through, and a Resistant Fact Finder, she isn't ever going to follow a day timer or keep her own filing system straight," says Sullivan. "She needs someone else to do it, or she needs some kind of unique system that works for her."

Sullivan counsels her clients to concentrate on their strengths and get other people to do the rest. "If you work against the grain of your natural instincts, it takes too much energy and causes a lot of stress," she says.

Knowing your strengths and weaknesses is especially important as your company grows, since the demands on you expand and change. Some of the behaviors that may have contributed to an entrepreneur's success in the beginning can lead to failure later on.

"Individuals who are entrepreneurial tend to be very hands-on, and that's what allows them to build something to a certain point from nothing," says Pearce. "But those same hands-on qualities that worked when there was no one to delegate tasks to are the very qualities in a growing company that will turn subordinates off and create a company of flunkies."

AN ENTREPRENEURIAL UPBRINGING

The way a person is raised influences the growth or suppression of entrepreneurial talent and interest. The child growing up in an entrepreneurial household has a tremendous head start over the child with employed parents. Her entrepreneurial skills and instincts are encouraged and shaped each day at the dining-room table. She is witness to the daily process of monitoring the health of the business, planning its future, and worrying about its problems. The business becomes a living thing. Its characteristics, strengths, and needs are understood by the child long before she ever sets eyes on financial statements.

When the children of entrepreneurs leave home, they will ask after the health of the business in their calls home, in the same breath as their inquiries about family members. For them, a company is not something you work for, it is something you live with and love.

BRENDA'S STORY

Brenda Schiedel is the president of Coyle & Greer Awards Canada Limited, located near Ingersoll in southwestern Ontario. Coyle & Greer is a leading manufacturer and distributor of awards and other forms of recognition. Now forty-four, Schiedel has been an entrepreneur since the age of five, under the mentorship of her father, also a lifelong entrepreneur.

"We had a jewelry store when I was little," she says. "Right from the time I was five, I was working with my dad in the store on Friday nights making boxes for cups and saucers." She quickly graduated from box making to her own entrepreneurial enterprises. When she was seven, she sold golf balls and lemonade to golfers on the green. As a teenager, she taught piano lessons and had a birthday party business: she would provide the food, cake, games, prizes, and party management for mothers on Saturdays.

Her brother, five years younger, showed no interest in their father's business, and has made a career out of a passion for snowboarding. In contrast, Schiedel didn't think twice about joining the business on graduation with a business degree in 1972.

Back then, the company had four employees, sales were around $100,000, and the company's market was primarily southwestern

Ontario. Schiedel's job was everything that needed to be done. Today the company serves a North American market, employees number a hundred, and sales exceed $8 million.

In the beginning, the challenge for Schiedel was keeping up with the growth. Her father took responsibility for external functions like marketing and sales, and she focused on managing the internal functions. Today she spends two days a week visiting clients and uses the rest of her time setting the strategic direction of the company.

Schiedel has learned that it's critical to maintain close contact with customers. "They want to meet the president. I give them a comfort level they wouldn't have if I didn't make the effort. I am the next person they can call if they have a problem or if they need something in a hurry."

In the late sixties and early seventies, Coyle & Greer's mainstay business was trophies for sports like bowling and darts. But it was an unreliable business. "You could give the best possible price and service, and the next year the league committee would change. They wouldn't remember where the trophies came from the previous year, and they'd go someplace else. So it wasn't a good business to concentrate on."

Schiedel decided to move the company's focus to the school market's academic and athletic programs. Coyle & Greer's full range of products — trophies, plaques, pen sets, and commencement awards — meant that teachers only had send in the information each year and their full needs would be met.

This new market fueled the company's growth, but growth brought with it a new problem. During April, May, and June the company couldn't keep up with demand; but come summer, the business died, creating havoc with cash flow and forcing employee layoffs. In response, Schiedel steered the company into the less cyclical corporate market and into organizations such as Optimists International, Lions International, Kinsmen, and Rotary clubs.

Throughout, Schiedel was adding new manufacturing capacity. When her crest business reached sufficient volume, she stopped subcontracting and bought the equipment to start producing it herself. In the same fashion, she acquired silk-screening equipment, hot-stamping equipment, and a jewelry manufacturing capability for sterling silver, tin, and gold pins.

Her market is primarily Canada. "We've been dabbling in exporting for ten years, and I'm not satisfied with the growth of our exports. But at this point, it's not a priority," says Schiedel. "The recognition market in Canada spends $750 million a year, so there's still a lot of market share we can grab from other companies. As companies downsize and cut back on salaries and big trips to Hawaii, they're looking at other ways to motivate their employees. Recognition and promotion items serve that need."

Schiedel's father has been retired for a decade now, but he comes into the company every day to have coffee with his daughter. He gave her his entrepreneurial passion, his company, and even introduced her to her husband, a self-employed consultant who helps turn around companies in trouble. "My dad provided everything for me," she says with a laugh.

DIDACTIC DADS

Monica Belcourt's study of entrepreneurial women found that half of entrepreneurs — both male and female — come from families in which the father was self-employed.

Fathers play an important part in the stories of many successful businesswomen, for they were the first source of learning about entrepreneurial skills and passions. Fathers, in their role as mentor or thorn, deliberately or accidentally infect their daughters with an entrepreneurial spirit.

"My dad takes food companies that aren't doing well and builds them up and sells them," says Janet Sinclair, a partner in Chez Soleil, a cordon bleu bed-and-breakfast in Stratford, Ontario. "I was brought up listening to him talk about companies and why they were doing well or weren't. I was always inspired by my dad, who loved what he did and talked about the possibilities with passion. Life is a series of endless challenges for him, and he is always learning something different."

Although Sinclair's warm relationship with her father is optimal, a negative relationship can actually be just as effective in creating an entrepreneurial spirit. Many highly successful entrepreneurs have troubled relationships with their families, where power is given and taken away, and a child is singled out and then rejected.[2] "Although there are, no doubt, several paths to entrepreneurship," Belcourt writes, "the literature suggests at least one of these paths involved an early experience with the unreliability of key people in the entrepreneur's life."

And when a disruptive relationship destroys the daughter's trust in authority figures, working as an employee in a hierarchical workplace becomes impossible.

In Belcourt's study, over half of the respondents felt that their fathers had not been there for them. Unable to rely on their fathers, the daughters became preoccupied with developing their own independence.

MARNIE'S STORY

When Marnie Walker was growing up, her father — a wealthy entrepreneur with a bus company, travel agency, and laundromat — involved all of his children in his businesses, but with different expectations. "From a very early age, I was conscious of the difference in gender roles," says Marnie. "Girls didn't need to be educated, and my father's vision for me didn't extend beyond driving and cleaning out buses."

Walker did not go quietly into her preordained future. She fought her father every inch of the way. Her mother and uncle quietly funded her university education, and on graduating, she worked in a variety of advertising and marketing positions. While in her thirties, she rose rapidly to a senior position in Bell Canada.

"I hadn't thought through the differences between a worker and an owner till I reached the age of thirty," she says. "Then I realized that in order to take a leadership role, I had to stop taking the 'worker' role. I had to stop being a 'good girl' — one who is always supporting men. And I had to start asking the question, *What's in it for me?*"

This new attitude helped her to reawaken her entrepreneurial interests and reevaluate her career goals. "I felt that if I continued the way I was going, I was going to have a gravestone that said, *If only I had ...* I became very restless."

Today, Walker's bus company, Student Express, competes in the same industry as her father's and has annual revenues of approximately $2 million. Father's and daughter's businesses are separate; their relationship is cordial and removed. There is a painful irony in the fact that despite her father's intentions to the contrary, he is the inspiration for much of Walker's significant entrepreneurial talent.

But where does Mother fit in all this? The women in Belcourt's study did not turn to their mothers for guidance. "The mother often served as a negative role model, a person not to be emulated because she was powerless or her life was a waste. Relations with the mother varied from indifference to disdain to hostility. ... The perception of the powerless homemaker mother may provide a negative perception of a traditional female role and influence her to choose a masculine, nontraditional role."

CONQUERED CRISIS

Women in the past who became entrepreneurs were deserted or widowed, and they had to do something. Today women still tend to become entrepreneurs when something in their lives pushes them in that direction.

— Dianna Rhodes

The fellow that I used to work with in the consulting company maintained that every successful woman he knew had a divorce somewhere in her immediate family. I don't know how accurate that is.

— Andrina Lever

A hard fall is painful, but it can make for a hard head, useful armor for an entrepreneur. Entrepreneurialism is a philosophy of life, and this philosophy may develop after a fall. The culprit behind the fall can be a family member (divorce or death), society (discrimination), or work (job loss). Suddenly, the risk of not generating enough revenues to meet the payroll or pay the mortgage doesn't seem as awful as being unemployed, without purpose, control, or money.

When Marnie Walker's first marriage dissolved, she was a senior executive with Bell Canada. The breakup was a turning point in her life. "It made me stop and reflect on my life. I sensed that what I had been doing for the previous five years wasn't enough. I wasn't unhappy, but I wasn't fulfilled."

Walker took stock of her life and decided what she was going to keep and what she wasn't. She formulated long-range plans for herself, both business and personal. Out of this process, she resolved to leave the corporate world and start her own business. "I was going to run down any rat hole for an opportunity," she says. "I took off my blinkers."

In the long and nasty list of traumas that can knock one's life off its course, job loss is right up there with death and divorce. "When men and women in senior positions lose their jobs, there's a period of unhappiness and anger in both sexes — it's not gender specific," says Marina Heidman, a career transition consultant. "Their anger is a function of delayed anger from the past. There is a period before the actual termination, which I call disengagement and disenchantment. Women get caught up in what's unfair. The guys might say, *This didn't work. I'm going to sort the legal side out, get my severance, and move on.* They seem to be able to move forward a little faster than women."

The reason for this difference may be an especially difficult environment for women in the period before termination. They may be embittered by the glass ceiling and grappling with the "stranger in a strange land" sensation that author Deborah Tannen describes in her work on differences in gender communication.

"When I was employed, I was a good corporation man," says Elizabeth Stewart, who started her own marketing consulting firm after being terminated from a senior position in the insurance business. "I bought the party line. There's a certain amount of loyalty and blindness that you take on toward the workplace that you inhabit, and there comes a point where you just can't do it anymore. You have to stop lying to yourself.

"I know a lot of women my age who have what we call the Peggy Lee syndrome: *Is that all there is?* They have fought the good battle, through hard work and learning the corporate behavior, and then they reach a certain position and they say, *My God, I'm exhausted. I've made it, but I can't imaging spending the next twenty years in this environment.*"

After the initial anger abates, Heidman finds that women pick up speed and overtake the men in identifying what they want to do and need to learn. "They're organized, systematic, tenacious. It doesn't mean they don't struggle, but they seem to get their heads around it. They take hold of their goals and move on."

Part of this learning process is the dawning realization that their values differ from their ex-employers. This realization spurs them to define exactly what they want for themselves.

Roz Usheroff, president of her own personal style consulting firm, used to work as a salesperson in the retail clothing industry, where "when the economy's good, you're a hero, and when sales drop, you're doing everything wrong."

During the recession in the late eighties, Usheroff got a firsthand taste of just how awful a retail sales job can be: empty stores, grim-faced bosses, and frugal shoppers. Then, in addition to the daily grind of a job she was growing to detest, her engagement to a man she thought she loved ended.

"I realized then that I had nothing. I had been living my life for the man in my life and now he was gone. I became very angry." She had always dreamed of having her own business. So she just did it.

THE RIGHT SKILLS

There is only one proof of ability: action.

— Marie von Ebner-Eschenbach, *Aphorisms* (1893)

NORA'S STORY

I say to myself, if I'm not going to shoot for the stars, I won't even get off the curb.

— Nora Forsey

"I don't think everybody can be an entrepreneur," says Nora Forsey, president of Corben Enterprises Inc., a company that brokers apparel design and production for other companies. "I look at my employees, and every one of them is strong. But they couldn't run a business. You have to be multifaceted. You can develop entrepreneurial skills if you want to, but you've got to want to. And you have to understand business and money, and that you're in business to make money."

Forsey had been working at Reebok for four years when she saw the writing on the wall. The first two waves of downsizing left her unscathed, but another, more senior person had the same design skills that she had, and she knew she was vulnerable. In 1993, her prediction came true and she was let go. Her response was to start her own business. That her business, whose sales soared $700,000 *above* 1995 projections, is a success is an understatement.

Forsey is an apparel designer with a strong practical streak. She's watched other people, whom she called *visionaries*, try to start businesses and fail. "They had great ideas, but just didn't know the step-by-step process of getting there. Those steps are boring, they're *really* boring, but you have to go through them.

"Your first many months, you'll probably be the only one at work, so you'll be doing the sales calls, the invoicing, the bookkeeping, the banking. Then you get to do the fun part — making the product and shipping it. That's the real high for me. But if you're not equipped to do the nitty-gritty, and your boyfriend or mother isn't willing to do it for nothing, it's not going to happen."

Thirty-eight years old and single, Forsey is no stranger to apparel design. During college, she worked freelance, taking designs from a number of small businesses in Toronto and cutting and sewing them to order, earning a couple of hundred dollars for every high-end custom design she completed. She loved it. "When I was doing piecework, I could make eight or ten dresses in an afternoon. I challenged myself to do it quickly while keeping the quality high."

Then she ventured into her own silk apparel line, targeted at women who wanted something comfortable to put on after work that looked good enough to wear in front of company. She sold her clothing, customized to each client, through monthly home fashion shows. She'd fit her design to the customer, spend the next two weeks making the orders, and the next two weeks selling. Forsey found it fun and lucrative, netting $3,000 to $4,000 a month.

But when the chance to work and learn at a well-known design studio arose, Forsey took it. She gradually made her way to Reebok as a production coordinator in their apparel division's private label program. Here, major retailers like Foot Locker and Athlete's World wanted products redesigned slightly so that their apparel line was different from other retailers.

She learned how to manage multimillion-dollar budgets. "It took any fear of large numbers right out of me. I liked doing it. My boss was often too busy to do the annual budget for the entire department, so she'd throw it on my table, and I'd put it together."

When Forsey was let go, she and her boss cried. But despite the stress, she knew she was ready to go out on her own. "I didn't have the freedom at Reebok that I have now. A lot of the design work there was dictated to me, and here I can conceive the whole idea and see it come to life."

Her first step on the road to building her own business was applying to the federal government's Self-Employment Assistance program. For fifty-two weeks, SEA participants receive unemployment insurance payments and in-class training on self-employment.

One crucial thing that Forsey learned in the SEA program was to be critical about expectations. Through working with experts on her business plan, she could see where her expenses were too high and her sales didn't justify them. "You learn all this as you go through the hoops of running a business. And you learn to take a lot of leaps of faith, like *God, I can't afford to lease this whole factory but I have to*. I had to have a place to hang my hat."

The SEA program helped her untangle her best business idea from a web of different interests. As an artist, Forsey was attracted to many business possibilities. "I like making print material like catalogues. I like doing patterns and detail work, where you don't sew at all. I like designing and helping other companies get a line going. And I have ideas for my own lines too."

Once she settled on a business that would meet the production and design needs of other companies, she took up her SEA instructor's challenge to go out and get a customer. Forsey took a deep breath and telephoned a sports equipment manufacturer. When the call was over, she had won the chance to bid on a project designing street hockey apparel.

This was just the boost to her confidence Forsey needed in her business idea. "I still haven't found another company in Toronto that does exactly what we do," she says. "We're unique in that we can do a wide range of apparel and related things like caps and bags. There's no one else around who can say, *Yes, I know the manufacturer for that product; yes, we can source the raw materials for you; and yes, we can give you samples of what you want.*"

The SEA program also gave her exposure to other would-be entrepreneurs, and she was skeptical about some of their motivations. "I *really* wanted my own business. I think others wanted another year on UIC or thought that if they couldn't get the job they wanted, they'd have their own business. But if you're not dedicated, you can forget it. It takes hours and hours. I'm often here till eleven at night, and I work on weekends. You get married to it. It's part of being willing to lay your life down for your business."

She doesn't expect her job to always be like this. "It's like raising a baby. The first two years are hands-on. At some point the business will be able to stand on its own. A lot of people have other pulls on their lives, like the husband who wants you to have a regular income. That's hard to live with. If the whole family's not behind your new business, you can't do it."

Learning as one goes is a necessary and sometimes discouraging aspect of early entrepreneurship. For example, Forsey learned to read financial statements on the job, as a business owner. It was a skill she felt she had to learn so that she could quickly access the financial information she needed.

Corben Enterprises Inc. was started without one nickel of financing. Forsey used her savings, her severance package from Reebok, and shared her first office with two other companies, an arrangement that reduced her rent to $150 a month. She borrowed a photocopier and paid $500 for a used computer. Eventually, Forsey took over the entire lease because of her need for more space.

Despite the frugal start-up, she struggled in the first year of business. Her revenues were virtually nothing, and her personal credit rating had sunk below sea level because she couldn't pay her bills.

"There's a salesman I deal with at a car company, and he laughs his head off now because he remembers me three years ago, signing my first lease for a car. I was shaking all over." Her father had to co-sign the lease because Forsey's credit rating was so poor. Since then, Forsey has replaced her car three times, and her hand is steady when she signs.

"No matter how often you phone in and say, *I can't pay — I don't have the money*, they still take your cards back. I paid it all off eventually, but in the midst of it you look like a dork from a credit standpoint." Forsey is proud of the fact that her company has no marks against it.

Her personal credit rating is now resuscitated. She has invested in a factory lease, factory equipment, an upgraded computer system, and office furniture. The factory space was leased in 1996 to produce Forsey's own line of golf wear, which will be marketed directly to consumers over the Internet.

"The Internet's a unique challenge because you have to make people think that they can see and feel the product. My line is going to be absolutely the best golf shirts in the world because of the fit, the material, and amount of detail we're putting into the patterns." She's also launching women's golf wear: "not just a takedown of men's, recoloured or something. It's flattering — something that women want to wear."

Forsey's golf line is a calculated move to reduce her company's dependency on several large customers. With the same goal in mind, she also has a licensed product line that is sold throughout North America through independent sales representatives.

A major blow to her company came from having too many eggs in one client's basket. In 1995, a major client was using Corben Enterprises exclusively for the manufacturing of fabric sleeves to package their product. "They decided to get greedy and shop around for the cheapest place to get these things made," says Forsey. "They ended up going to someone else and cutting us totally and not telling us, although we did figure it out when we stopped getting paid."

The client owed Corben $50,000 for goods received, and there was additional work in process worth approximately $90,000. "It was a $140,000 hiccup that you sure don't count on," she says. "I was familiar enough with the company to know I'd land flat on my back if I used a lawyer and went after them."

Forsey got her product returned and sold it at liquidation prices. Then she sat back and waited. The cheaper supplier gave the customer what they paid for, inferior product, and the customer eventually returned to Corben. "Funny, but our prices went up," says Forsey wryly. "Now we're doing their warehousing, shipping, everything."

Her company remains debt free, and Forsey is loath to take on debt because of the stories she hears from other companies. "As soon as they get into any kind of trouble, the banks become a burden. These companies are so controlled by the banks that they're under terrible stress. I've had financial problems too, but I couldn't imagine what I'd be like under that kind of stress. To know that at any time the bank can decide to call in your overdraft — I just don't think I could take it."

Forsey misses her first bank manager. "She was great. Anytime I had a hiccup of some kind, I'd tell her that a cheque was going to go through, and she'd cover us for a couple of days. It just wasn't an issue. But our new manager is after us all the time to register at the business banking center with all the information they require — all our financial statements, all my personal information. It's so much more information than they need. I feel an incredible invasion of my privacy. I don't know if it's different for anyone else, whether it's a man or a woman thing or an age thing, but it makes me feel as if I'm being raped. I can't sell my soul for an overdraft."

Strong words, but Forsey's experience with banks has been consistently rage inspiring. In November 1996, Nora Forsey applied for a personal mortgage and discovered that being self-employed is like "having the cooties." Her bank manager refused her.

"So I went to another bank and they put me through the wringer," she said. "I gave them my 1996 T4, which showed that I earned more than $54,000; my company's financial statements with revenues of more than $800,000; and a letter from a client. I didn't qualify because I was self-employed. I would have if I'd had a $45,000 salary."

In the end, her father had to guarantee the mortgage and she had to prove that her downpayment wasn't in fact a loan. "Once again, I feel as if I've been personally violated," says Forsey. "Banks haven't caught up with the fact that there is a huge increase in the number of self-employed. I understand that their interest is in my ability to repay, but the way I see it is that employment is no security for banks anymore. If I were employed I could be fired tomorrow. At least I'm self-employed."

Since Forsey doesn't have a credit line — unusual for a company with revenues approaching $1 million — she manages her cash flow by negotiating terms from suppliers and customers. For example, if a supplier expects cash on delivery, she asks the client for a deposit.

While this works well, there is little money left over for expansion capital. She has had discussions with a venture capital firm regarding an equity investment, and is willing to give up 10 percent of her equity. Her business plan shows how a venture capital firm can make an excellent return and exit her business within five years.

Forsey and three other people generate sales of just over $800,000. "We had a major shock in 1995, a big lurch forward. I had projected less than $100,000. I didn't know that people would be that receptive to this kind of business."

The other thing Forsey didn't anticipate was the company's demand on her time. "I'm getting pretty bogged down. Design takes time, and although I enjoy it, I also have to run the business."

To ease the load, Forsey hired a part-time designer and an administrator. One large drain on her time was visiting manufacturing subcontractors to ensure jobs were being completed to specification. "By the time I'm back at work, it's six o'clock, and I still have to do my work. The designer will offload quite a bit of that."

The four people who make up Corben Enterprises — Forsey, the sales and marketing manager, the administrator, and the part-time designer — work as a team.

"Everyone is strong in different ways; we need each other. I don't know half about sales and marketing that the fellow we have here does. I might come up with a strategy for the company in terms of the big picture, but he'll put together all kinds of detail that I couldn't. And the administrative person would put together even more details. My ideas and strategies are still subject to change, depending on what the others think."

Forsey hasn't found her gender to be an obstacle as much as her appearance is. "I'm thirty-eight, but I look about twenty-five. I put my hair up in a bun and try to look older, but sometimes people don't take me seriously. They don't think I have enough experience to meet their needs."

Gender still has an impact, in that she senses she manages differently than a man would. "I'm more sensitive to people and my customers. My sales and marketing guy will say, *Cut them off* or *just fire them.* So maybe I'm a little softer. I don't think it's a negative or a positive, just different. I'm very concerned about affecting people's lives. Men are a little more cut and dried."

THE RIGHT IDEA

Market

There must be a market for the product or service. If you are having difficulty finding a job in your particular area of expertise, it may be an early warning that there is no market for either an employee or an entrepreneur. Should that be true, turning an employed skill into a self-employed service may not be wise. For example, SEA program's Wilson points to the problem facing once-lucrative small printing businesses, which are struggling with shrinking market demand as personal computers and desktop publishing become more widespread.

Or there may be too many people with the same service. Wilson has found that many people being downsized from government have similar skill sets. "So we see a glut of desktop publishers or suppliers of clerical skills. The question is, is there enough of a market for these businesses?"

Production Skills

If you want to start a business that makes children's wooden toys but don't know how to make them, the risk of failure is high.

Financing Ability

Sometimes the obvious has to be pointed out to an impassioned entrepreneur. If you have to raise $500,000 to get your business going and, in Wilson's words, "don't have a snowball's chance in hell of raising even $50,000," it is unlikely that the venture will succeed.

TO CREATE OR ACQUIRE?

Sometimes an entrepreneur will choose not to build a new business from scratch and instead buy an existing one. Keith Pugsley, who works in the Ontario Ministry of Economic Development, Trade and Tourism matching investors with manufacturing companies looking for expansion capital and management skills, recommends the Four of Seven Rule to help an entrepreneur identify the company that can best meet her needs and abilities. In Pugsley's experience, a buyer typically has seven criteria describing the ideal business. "If an opportunity is identified where four of these criteria are met, then the buyer should give that opportunity maximum consideration before rejecting it," he writes. "The reason for this is that opportunities which have five or six criteria right sell so quickly that they are rarely seen on the open market."[3]

To help you make a purchase decision, Pugsley offers this list of criteria and suggests you identify seven that are the most important to you:

Location

Is the company located near you, and is that important?

Size

What is the sales volume, and does it fit with your goals? (Many of the companies that Pugsley helps have sales of less than $1 million.)

Price

Is the price too high? If it is, are you interested enough to monitor the price over time to see if the seller reduces it to a more reasonable level?

Product or Service
Are you knowledgeable and interested in the company's product or service?

Complexity
Does the complexity of the technology fall within your interests and capabilities?

Financing
Will you need the seller to help you finance the purchase price?

Capital Equipment
Is the company capital or labor intensive?

International Markets
Do you want a company that exports?

Sectors
What industrial sector do you want the company to be in?

Financial Condition
Will you consider a company in poor financial condition, or does it have to be profitable now?

Equity and Ownership
How much of the company do you want to own? Do you envisage a partnership? Are you willing to take a minority position?

Income Requirements
Do you need a certain salary immediately, or can you survive on a minimal income from the company for a period of time?

Brokered Deals
Would you consider working with a mergers and acquisitions consultant — who usually charges a contingency fee — to identify the best acquisition?

Markets

What markets do you want the company to be in?

Timing

Do you have the time to close the deal that the buyer requires to sell?

SHELLEY'S STORY

In 1994, at the age of thirty-seven, Shelley Fisher built a new niche in an old marketplace, thanks to the specialized experience she gained with her last employer, the Workers' Compensation Board (WCB) in Ontario. Her departure from the Board ended a government career that began when Fisher was nineteen.

"I never lasted in a job longer than two years except for WCB because I'd learn the position and get bored," she remarks cheerfully. "Once I learned it, I'd move on." In this fashion, she moved through Transport Canada, the RCMP, Agriculture Canada, UIC, Canada Pension, and finally Workers' Compensation. "If I wasn't a risktaker, I'd probably still be sitting at Transport Canada, typing. But when I get bored, I have to do something about it."

At the Board, Fisher worked as a senior adjudicator, resolving the compensation claims of injured workers. Then she was terminated while in the hospital with pneumonia.

"I had a personality conflict with my supervisor, who sent me a letter demanding a doctor's letter within five days or he'd terminate me. I got the specialist to send my medical to the head doctor at WCB. The guy terminated my position anyway because he never checked to see if WCB had received my medical. Instead of calling him back and saying my medical was there — he has no access to my medical anyway under the Privacy Act — I just called a Bay Street lawyer and sued them. They paid $20,000 a week and a half later and extended all my benefits for eight months after I left. I used the money to start my business, Fisher & Associates."

This business is for-profit assistance to injured workers who need their claims resolved. Fisher's competitive advantage is that she can provide faster and better service than the government can. "The WCB advisers are there to help them, but they're backlogged two years and being downsized," she says.

This backlog is exactly why her business works. Many of her clients can't wait to have their claims heard, or they have been turned down, or their cases have become mired in bureaucratic goo. Fisher's promise is to barrel through the obstacles and get the compensation her clients want. She claims a 97 percent success rate because she looks long and hard at every case to assess the chances of winning, and because there are a lot of winnable cases languishing for lack of attention. "There's this big misconception that people on Workers' Compensation rip off the system," she says. "But when I was working at WCB, 90 percent of the claims were legitimate."

Before actually starting her business, Fisher enrolled in the federal government's Self-Employment Assistance program. As part of the training, she presented her business plan to two lawyers and two bankers. They told her it was a great idea that wouldn't work because injured workers couldn't afford it.

That was when Fisher was proposing to sell her services for a flat fee of $425 and 10 percent of any compensation due the claimant. She ignored the experts and since then has raised her prices three times. She now charges $995 and 10 percent for any back pay she wins. "There are para-legals out there who charge more than I do," she says with a snort. "And there are only three lawyers I know of who can match my expertise."

She points out that her competition is not only thin but ailing. "The Ontario government is getting rid of offices across Ontario that help injured workers. If you needed someone, you would have go to a lawyer and pay $250 an hour. I win cases against lawyers. One lawyer told a client of mine that his case would take five years and cost $10,000; another lawyer wanted a lien on his house."

One of Fisher's victories was a construction worker in Welland who in 1956 injured his knees in a fall from a scaffold. On the same day, in another part of the province, another man bruised his knee with a wrench. "So the Board in their wisdom mixed up the claims. The guy in Welland has been after the Board for the last thirty years. We over-turned that one in the summer of 1996, and he got a nice pension. Another old guy up in the boondocks had been fighting Ontario Hydro for years and years. We got him over $30,000 for hearing loss."

A sense of outrage at some of the disputed claims she represents is mixed with clear enjoyment at the prospect of winning big on behalf of the "little guy." "One man worked for this little hick township for nine years, and one day he gets injured. They hold a town council meeting that night and decide to give him a nine-month contract job and then whoosh him out the door. I won the case.

"Then there was another case with the same township, where a 450-pound tailgate on a dump truck fell on an employee's head. He had brain damage, and they got rid of him. He's been on welfare for the past ten years. I found this guy in a home and won the case. That's just one of many stories."

Her market is wide open. Although Workers' Compensation falls under provincial jurisdiction, Fisher is able to serve claims in other provinces because regulations allow anyone to represent the claimant, and claims policies and procedures are similar. However, she is focus-ing on the Ontario market.

Finding injured workers was initially quite a challenge. If her marketing efforts flag, even for a short time, she feels the consequence the next month in low sales. She started out conducting free seminars in cities all over Ontario. She would book a room in a hotel, advertise the seminars, and create interest by explaining the ins and outs of getting Workers' Compensation to the crowd that signed up. "I was nervous giving seminars at first, but not anymore. I'm very confident with my technical knowledge, and injured workers have no idea what's going on. I'm educating them — in layman's terms."

But the seminars were expensive and time-consuming. Trade shows were even less appealing, since many employers attend them. Fisher's activities result in increased claims and compensation premiums, so employers are not Fisher's biggest fans.

Given the drawbacks of trade shows and seminars, Fisher tried radio advertising on a pay-per-inquiry basis. The station would air commercials, and for every call that came in on a special 1-888 number, Fisher would pay the station $100. "I took a chance because commercials are about $400 for a thirty-second spot. We needed the exposure." In August 1996, the bill came to $6,000, which Fisher negotiated down because there were a lot of hang-ups, which she successfully argued shouldn't count. All in all, it was a break-even venture.

Then one day, she was driving from one seminar in Sudbury to another in North Bay when the realization hit her that she had been targeting injured *individuals*. Why not go after the big associations like the unions and the police and firefighters' associations? She picked up her cell phone then and there and called the Ontario Provincial Police association. Once she got through to the person who handles Workers' Compensation claims, she rambled on excitedly for five minutes into her phone. "There was this silence. Then he said, *Well, okay, I guess*. I met him in Toronto, spent two hours with him, and offered to represent one of his claimants, free of charge. He gave me a cop who was trying to get twelve years' worth of back benefits. I won, and the OPP started sending us their files."

Today Fisher's company represents cases on behalf of nine police associations and the Brewers Retail union in Ottawa and Sudbury. "I show them what I'm capable of doing. For example, the London police gave me a case that had been out-and-out denied. I made three calls, and three days later they flipped it — the guy got everything he wanted. News spreads."

Fisher moved to Pembroke, Ontario, in early 1995 to better manage a surge in business in the area. She talked a high school buddy whose marriage had recently disintegrated into quitting her permanent job in the insurance industry, becoming her business partner, and moving to Pembroke with her three children.

The partnership works because the two women's personalities complement each other. "Laurie has strong administration skills and is an organizer plus. I'm usually all over the place, saying, *Let's try this* or *Let's try that*. Together, we hash it out."

The two women also share responsibility for a total of four children. "If I'm on the road, my daughter is with Laurie, and if she's on the road, the kids are all with me."

She believes that her daughter has benefited immensely from having an entrepreneurial mother. "I'm raising my daughter to roll with the punches because I see that the people who can't are having a much harder time with life. 'Whatever will be will be' is my philosophy, and she understands that totally. If something ever happened and it didn't work out, we'd just do something else."

Fisher loves her life: her business, her friendship with Laurie, and her new home. "Some people go to cottages on the weekend; I go home. I sold my home in Scarborough for $200,000 and bought a renovated, century-old house in downtown Pembroke for $130,000. It overlooks the Ottawa River onto Quebec. It's not only picturesque, it's a different way of life up here. It's half the pace, and the people are so different. You walk down the street, and people say hello even if they have no idea who you are."

Initially, Fisher's company had low overhead, but now with two associates on a retainer basis — "we pay them every month whether they have files or not" — and a phone bill that averages $1,000 a month, costs are an increasing concern. In 1995, Fisher & Associates was two to three months behind in its payables and had revenues of $60,000. In 1996, the company kept on top of its bills and revenues doubled; 1997 is the year that profits are anticipated.

Fisher didn't get any financial backing, and she regrets it. "I should have gone to the Federal Business Development Bank, but I used my severance package instead. We've got a business bank account, but we've never asked for a loan. I'm thinking now of approaching the FDBB for a loan for advertising because I don't think you can get it through the banks."

Fisher's clientele is almost entirely men. She finds that being female can be an issue in rural areas, where they aren't used to dealing with females in positions of authority. "They're very leery at first, but once the case is won, all of a sudden their buddies are calling me."

Many of the men she meets are single. "But no dating clients, even the uninjured ones. It's one of the hardest policies we have, but we absolutely do not date clients. Wait till we get into the firefighters' association ... oh God," she groans.

Fisher doesn't belong to any networks, male or female. "A lot of people don't understand Workers' Compensation, so it's not only, *Why are you doing this*? but also, *What are you doing?* and *Are you nuts?* If you phone up my mother, she'll say, *I have no idea what that woman is doing.*"

Fisher firmly believes that she manages her business differently from men, and the main difference is her larger appetite for risk. "Men don't like change. They will take a risk to a certain degree, and then they panic. If something is falling apart, they can't seem to handle it." She points out that she pulled up roots and moved to an economically depressed region of Ontario.

"Here I am up in the boondocks. If I'd stayed in Toronto and my business fell through, I would have a better chance of getting a job. Up here, there's no fallback, but I threw caution to the wind and moved up here anyway. Not many men I know would attempt that."

Her self-confidence keeps her going. "I never lose sleep over this business. I can't stress how confident I am. My goal is to have an office beside every WCB office in Ontario, where people can just come in and I don't have to do quite the amount of travel."

Fisher could have chosen to work for an employer, fighting employee claims for compensation. "I would be richer — a nice plush office, sixty-plus salary, nine-to-five job. It's not that I'm a saint — maybe a little stupid sometimes," she says. "But all I'd be doing is trying to keep the costs down. I wouldn't have my heart in that, simply because there are a lot of legitimate claims out there."

CHAPTER 3

THE AGONY ...

The number of things that can plague the business owner in the wee hours of the night can be overwhelming. A 1990 Quebec-based study[1] found that the most frequent obstacles women encountered when launching their own businesses were:

- lack of confidence shown by banks, suppliers, and clients;
- lack of start-up capital; and
- their families.

And after the business was launched, a whole new wave of knuckle-gnawing obstacles blossom:

- marketing problems;
- problems with associates; and
- difficulties in recruiting and training competent employees.

Any experienced entrepreneur can readily add to this list. Isolation, lack of knowledge, dishonest employees, customers who change their minds, resentful family members, gouging landlords, unreliable suppliers, and ruthless competitors are just a few of the problems that can present themselves on any given day of the week.

Judy Byle-Jones, who sells financial planning and insurance, brims with energy and good humor as she describes her business as "100 percent negative."

"I'm constantly marketing my services to people who don't understand what I do, and I'm constantly dealing with rejection. I have days and sometimes weeks when I don't do business. But experience has helped me realize that I have to have negatives in order to experience the positives. It's not always an uphill ride. Sometimes you're down in the trough. To cope, I keep physically fit, I surround myself with positive people, and I always see the glass as half full, not half empty."

Many of the negatives an entrepreneur faces are stared down by sheer will and a determination to find the positive side of an often difficult reality.

ISOLATION

It's like being in the middle of a twister. You can't get out of it. There is nowhere to go for the solution.

— Marnie Walker

I hear the sentiment often that women entrepreneurs are isolated, and I think it's partly true. There's no other businessperson that I can spill my guts to and feel that I can trust their answers.

— Tracey De Leeuw

Wanda Dorosz, president of Quorum Growth Inc., a venture capital firm, received a distraught phone call on Christmas Eve from the entrepreneur whose company she had invested in. She agreed to meet him at her office. He burst into tears and told her that his wife had just learned that their baby would be stillborn. He needed to talk.

What has that got to do with being an entrepreneur? To Dorosz, it's compelling evidence that they have almost nobody that they can be weak or sad with.

Isolation is a real problem for women entrepreneurs because their peer group is especially small. Paula Jubinville, whose company, Aqueous Advisory Group, provides consulting services to entrepreneurs, is conscious of this feeling of *otherness* even when she and her husband socialize. "We go out with our friends, and most of the wives have jobs and kids, but they're downstream from bringing the business in the door. They still get a paycheque, whether they're there or not."

Many of Jubinville's female clients, only half joking, call her their chief psychiatric officer. "I get calls saying, *Just tell me I can get through this. If you tell me, then I'll believe it.* They don't have a peer. It's almost like being a single parent. You can talk to others, but they're not there when you're disciplining your kids or juggling work and your child."

Having partners is crucial for Ellie Rubin, president of the Bulldog Group Inc., a high-tech media asset management company. "When you're by yourself, everything's your problem. Your employees work for you, no matter how many parties you invite them to. That's how business works: you have to have that separation, and it can be really lonely."

Rubin had a taste of isolation during the four months she spent trying to find investors in Silicon Valley, California. "Being alone; not knowing anyone; every day meeting a new person and selling; no office colleagues to talk to; my husband 3,000 miles away — for days on end, I had no one to talk to."

Isolation can become so woven into an entrepreneur's life that it affects the way she deals with other people. "You're always 'on,' and you're not sure who to trust with the 'off,' " says Rubin.

"I wish I had someone to call when I had a problem," concurs Sarah Band, a single mother who owns and operates a retail store. "But I don't. I get into a slump and hunker down, and then I go back up and get totally overstretched and say yes too often. Three weeks later when I'm about to break down, I'm telling everyone: *I can't do* everything!"

Having a spouse or significant other may be personally enriching but doesn't ease the entrepreneurial isolation. Marnie Walker's second husband is Bill Fahey, a chartered accountant with his own tax practice. Walker spends nearly all of her free time with him. In her previous marriage, Walker often felt insecure and inadequate, in part because her first husband was an imposing authority figure, strong on advice.

"Bill is one of the reasons I've done as well as I have," she says. "He doesn't coach me, and he gives me the space to do what I need to do. I don't get heat from him if I can't make it home for dinner. He'll pick up the slack because he knows that once I get through the peak, I'll get my balance back. He listens to me and offers suggestions. I may not take them, but he gives me the confidence and support to keep on trying. He isn't jealous of me. He's confident in his own life and doesn't compete with me. He doesn't care if I'm different. He loves me unconditionally. When I'm with him, there's room in the room for me."

"I don't have anybody at home saying, *It's okay if this business doesn't do well*," says Helen Sinclair, whose husband is a partner at a public accounting firm. "It's not this rosy picture where you go home every night and lay your problems on the table, and he very patiently helps you run through them.

"On Sunday afternoons, I wrench him away from the TV screen and say, *Do you mind looking at these cash flows and telling me if there's anything grossly wrong?* He growls, but he goes through them with me. That's just to say that he's busy too, I guess. And he's saying to me, *This was your choice. You don't have to do this.*"

"The contract that my husband entered into was with a person who doesn't exist anymore," says Giselle Briden, president of the Magellan Group. "A woman becomes an entrepreneur and it changes her.

"I had big fluffy blond hair and just wanted to go to my aerobics classes and be a good wife and cook dinner and have 2.5 kids, and just look at what happened! I said, *C'mon honey, let's go try this*, and we ended up losing everything and living in a storage room."

Now that Briden is a success, they have moved into more affluent accommodations. And Briden continues to be impressed with her mate. "That he doesn't let his ego and male conditioning get in the way is awesome. I take my hat off to him."

Tracey De Leeuw is a single mother and president of ManGlobe International Exchange, a company that provides turnkey solutions for companies that want to transact business on the Internet. "Am I lonely because I'm an entrepreneur, or am I lonely because I don't currently have a date? It's probably more the latter. Men don't understand that I'm not free till one in the morning. They don't get it.

"I call myself the One-Date Wonder. I'm great at getting one date, but pretty much by the second one they've said, *Whoa, this is more than I can deal with.* I work eighty hours a week, and I'm rarely available. When I *am* available my kids are first, my business is second, I'm third, and they can only hope to be fourth.

"And I don't do *coy* well. I say, *Here are my cards — they're on the table. Do you want to have a second date?* We usually end up friends. All of this is okay. I've pretty much said to myself that when I'm where I want to be, I'll know who I want to be there with, and that's all right."

Claire Cobourn, in her early sixties and president of Comfort Care, a three-year-old company that provides in-home care for the elderly, has been living with a retired business teacher for a year and a half. "He's turned my life around. When I get down and depressed about work, he has good things to say and encourages me. I'm blessed."

"My first husband wasn't the best match for me," says Judy Byle-Jones. "He was more unstable than I am, and he had a low self-image. The more successful I became, the harder it was for our relationship. I'd say, *Oh, I made a good sale today.* And he'd say, *At least somebody in the family is making money.* Being around someone who is negative, even though he wasn't negative all the time, brings a positive person down. I now have a positive husband, and because of that I believe I can be that much more successful."

Bonnie Bickel, the president of B. B. Bargoons, doesn't talk to her entrepreneurial husband at all about her business, and he is equally reticent about his own. This arrangement effectively prevents one from pointing out the other's mistakes.

LACK OF KNOWLEDGE

I tell people, Today I don't know whether to shoot myself or go bowling.

— Ingrid Mueller

To the novice, entrepreneurship is a tricky balance between dizzying horror at how little you know about growing a business and the determination to learn fast enough not to fail.

Just how important is it for you to have industry-specific skills *before* you start a business? Very important. Consider these facts:

- The Canadian Advisory Council on the Status of Women found in their 1991 study that 40 percent of women entrepreneurs started businesses with no related experience, and that their businesses had significantly lower profits than those headed by experienced women.
- In a study of the management practices of successful female business owners, the majority of women cited experience as the best preparation for running a business, far greater than formal education.[2]
- The federal government's Self-Employment Assistance program, which gives would-be entrepreneurs training in how to start and manage a business, tries to bring people into the program who will generate the best return on taxpayers' money. This means they focus on people who already have the industry-specific skills and need help developing their business management skills.

Marnie Walker recently led a seminar on entrepreneurship for female university students and was perplexed at the lack of "how to" questions. "The questions were more abstract, like: *Where did you get your idea?* and *Where did you find the courage?*" Her conclusion was that many women are naive about the knowledge, time, and focus required to succeed: "For many of them, entrepreneurship is just another course."

She supports mentoring programs because of their potential to teach women how to be effective faster and avoid mistakes that others have gone through, but is critical of the emphasis on what she calls "touchy-feely issues" at the expense of content.

Angela de Martigny is an aboriginal designer who is building a second company after having to close down her first one. To her, what is most important is having experience in the field you want to have a business in.

"A lot of people think, *Oh, I'd love to own my own business* or *I'll open a franchise,* even though they know nothing about the industry they're interested in. You *have* to know what you're doing and what your market is. You can't just go in cold. That's basically what I did the first time, and I made a go of it, but I was naive and it was difficult."

The idea of a shredding and recycling business came to Wendy Banting, president of Secural Environment, when she worked in executive search. "I felt that all this confidential stuff we were generating shouldn't be going into an open waste stream. I had this horror that one of the garbage bags on the curb would split open and all these résumés would go drifting down the street."

Her mistake was starting a business she knew little about. This meant no business contacts to begin with, and the need to build each client brick by brick. She also had no idea that margins in the paper-shredding business were slim and that low volumes per client were so prevalent. Today, with sales under $1 million, she has come a long way in dealing with these initial problems. "Now I'm focused on the $1,000 sale rather than the $10 sale," she says.

She has introduced a whole new line of products, and thanks to a friend who sat her down and told her that many clients were not aware of all her products and services, she is taking more time to communicate her company's capabilities. "We're doing cross marketing among our shredding clients, sending out product literature and tapping new clients. I don't look at my shredding clients as solely shredding clients but as potential business for other types of material handling equipment."

Sometimes an entrepreneur needs to be told that the glaringly obvious is staring her right in the face, and that's where mentors are invaluable. The difficulty is breaking out of the isolation so common to entrepreneurs to find that source of wisdom.

Bonnie Bickel is a mentor with the Step Up program. One of her protégées had money in the bank, a good business, and no bank line. "She designs and manufactures T-shirts, which requires creativity, and she has a lot of talent," says Bickel. "But she would spend an hour or two each day sweeping her warehouse." She told the woman to stop sweeping the floor and spend the time being creative. When the woman did so, her business expanded.

Knowledge is important because it keeps the mistakes down and creates a competitive advantage. Lack of knowledge births and feeds mistakes and misses fleeting market opportunities.

INGRID'S STORY

For Ingrid Mueller, her first year in business was a year of learning. She learned that the experts aren't always all-knowing, and that lack of knowledge can hamstring a company that is still struggling to stand.

Mueller knows the advertising industry for publishers inside out, having worked in the industry for fifteen years. But while she knew a lot about magazines with controlled, paid circulation, she knew little about newsstand sales and distribution issues. It was a whole new ball game that she's learned to play, in mid-game.

In 1994, Mueller created TMT Communications, after a frustrating job search in advertising. She had been laid off, and her job search delivered nothing but the repeated comment that she was overqualified. "I felt like saying, *What would you like me to forget?*" she quips, laughing.

TMT began as a publishing company for the *Women's Survival Handbook*, a directory of products and services for women in the Toronto area.

When she was creating the handbook, she worked eighteen hours a day. "I got very little sleep. That was my first issue, so I had to. I researched it, wrote it, sold the ads, produced it, everything." But her three children, ages six, eight, and nine, are her top priority in life. "I work my butt off, but I stop working when my kids come home, and I start again when they go to bed."

She targeted over 100 corporate advertisers and cold-called them, avoiding small businesses. "They can be very unreliable in terms of collections, and I wanted to get quality advertisers who would pay their bills and could afford to become involved in a new venture."

After the handbook's launch, Mueller discovered two serious problems. The first arose in the definition of the publication. Mueller wanted it to be sold as a book but was advised by her distributor that she couldn't because it contained advertising. Positioning it as a magazine meant a short shelf life. "Some of the retailers had a real problem figuring out where to put it — in the magazine section or the book section," she says. "It was heartbreaking when I found out that some retailers took it off the shelf at the end of June 1996." Later, she found out that if she had only removed the advertisement from the back cover, she could have sold it as a book.

The second problem arose in the dating of the publication. Mueller had planned to present it as a 1996–1997 issue, but her distributor told her it would confuse the retailers. He talked her into making it a 1996 issue.

Because it was launched in April of 1996, it could have sold well into April of 1997, and Mueller wouldn't have had to republish it until 1998. However, virtually all the retailers returned their copies in November.

"It was on the shelf for eight months," says Mueller. "It was my mistake. I took some bad advice."

By industry standards, the first issue did well in terms of paying for itself. Advertising paid for half of production costs, and she paid for the other half through a $50,000 credit line she and her husband took out on their house. "It has not supplied me with an income, so I'm looking for other work for my company," says Mueller. Since then, the company has expanded into publishing and consulting services, and advertising and promotion seminars.

Mueller remains optimistic, because of her belief in the inherent value of the handbook and because optimism is intrinsic to her. "My philosophy is that you have to maintain your sense of humor. When things seem to be hitting rock bottom, you just have to sit back and say, *Well, it can't get much lower, so it has to go up.* I have to have a sense of humor, otherwise I'd go out and shoot myself."

Mueller is now looking for a joint venture partner with the resources to invest in the handbook. "I have to make a decision about whether this is going to grow huge or whether it's going to stay a home-based business," she says. "I think there is enormous potential in this publication because the information it provides is so necessary for women everywhere." She would like to see it franchised right across Canada and is also looking at creating a Web site on the Internet, where advertisers would pay her to appear on her Web pages.

If she doesn't find a joint venture partner, she'll continue to publish the handbook herself. She is heartened by the prospect of a second round, which will be an easier labor of love. "I have all this information now. All I have to do is update it. I can just call them up. I don't have to go through process of explaining the concept again.

"This is an effort from my heart. I'm lucky to have a husband who's so supportive, morally and financially," says Mueller. "And I've learned that I have the will power and drive to accomplish things on my own without anyone hanging over me. Initially, I got really disgusted by the three inches of dust on the furniture — I'd want to go and dust it. Now I'm beyond that. I can handle the dirt. I know it'll be there tomorrow."

When she first started working from home, Mueller used to dress in a business suit. Now she sits down in front of the computer in her nightgown. "I'll just pull my jeans up over my nightgown to walk the kids to the school bus," she says, laughing.

Although she finds working by herself lonely, she is happy to be so accessible to her children. "Even though they're at school all day, they love that I'm home. If somebody gets sick or gets their lights punched out, I can be there very quickly.

"I'm bound and determined to keep this going," she says. "I believe it's a good thing. It can make money, and it's a good thing to be doing for women."

PROBLEM: OVERWORK

Tracey De Leeuw, president of Winnipeg-based ManGlobe International Exchange, doesn't stop until something she has decided to do is done. In other words, sleep deprivation. When she's not traveling, she comes home at five o'clock "like a normal Joe. I hang out with my kids, avoid my housework, and then I put my kids to bed and work from nine till about four in the morning." Her day begins again at 8:30 the next morning.

Entrepreneurs have an elastic definition of work and overwork. And according to Eva Klein, a clinical psychologist, women entrepreneurs have a particularly difficult time knowing when they've exceeded their limits. "Women are especially vulnerable to burnout because they aren't as comfortable asking for help, saying no, and putting themselves first. Unless you nourish your needs, you *will* burn out."

Many women entrepreneurs are in the service industry, and this presents a slippery slope into overwork. Elizabeth Stewart, owner of a marketing support services company, explains by pointing out two basic facts. First, the business is inseparable from the owner because the owner *is* the service. "This has a big impact on you and your sick days, vacation days, and child-care obligations," says Stewart. "In service, you won't take a vacation for the first few years; even so, you'll always feel guilty." And because the owner is the service, there is the struggle to deliver the same quality of service and conduct yourself accordingly, every day.

Second, the business is perishable. "If a client wants to see me within a specific period of time, there's often no alternative. This creates enormous peaks, where you work twenty-four hours a day and you're using toothpicks to keep your eyes open. And then there are the enormous valleys, where you have no business and you're *worrying* twenty-four hours a day."

But sooner or later, by choice or necessity, overwork gets managed down. Wanda Dorosz finds that her capacity for work today is five or more times greater than it once was, with far less strain on her health. "I never imagined that I would have the bandwidth in terms of sheer capacity," she says. "Some of that is truly being far better organized; some of it is getting better at problem solving; and some of it is simply making decisions faster and reacting more quickly."

ANGELA'S STORY

Angela de Martigny is a clothing designer who has little time left in each hectic day to do design. She works long hours, seven days a week, and has done so since she started her company, Spirit Ware, in 1995.

"I'm not working for a big designer because I didn't want to design ugly little dresses," she says. "I have my own vision of how I think people want to dress these days. I don't like what's out there, which makes me wonder who these people are designing for."

Marketing and sales consumes most of her time — from creating and sending mailouts, answering requests and sending out catalogues to traveling around North America to drum up interest in her designs. Through 1996, pregnant with her first child, she traveled in Quebec and Ontario, and the United States.

"I don't mind the hours because it's not really like work," she says somewhat wistfully. "But the lack of free time kind of gets to you after a while. It would be nice to take a weekend off."

Originally from British Columbia, Angela de Martigny came to Toronto to undertake a six-month internship with the Canadian Apparel Centre. Four years later, she is living with her partner on the Six Nations Reserve in Ontario, managing her company, and taking care of her baby, born in December 1996.

De Martigny is quick to point out that her work does not fall into the category of native arts and craft. Her unique designs incorporate the spirit of aboriginal culture, however. In addition to deer hide and fur, she uses natural fabrics like cotton. "I find that people expect every-thing I make to look extremely native, but what I do is subtle," she says. "I don't want to be 'in your face' about it."

For example, de Martigny's designs include a two-piece vest and long skirt with wood buttons down the front and front pockets. The skirt has a small embroidered native symbol on a pocket, as do the pocket flaps on the sleeveless vest. "It's very tasteful and modern but comfortable, and you can wear it anywhere," she says.

De Martigny believes that Canada is one of the most difficult markets in the world. The United States has been a prodigious consumer of her designs, far outweighing the demand in Canada. "Canada is an extremely conservative country, and people right now are not spending money on anything," she says. "The difference between Canada and the United States — as far as the appreciation of native products, people, and culture is concerned — is like black and white. It's as if you don't acknowledge what's in your own back yard." Europe also has a huge interest in native culture, and her goal is to expand into that market as well.

Her business and emotional partner is a Mohawk artist and computer whiz, John. He helped de Martigny begin selling clothing through their Web page in May 1996. While queries and orders have come from as far away as Kuwait and Germany, the Internet is still an insignificant source of sales for Spirit Ware, which sells through retail stores with the support of three sales representatives in Western Canada and Ontario.

De Martigny would like to reduce her travel commitments to spend more time on design. Her ability to do this is contingent on finding good sales reps, which is a process of trial and error. "You have to go through a few to get a really good one. And it's more difficult because there is more to the product than just being a garment. There's a whole culture wrapped up in it: details like the embroidery design are part of our culture, which needs to be explained," she says. "If you don't have the right person, someone who understands the philosophy, then it's not going to work."

De Martigny's line is also fighting with the other lines the representative is carrying. It's human nature, she says, to push the lines that are already established with clients. "If they make extra money on your stuff, that's great; if not, it just sits there. You don't know whether they're showing it. In that sense, it's frustrating, especially since I know if I were doing it, I'd be doing a much better job. But then I'd have to do all the traveling."

With the same intensity that de Martigny loves design and marketing, she hates the financial end. "Usually when I get depressed, it's about financial things. Then John reminds me that we've done quite well so far."

She operates more on instinct and intuition than facts and figures. "I'm someone who believes in capitalizing on opportunities as they come up. I'm not quite sure how it's going to work out, but I have a gut feeling that I should be doing it. Then it usually works out."

For example, de Martigny moved into designing fur when the opportunity came up to produce a coat in a week for the Canadian Fur Council. She had never worked with fur before and sought out a furrier to help her. They forged a strong relationship, and out of this she was able to participate in one of the largest fur shows in the States.

Despite her emphasis on gut instinct rather than hard, cold numbers, de Martigny has a business plan. "I did it mostly for myself. The one we're working on now is an expansion of it. There's nothing in it that's not going to be achieved as far as I can see. It's very practical and ambitious, but I know that we can do it. We've actually exceeded what was in our original business plan already. To achieve what we have with the small amount of money we had is quite a feat."

Her biggest torment today? "I dislike the dishonest way many Canadians do business. There are people who blatantly rip you off." Because many suppliers refuse to give terms for payment to anybody these days, de Martigny is forced to pay on receipt of goods. She, in turn, tells retailers that all orders are COD. "But many retailers are in a bad way, so what they're doing is taking the merchandise, handing over a cheque, and then stopping payment on it. When somebody does that to you, it really puts you back. I'm not sure whether it's something in the fashion industry or something that's happening everywhere. I'm not seeing this in the States. The economy seems to be worse here."

She is also frustrated by the ease with which companies go bankrupt and then resurrect themselves. "The supplier has no recourse," she says. She's been forced to give an unknown retailer thirty-day terms in order to get her clothes in the store. "They receive the merchandise and sell it, all along planning to go bankrupt before the thirty days are up. So they've sold your stock for cash, and you can't retrieve that. And then they go and set up under another name somewhere else. It's really horrible. As far as I know, there's nothing you can do. I just take it as a loss. You can find out who the bailiff is, but you'll only get ten cents on the dollar, so it's not usually worth it."

While de Martigny finishes the leather items herself, she relies on others on the reserve to do the beadwork and embellishments and uses a number of contractors to produce the leather goods, fashion wear, and gift ware like deer hide pillows, address books, diaries, and cosmetic bags.

Her contractors have the capacity to do large volumes, which may come in handy if one of her marketing efforts pans out. "We have an opportunity to sell to a catalogue in the United States that has a distribution of eight million. We're sending them four samples. Even if they choose just one, they'll order thousands of units. And we won't have a problem doing that. In fact, my manufacturer will be quite happy."

Her dream of owning a factory is proving more elusive than she had originally anticipated. There are no existing facilities on the reserve, so she would have to build from scratch. Given the large capital and equipment costs and the lack of a skilled, available workforce, it makes more sense now to subcontract.

Spirit Ware, with 1996 sales of approximately $60,000 and 1997 sales projected at $200,000, isn't de Martigny's first business.

De Martigny grew up in British Columbia not knowing very much about her native background. Her father believed his children would have a better way of life if the family assimilated and tried to live "like normal Canadians."

The first six years of de Martigny's working life were spent as a secretary. "One of the most liberating things I've ever done is quit and become an entrepreneur. I found out what I was capable of, and it was much more than I had first thought. I hated being a secretary," she says, laughing. "I thought, *If this is what I'm going to be doing for the rest of my life, I might as well end it now*." At age twenty-four, she and a girlfriend quit their jobs, sold all their belongings, and signed up to work in Saudi Arabia. Then at the last minute, the Saudi government refused their visas. "I thought, *I have to have a plan B here*. Hand-painted clothing was in vogue. A Vancouver company had started doing it, but I thought I could do a better job than they could — so I did."

Her clothing design business in Vancouver lasted for about four years, selling casual funwear, hand-painted clothes, and custom graphics, artwork, and promotional garments for resorts and companies. Her contractors were her downfall. "Unfortunately, I was very small and very young and naive, and the people who were contracting my work were much larger," she recalls. They undermined her success by delivering orders late and wooing away her clients.

De Martigny folded the company and paid off all her debts. Far from warning her off, the experience helped her lose her fear of failure. "I've already been there, and it's not a big scary thing, really. I was more terrified of it then, but after you experience it, it's not frightening anymore."

She worked for a high-end retail chain for a year and a half and then seized the opportunity to enter an aboriginal design contest sponsored by the Canadian Council for Aboriginal Business.

"It was the first time the Council created a public awareness of aboriginal designers," she says. "The fashion show at the Art Gallery of Ontario blew a lot of people away because no one knew we did that kind of stuff."

While de Martigny didn't place in the contest, she had the opportunity to take a two-year internship in the design division of the Canadian Apparel Federation, an Ottawa-based organization that promotes Canadian designers nationally and internationally. Then she decided she'd had enough promoting other people's designs.

De Martigny is happy about her progress. The only difficult part has been dealing with bankers, whom she finds patronizing. De Martigny faces an extra hurdle in obtaining financing because she is based on a reserve, which means that there are no assets for the bank to secure.

Her bank addresses all materials to John, much to de Martigny's annoyance. "And when I do go in to talk to our manager, it's clear that the bank expects us to be making a huge profit. I say to them, *How many businesses do you know that are making money in the first year?* And the response is, *Well, that's not the point. The point is that's not how we finance things.* Their service charges are just about killing us. Clearly, they make no effort to help us."

De Martigny believes this attitude is a stew of racial discrimination, gender discrimination, and bank policy. "Their policies are not there to help small business. The amount of money we have with them is ridiculously small. It's an inability on their part to see the larger picture. They just want as much profit as they can possibly get. If they can bleed a small company dry, they will."

To start her business, she received $30,000 in debt financing — half of what she asked for — from an aboriginal new ventures loan and a small business loan for equipment. Aboriginal Business Canada also helped finance some small marketing projects and helped Spirit Ware get on the Internet, but the funds were designated for marketing, not capital. "There's money to market yourself to death but you need capital," says de Martigny.

"When an article came out about us in the community paper, a private investor saw it. He was trying to find a local business that needed his help, and he showed up on our doorstep. I almost fell over when I found out what he was here for."

She loves being an entrepreneur because of the opportunity to travel and the sense of self-worth that it gives her. "You're doing this on your own, and you can take a lot of pride in what you've accomplished," she says. "I've had a lot of lousy managers and bosses in my lifetime. Not having someone stand over you and criticize you — I just love that part of it."

Her goal is to make a comfortable living and to be recognized for her designs. "I'm not where I want to be, as far as business goes. I'd like us to be making more money and be more established. I'm really impatient in that respect, even though people say, *Look what you've done already*. It's not enough." She's aiming for half a million dollars in revenue a year; then she can pay her bills and take a holiday.

Being female is an advantage for an entrepreneur, she thinks. "Women get far more done in a day than men can," she says. "I can have ten different things on the go. Men just don't have the capacity to that. And as wonderful as John is, if I had to hire him, I wouldn't." She laughs. "But I didn't have his baby because he's a good worker."

PROBLEM: STRESS

Being an entrepreneur is like setting your head on fire and trying to put it out with a pinhead hammer.

— Anonymous

Having your own business is serious pressure.

— Ellie Rubin

I've had sleepless nights, but I'm still here.

— Sarah Band

Employees quit suddenly. Your bank makes worried noises about your accounts receivable. An important client stops buying. The landlord doubles the rent. Your partner complains that he never sees you. You have unexplained inventory shrinkage. You go from being overwhelmed to immobilized. Suddenly, nothing is going as planned.

For Louisa Nedkoff, who has been an entrepreneur for three years, it's one thing to make the jump into entrepreneurship, but once in, there's the stress and fear of constantly facing new challenges.

"You're operating outside your comfort zone all the time, doing things you've never done before," she says. "That was the thing I found the most difficult to get past — the fear ... even identifying it. As soon as you know that you're scared out of your mind, then you can deal with getting past the fear."

Once stresses like these wreaked havoc on Brenda Schiedel's peace of mind, but now they're simply tugs on her sleeve. When she was twenty-five years old, stress had far more authority in her life than it does today, even though her company was a molehill compared to the mountain it is today. "The stress came from not knowing how to deal with problems," she said. "Things bothered me more then. But as you get older, you learn how to deal with problems and forget them and go on, instead of going over and over them in your mind."

What causes stress is dwelling on mistakes and undertaking multiple tasks that you couldn't possibly complete in a twenty-four-hour period, and sleep too. Schiedel is philosophical about her past. Frequently, her life was out of balance. "Now I have far more responsibilities. In my lifetime, I couldn't possibly pay back the money I owe if something happened to the business. But I don't feel the stress nearly as much."

Her learned ability to deal with stress has helped her manage staff more effectively. Schiedel knows which employees are feeling stress, and it's usually the younger ones. She helps them learn to segregate and prioritize tasks under A, B, and C categories. "Anything under C, you're not ever going to do, so just forget about it," she advises.

Ellie Rubin has developed her own way of sorting the straw from the stress: her "postcard." "Your postcard is what you want to achieve in one month, two years, and five years. Detail it. Paint your postcard. See your postcard," Rubin advises. "When you're sitting there in a meeting that's not going well and everything's falling apart, just remember your postcard and walk toward it. It sounds ridiculous, but it really works. Every time I don't do it, things don't turn out the way I want. Every time I do it, I get there way faster."

In short, stress is something that with practice, you can choose to rake away from your line of vision. Once it's cleared away, what's left is opportunity and, if you dig a little deeper, an incredible sense of satisfaction.

JULIE'S STORY

Julie DiLorenzo, thirty-three, describes Devon International as "specializing in difficult work." Devon is a Toronto-based real estate development company with a specialized skill in concrete structural work. While this specialty produces only a small part of Devon's overall revenues, it has given the company a high profile in a valued niche market, resulting in projects like the angled concrete skeletal structure for the Bata Shoe Museum in Toronto.

The company's mainstay business is development: land is purchased and developed, then marketed. Once clients are secured, commercial, industrial, or residential building begins. Development revenues approximate $40 million over a two- to three-year development cycle.

Julie incorporated her business when she was eighteen years old, as soon as she graduated from high school. She reasoned that she could handle a full-time job running her company while taking a university degree in medieval history and philosophy.

"But when it came to finishing an assignment or dealing with a bank manager who was calling my loan, I always picked the bank manager," she says. She stopped attending classes altogether in the third year of her degree.

"I still feel insecure about my lack of education," she says. "But the boom in real estate had started, and my business needed me. I couldn't let go."

Julie's workday starts at eight in the morning and often goes until ten o'clock at night. In certain critical phases of a development project, like marketing a project to prospective customers, she works seven days a week. "Socially, I need a lot of patience from my friends," she says, referring to her reputation for canceling engagements at the last minute and "no showing" on others.

Julie is a business partner with two men, one her ex-husband. "I'm very lucky," she says. "We weren't compatible married, but we make great business partners."

The three have clear divisions in responsibilities. Julie's job is financial management. "I'm accountable for what we're doing tomorrow. I draw the box, and they fill it in." Her ex is the project developer. The third partner is the on-site manager. Together, they employ forty people, twenty-five of whom are currently working in Taiwan on a 400-unit residential condominium.

She has stayed on the stomach-wrenching roller-coaster ride through the real estate boom in the eighties and the bust in the bleak nineties. In the eighties, she earned a six-figure income; but since 1991, she hasn't drawn a paycheque. The villain was a promising development project that went belly up and proceeded to lose several million dollars.

"Once a project starts bleeding, the hemorrhage continues for years," says Julie, with the practiced calm of a surgeon. "But I've learned that when you're in trouble, you have to keep the negatives at 50 percent of your energy or you can't stay afloat. Now we're in the position where 80 percent is positive and 20 percent is negative. It's getting better."

PROBLEM: GETTING FINANCING

All they can do is take my home.

— Marnie Walker

Expect nothing from the banks. They have imbeciles working for them.

— Bonnie Bickel

Despite the growing number of women entrepreneurs and their reported success rate, you must be prepared for the possibility of a refusal based on discrimination alone.

— Business Development Bank of Canada

Bankers, lawyers, and accountants are not businesspeople. Don't let them tell you how to run your business.

— Carol Denman

When banks suggest that one of my clients bring in an equity partner, it's like suggesting to a single woman that she get married so she can buy a bigger house.

— Paula Jubinville

When Carol Denman, president of Atchison & Denman Court Reporting, was asked by a bank to speak about what she would do differently if she had to do it all over again, she told her audience that she would start her own bank: the Little Ladies Bank for Ladies' Little Businesses.

She was alluding to her frequent experiences of being on the receiving end of comments like *Oh, you have a little business!* When the moderator, a bank employee, stood up to thank her, he acknowledged he could relate to her story, since his wife also had a "little business."

Today, as owner of a company that generates $2 million in sales annually, Denman takes great delight in asking her bank manager how things are going at his little bank.

Joanne Thomas Yacatto, president of Women and Money Inc., had a similar experience. She recently put together a business plan asking for an operating line of credit of $40,000 for business expansion purposes. "I sat back with my arms folded across my chest, waiting with bated breath for discrimination. I've got one of those kinds of businesses that banks hate with a passion: no assets except the ones between my ears. If I crap out, then what are you going to do, honey?"

Within forty-eight hours, her request was approved, not by her account manager but by a credit manager from risk management. The credit manager happened to be in the branch, and the account manager introduced him to Yacatto.

"I thanked him for his vote of confidence and said I understood that mine is the kind of business that banks don't feel comfortable underwriting. He turned to me and said, *No problem. That's quite a nice little hobby you got going for yourself there.* Discrimination? Clearly not. Instead, pat on the head. Cute little girl. Nice little hobby."

Yacatto was rendered speechless. "My account manager stood there with her mouth open, she was so stunned. He walked out of the office, not knowing that anything had taken place."

The credit manager's behavior is what Yacatto calls gender bias — an attitude that individuals develop from the cumulative experiences of their lives. Often, people aren't conscious of their bias. Yacatto learned in one of her training sessions with bankers that a "leg loan" is a term used for a loan given to an attractive woman, confirming that gender bias was so prevalent that a label had been created for it.

According to a 1996 study prepared for the Canadian Bankers Association by Thompson Lightstone & Company Limited, the types of businesses most likely to report that they do not have any business financing include businesses owned by women. "I love it when people say to me, *Women don't go into manufacturing*," says Karen Fraser, author of *Women Like Me,* an entrepreneurial networking directory. "Give us some money and we would. It's kind of hard to open a manufacturing plant with $10,000."

> Female entrepreneurs are less likely to borrow from banks or other financial institutions (25 percent) than male entrepreneurs (36 percent), and rely more heavily on personal savings (69 percent) and credit cards (52 percent).[3]

She indignantly recalls a conversation with a vice president at one of the big banks who questioned Fraser's assertion that women-owned businesses have a stronger survival record than men's. "I won't use names, so we'll call him Mr. Pompous," she says. "He said, *Women aren't that much better than men.* I pointed out to him that the banks don't give us enough money or advice; our friends and family think we're nuts; and suppliers won't take a chance on us. Still, we do better than the men. What would happen if you *helped* us? He said, *I didn't think of that.*"

Small and medium-sized enterprises, defined by the Lightstone study as companies with revenues of $50 million (although most of these companies have sales under $5 million) do not borrow large sums of money. In 1995, almost half of these businesses sought less than $25,000. The difference between men and women entrepreneurs in their appetite for debt is startling: the average dollar amount requested by women entrepreneurs was $40,000, in stark comparison to their male counterparts' average request of $280,000. The study suggests that this disparity is due to the smaller size of women's businesses.

Despite the furor in recent years about the reluctance of banks to lend to small business in Canada, statistics do not back up the assertion that banks have turned their backs on this market. The study found that 73 percent of small and medium-sized businesses had their financing requests approved in full. However, women-owned businesses were less likely than men's to receive approvals: only 69 percent received the financing they asked for, despite account managers' claims that they approved female entrepreneurs' financing requests as frequently as they did those of male entrepreneurs.

Why is this? Not because of discrimination, says the study, but because of the characteristics of women-owned businesses. They tend to be new companies, smaller by sales volume and employee numbers, and concentrated in the accommodation, food, beverage, retail, and "other services" sectors, which experience lower financing approval rates because of the risk banks associate with them. "In other words," says the study, "the higher turndown level is related to the business case merit of the application and not to the gender of the owner."

In light of this higher turndown rate, one of the most surprising findings in the Lightstone study was that women entrepreneurs express greater satisfaction with their primary bank contact than do their male counterparts. It appears that this satisfaction exists despite lower service levels: "While females receive fewer contacts from their account manager or officer to discuss business or banking matters, female owners are mostly satisfied with the number of calls and visits they receive and do not request more."

"I think women have a double whammy," says Paula Jubinville, whose company, Aqueous, provides consulting services to entrepreneurs. "Entrepreneurs aren't taken seriously by banks because in many cases their business proposals are being evaluated by people who have a job. There's no shared reality. It would be like me looking at Greek, which I can't read, and offering editorial comments. On top of all this, women aren't taken seriously."

Charlie Coffey looks like a banker — the archetypal fifty-something, gray-haired Royal Bank executive — but the differences become noticeable when he takes from his pocket a small slate rock, painted by Natalie Rostad. With the coaxing of ink and paint, the lines of the rock have offered up the outlines of a native woman and her baby, and the outline of a bird. It is wonderfully tactile, and Coffey is smitten with both it and the artist.

Coffey actually chuckles sympathetically when Christina Temple, a woman entrepreneur, makes a snide joke about banks and their ineffectiveness. He adds that "bankers do have some trouble with — "

"Creative types like me," interrupts Temple, and Coffey bursts out laughing, his enjoyment evident.

Coffey's interest is moving entrepreneurial businesses from their early stages into commercial enterprises, and ultimately to an initial public offering. He's especially interested in the women's market because of its growth, and because he believes that the banking industry has not done a very good job in meeting this niche market's needs.

To date, only the Royal Bank and the Bank of Montreal have openly targeted women entrepreneurs as a niche market. Kelly Shaughnessy, senior vice president of small business banking at CIBC, says that his bank doesn't distinguish small business needs by gender. "I've been working with small and medium-sized businesses for twenty-five years," says Shaughnessy. "And all the successful women I've met say that they don't want to be treated any differently."

Which is just fine by Charlie Coffey, who sees the market as having both special needs and potential. In his view, women face different problems in obtaining financing than men. "I've heard too many stories and heard from too many entrepreneurs who have had difficulty for one reason or another," he says. "Women are subject to language like *Dear* or *Get your husband or father to sign* and other patronizing stuff."

Coffey has hard cold business reasons to be concerned about this. "Let's not forget what my reason for existence is," he says. "To enhance shareholder value. The issue for me is that more and more businesses are being started by women. We've got to be there, and we're not going to let Bank of Montreal or any other organization dominate that market or that issue," he says.

Coffey's value is his networking skills and his ability to connect women entrepreneurs with others who can help them. While attending a function at the Canadian Youth Business Foundation,[4] Coffey bumped into retailer Sarah Band, and they started talking about issues facing retailers. Coffey suggested that they host a dinner for a group of women retailers and that he would supply an adviser who could talk about retail market strategies. Other than a bout of bank-bashing from the audience — Coffey winces at the memory — the evening was very well received.

He also refers women to organizations like Business Centurions, a group that connects investors and advisers with entrepreneurs. "It's very simple stuff," he says. "It's called networks. When I make an introduction, it may not have a direct impact on her bottom line, but we're seen to be adding value, and networks are really what it's all about."

The Royal Bank and CIBC are co-founders of the Canadian Youth Business Foundation (CYBF), whose goal is to help youth create their own businesses by creating the rare opportunity for entrepreneurs to access what CIBC's Shaughnessy calls "patient capital." "If you're starting a new business, the last thing you want is a bank or anyone as an equity partner. Most small businesses want a five- or seven-year loan with no payments for the first year or interest only. That's what I mean by patient capital. We're attempting to address that need through the CYBF."

"Banks are useless," says Louisa Nedkoff. "I wanted a $5,000 line of credit, and the bank said, *Sure, we'll give you a $5,000 line of credit as long as you give us $5,000.*" Furious, Nedkoff argued back and won her $5,000 line without depositing the required amount.

Canadian banks have consistently received bad raps and bum reviews from small business owners, including women entrepreneurs. But sometimes these negative outcomes can be mitigated and even prevented by the financing applicant herself.

"I think some women do themselves a disservice when they go for bank financing," says Dianna Rhodes, head of Rhodes Accessories and president of the Canadian Association of Women Executives and Entrepreneurs. "They don't prepare themselves well enough, and sometimes they're not optimistic enough about their business."

Jo-Anne Raynes is CIBC's vice president of knowledge-based businesses, with extensive experience as a corporate lender. Today she deals exclusively with companies whose assets are expertise (often a technology or technology application) rather than hard assets. Although women migrate heavily to service-based industries, Raynes knows of very few women entrepreneurs in the technology sector, which is treated differently from a financing standpoint because of its burgeoning need for equity capital. To meet their needs, Raynes uses her network of venture capitalists, her debt-financing capability, and a $100 million equity fund that CIBC has established for this sector. This is her summary of what banks need to see before they can approve financing:

- a business plan;
- a marketing plan;
- a real sense that the people know what they're going to do;
- management skills; and
- the ability to build a management team of good people.

If the company is technology based, Raynes wants to know about the technology — what market niche it fits into, what makes it different from other technologies, how "mission critical" it is to customers, how innovative the technology is, the company's research and development strengths, and plans for growth and accessing equity capital.

Tracey De Leeuw, who is in the extraordinary situation of having a major Canadian bank as an equity partner, received no financing from banks to start up her business. "I had a knowledge-based business before banks had ever heard of the term," she says. "Now that I know what they're looking for, I realize I wasn't giving information to them in a way that they're used to seeing it. I didn't know that then, nor could I have put it in that kind of format."

She says she never walked away from a bank or financing opportunity thinking that she didn't get financing because she was a woman. "They didn't understand my business because it didn't fit the mold," she says. "I didn't have a formal education, and my credit rating was getting messy because of my divorce. When my husband went bankrupt, the bank had my signature on those debts, and they came after me. I ended up with 100 percent of the debt."

How Small and Medium-Size Enterprises Finance Their Businesses

Financial institutions	51 percent
Credit cards	44 percent
Retained earnings	40 percent
Personal savings	39 percent
Supplier credit	38 percent
Personal loans	28 percent
Government loans/grants	15 percent
Loans from friends/relatives	12 percent
No business financing	9 percent
Other private loans	4 percent
Public equity	1 percent
Export financing	1 percent
Venture capital	1 percent

Source: Lightstone Study (1996), Canadian Banking Association

Women appear to be more averse about taking on debt than men, particularly in the formative years of the company. This aversion may explain in part why women-owned companies are smaller: they are preoccupied with avoiding or getting rid of debt. This aversion can actually stunt a company's potential if it takes the owner's attention away from growth opportunities.

Audrey Vrooman, a banker with Scotiabank, has worked with commercial businesses for the past two decades, and believes that the main challenge for women entrepreneurs seeking financing is to understand what banks can and cannot do, and how they make lending decisions. Banks, she says, can't meet the financial needs of all businesses. They typically extend short-term credit in the form of loans, revolving credit agreements, and lines of credit. Often a fledgling entrepreneur is better off relying on "angels," private investors acquired through the entrepreneur's own efforts. Venture capital firms are another, rarer alternative, interested only if they see the opportunity for substantial profit.

Why not banks? "Because banks lend within a very narrow band of risk. We have to because we're lending depositors' money," Vrooman says. "For every hundred lending decisions we make, ninety-nine have to be right." A venture capital firm, in contrast, may be content with thirty successes out of every hundred investment decisions, she suggests, because of a higher payback.

Most account managers can approve loans of up to $50,000 independently, but they know that they will be second-guessed on their decisions. And so if you are faced with a negative account manager, know that it is his or her decision and not necessarily the view of his or her superior or that of another bank. Go up the bureaucracy. Ask to speak to the small business advocate. Or go elsewhere. One person's risk assessment is not law.

Entrepreneurs can reduce the bank's assessment of risk and improve their chances of receiving financing by understanding what banks call the Five Cs of Credit. This, explains Vrooman, is the internal checklist a bank compares the entrepreneur against in making a financing decision.

Character

Good character indicates that you will repay your indebtedness. It is expressed by a professional presentation of yourself, your business plan, and no sign of desperation. Wanting a loan in order to reach greater pinnacles of success is more attractive to banks than needing it to survive.

Credit History

Some women with new businesses don't even try to get financing from banks because they believe they have to have a business track record to set foot into an account manager's office. Not true, says Vrooman. To a banker, an individual's management of her personal financial affairs is an important consideration in the decision to extend credit to her business.

Many women begin their businesses with no personal credit history because all loans and credit cards have been issued in their husbands' names, or they may have a poor credit history because of job loss or marriage breakdown, both infamous for disrupting one's credit rating.

"These are very common situations," says Vrooman. "So even if you're happily married, get your own credit rating. If your marriage ends, take care of your own financial obligations first and handle your joint obligations the best way you can." Although failure to meet joint obligations negatively affects your credit rating, the fact that you have a separate, healthy record of repaying your own obligations goes a long way to validating marriage breakdown as the cause of your current credit difficulties.

Job loss through downsizing has huge financial impact during an individual's transition from employment to self-employment, and Vrooman says that banks look for people's best efforts in finding a solution. "Bankruptcy, however, is a lot harder for banks to overlook," she adds.

When seeking to establish or reestablish a credit rating, don't overlook your suppliers. "If they give you credit, use them as a reference," suggests Vrooman. To establish a credit rating, she also recommends saving several thousand dollars and then using it as collateral for a credit line for the same amount. Of course, in typical Catch-22 fashion, this tactic is best used when you have no need for a credit line.

Capital

Capital is the money already in your business and the sum of your company's debt and equity. Debt is a loan. Equity is the money supplied by you, the owner. Banks will look to your financial statements to see how much capital you have — and the more, the better.

Banks want you to invest in your business. If you don't want to risk your own capital, it makes it difficult for them to stomach the risk of a loan. "Fundamentally, risks are for the entrepreneur to take, not the bank," says Vrooman. "After all, the entrepreneur is the one who stands to benefit, and it's the entrepreneur who controls the business. Banks are there essentially to finance timing gaps."

Cash Flow

Cash flow summarizes where your business's money has come from and where it has gone. It is important to banks because it is the source of loan repayment. Banks look at cash flow generated in the past, what is projected over the next twelve months, and the business plan to back up the projections.

Banks are good at separating the hope from the reality, the straw from the chaff. "We see a lot of businesses and business plans," says Vrooman. "So we know a lot about the entrepreneur's competition and their revenues and costs, and we look for a margin of error. If some projections don't happen, and the margin of error is slender, that's a riskier proposition. If it's slender but the entrepreneur has deep pockets (well capitalized), then it eases our concern somewhat."

If the business is growing and needs more capital, it is better to approach a bank when the company is not completely tapped out of capital.

Collateral

Collateral is the bank's assurance that if your company fails, there are assets that can be sold to pay off your indebtedness to them. A secured loan has collateral behind it. An unsecured loan does not, and is not usually available to entrepreneurs.

Liquidation of assets is rarely at face value. By the time the bank has to realize on its collateral, it will have lost much of its value.

"Banks don't want inventory. They want my house and my child," says Sarah Band, only half joking. For most people, their largest asset is their home, and if the woman is married, the husband must also pledge the home as collateral.

Vrooman finds that many women are offended when banks ask for the husband's signature, but the request is necessary because the home is a matrimonial asset. "But you won't get a loan simply based on the equity in your home because banks do not want to realize on this asset," says Vrooman. "You should have cash or personal assets or business assets."

Conditions

Every loan agreement has conditions set out, which the borrower is expected to comply with. "They're necessary to the bank to stay informed of what the business is doing. They're an integral part of our monitoring and risk assessment process," says Vrooman. "A lot of customers don't attach importance to them. You should read them and feel comfortable that you can comply with them. If there are conditions that are too onerous, by all means negotiate, but don't ignore them."

Banks expect debtors to communicate with them regularly so that they are assured that the conditions are being met. To them, silence is ominous.

Brenda Schiedel, who has a positive banking relationship, overcommunicates with her bank. "We've always given them reams of information. They know the new products that are coming down the tube; they know the markets we're going into, our big orders and our success stories. So there have been no surprises, and they stuck with us through thick and thin, through three major crunches."

The first crunch was an inventory problem. A significant inventory waste was not recorded, and at the end of the year, she discovered $100,000 less in inventory than she had expected. At the time, this was a huge blow, cutting $100,000 cleanly off the bottom line. The other two crunches came when her business growth exceeded her cash flow: "We didn't have enough cash, and we had to cover our payables before our receivables came in. In response, I had to give the bank a lot of information, tell them why it happened and why it wouldn't happen again."

Sherry Fotheringham of the Royal Bank offers the following tips to maximize your chances of getting a loan.

Make sure your personal finances are in order and your credit record is clean

A black mark on your credit record can reduce your chances of obtaining a loan or credit card. Fotheringham suggests checking your credit record at least one month before applying for a credit card or loan. If you find a black mark or inaccuracies, talk to the credit bureau about how you can fix it. Be prepared to provide your lender with information about the cause, extent, and resolution of the problem.

One way to elevate your credit score is to make payments promptly. Department store cards are not as highly regarded as bank credit cards because approval standards are less stringent. But they are better than no credit history at all.

Be discriminating about credit

The more loans and credit cards you apply for over a short period of time, the lower your credit score will be. Lenders interpret frequent requests as a sign of desperation, says Fotheringham, and will see you as a high risk. Six or more applications over six months is considered excessive.

Deal with a lender who understands your business and is genuinely interested in you

Shop around until you find a lender you like and respect. Update him or her about your successes and setbacks on an ongoing basis. Try to anticipate your short-term needs and discuss them before you actually need the loan.

Learn to read financial statements and understand business concepts and develop a business plan

In Coffey's experience, the entrepreneur's weakness is generally finance. There is an abundance of courses available through local community colleges and university business faculties. Ask other entrepreneurs which courses they recommend.

Limit the use of your personal savings to finance the business

Although injecting equity into your business is a general requirement, women tend to use the majority of their savings to start their businesses before approaching a lender for outside financing. You may need to use your savings during the start-up months when you won't be able to draw a salary, or during the low periods of the business.

Establish a credit history for the business as soon as possible

Using personal credit cards and credit lines to finance business expenses does little to establish the credit rating of the business. Establish a business credit history to increase the success of future requests to lenders and investors.

Be flexible and consider alternatives to your initial loan request

No matter how skilled or impressive their business ideas, many women face obstacles such as the absence of a credit rating, poor credit status due to divorce or other setbacks, or recent arrival in Canada. These circumstances make it difficult to obtain credit without a co-signer. Find out about existing programs that offer alternatives to traditional bank lending (see Resource Directory).

Do banks discriminate against women? No, says Yacatto. "The media go a long way to perpetuate the idea that banks discriminate against women, but we don't know if it's true or not. I don't believe it is."

Indeed, much of women's dissatisfaction with banks seem to focus on financial rather than gender issues. Bonnie Bickel, of B. B. Bargoons, is contemptuous of banks, but this feeling blossomed after her much-liked bank manager retired after representing her needs for fifteen years. In fact, it was during this positive relationship that Bickel agreed to be a spokesperson for her bank in an advertisement. But times change.

"My bank is awful," she says flatly. "And it costs too much to switch to another." Her two bankruptcies did not cost her bank a cent, but the relationship seems to have been irreparably damaged. Recently, when Bickel asked to set up a $25,000 letter of credit for her suppliers, depositing the money in full to back the request up, the bank wouldn't okay it.

The retailer Sarah Band has made her peace with her bank and believes that it is a level playing field for both men and women entrepreneurs. "All banks really want to do is to make certain that their loans are going to be covered, that your bank overdraft is going to be paid off, that you know what you're going to do, and that if you do go T-U [tits up], you have a house they can claim."

Band helped create this peace through a scorched-earth strategy. One day, the account manager called Band to tell her she was in overdraft by $400. "I just screamed at her. I said, *Do you guys really think I'm going to take off for $400!* I just went after her. I told her to get a grip. She said, *Well, it's my manager,* and I said, *I don't give a shit about your manager.* And she backed right off.

"The other day she phoned and said, *You're over your line. Can I take some out of this account and put it in there?* I said sure. You have to find somebody who understands. These guys never come out and see what you do. They don't see how hard you're working. Bankers should hit the street and see what people actually do."

DELORES'S STORY

Delores Lawrence is the president of two Canadian companies: NHI Nursing and Homemakers, created in 1983 when she was twenty-nine, and NHI Personnel, created in 1994. Lawrence has 1,200 people on her regular payroll and employs fifteen people in head office.

NHI Nursing and Homemakers provides home care and respite care in private homes. "Respite" means that exhausted family members get a break from caring for a family member. The company also provides supplemental staff like nurses to hospitals on a per diem basis.

Lawrence, a nurse by training, wasn't worried about the risk when she started her business in 1983. "I saw an aging population, and I knew there was no way the government could go on without making home care part of the health care system. I *knew* it would be successful." Her bank, however, was less optimistic.

Lawrence was raised in Jamaica. Her parents owned a small grocery store, a tavern, a restaurant, a dry goods store, and a haberdashery. She saw little of her entrepreneurial father, an importer/exporter who traveled extensively, while her mother ran the businesses and impressed her daughter with her know-how.

Lawrence's self-confidence is huge and unshakable. In grade school, she was always the first person to put her hand up. She excelled in sports, always wanted to be captain, and was convinced she could do anything.

"I'm a leader," she says. "If I'm going to get involved, I have to be one of the decision makers. To my mind, everyone is either a leader or a follower. If I were in politics, I wouldn't be happy being a back-bencher. I'd have to be premier or prime minister. What thrills me is being my own boss. I hate people in power unless I'm one of the them."

The family moved to Belleville, Ontario, when Lawrence was fifteen. She was popular and outgoing, and won the title of Snow Queen one year, a victory Lawrence enjoys recalling immensely — the first black snow queen in white Belleville.

After graduating from high school, she obtained a nursing degree. Four months into her first job, she knew she detested staff nursing. "I didn't like the patients talking to me," she says. "So I went into intensive care, where the patients are ventilated and sedated and you totally control them."

During the four years that followed, Lawrence took her bachelor of arts degree, married, and had her first child. Then she was offered a position at Sunnybrook Hospital as a nursing supervisor. "I was considered a whippersnapper. I got the job when I was twenty-six years old, one of the youngest administrative personnel in the country. I worked there for six years, although I was bored after the first three. I thought, *There's got to be more to life.* I'd almost reached the top of my profession, but I didn't *like* nursing. Doctors are always making the decisions, and I resented the way they treated nurses. I decided I had to move on."

Knowledge is opportunity, and her supervisory job dropped a gold nugget into her lap. Lawrence realized that there were not enough home care agencies and that she was always struggling with fewer staff than she could have used. "I went home and told my husband about my idea to start my own agency. He thought I was crazy, but I did it anyway."

Lawrence told her employer she was setting up an agency on the side; initially, there was no negative reaction. "But then I started ticking off the people in the hospital. They had thought I was going to be doing something little. Instead, they saw me making a lot of money. The revenues my first year were $250,000; my second year's were $500,000; and I had margins of over 35 percent."

Lawrence operated this burgeoning business out of her home in Markham until neighbors called the municipality to complain about the number of cars parked on the street from employees coming to pick up their paycheques. Lawrence moved the business to a commercial space and hired a manager. For the next two years, she burned the candle at both ends: working full-time, managing her business, and trying to maintain her sanity. Finally, her accountant said, "Delores, you've got to make a decision. You have to give up your job or give up your business." It was an easy decision.

Lawrence loves her job because she is accountable to no one, which may be why dealing with the bank has been so difficult for her. But her biggest challenge has been racial discrimination. She has found that women of color have an especially difficult time getting clients and access to capital.

In the early years, she needed the bank's facilities more than the bank needed her, so she had to play ball. By putting up $25,000 in bonds as collateral, she received a $25,000 credit line. It's only been in the last three years that the bank even considered her receivables as collateral.

Her banking relationship today is to her liking, but Lawrence put a lot of energy into making it that way. "I have had to be strong willed because they weren't always nice. And I had to constantly prove myself to keep my line of credit, in spite of giving them all the collateral they wanted."

At one stage, when her revenues escalated almost overnight from $200,000 to $500,000, Lawrence asked for an increase in her line of credit. "The bank wanted every single thing I ever owned," she said. "They asked for $1 million more in guarantees that they didn't need, and I had no choice. I gave it to them. They were oversecured; it was embarrassing."

Since then, the bank has reduced its talon hold on her assets and deals mainly with her receivables. "I had to prove myself, and until I did that, they treated me like a second-class citizen," she says. But Lawrence is not one to suffer fools gladly. No doubt she has been the cause of some wound-licking at her branch. "I've been called aggressive," she admits cheerfully. "If I were a man, I'd be called assertive."

Lawrence's biggest complaint is the bank's lack of understanding of her business, and their cold feet, which can turn into ice blocks within seconds. In the late eighties, when Lawrence needed money to meet the payroll, the bank balked and a couple of good friends lent her $50,000. "The bank didn't understand why I needed a cash flow in the business I was in," she recalls.

Her account manager changes every year, and every year she sits across from someone new who doesn't understand her business. She solved this problem by insisting the bank keep her business plan on file, and that each account manager read it before he picks up the phone.

And it's always a "he," since Lawrence had a series of negative experiences with female account managers. "They were pushy and jealous. They'd ask, *Why do you need all these properties?*"

RISK

When people look at women entrepreneurs, they see something they don't understand. They ask, Why would you want to do this, and how could you do it with all of these other commitments that you have?

— Paula Jubinville

Accept that this is something you have to do.

— Susan Steinberg

Companies throw you out when you turn fifty.

— Marnie Walker

To fear is one thing. To let fear grab you by the tail and swing you around is another.

— Katherine Paterson,
Jacob Have I Loved (1980)

If entrepreneurship is risky business, then a hell of a lot of people have developed an affection for financial bungee jumping. Ralph McLeod, an adviser with Business Centurions, helps individuals find equity or employment opportunities in small to medium-size enterprises. He notes that approximately 20 percent of outplaced persons end up as entrepreneurs — either out of necessity or desire.

The fact is that after the tenth time on the roller coaster, those sheer drops, shifts, and upturns in a business lose their sickening hold on one's stomach. Risktaking is implicit to success. Successful women accept the risk as part and parcel of life. They don't succumb to their fears of inching out on a limb by themselves, often without a husband, a guaranteed job, or other security blankets. Their philosophy is that all of life is risky, that security is a myth, that if you wait until everything's safe, you'll never do it.

Paula Jubinville goes blank at the suggestion that entrepreneurship is risky. "I feel more out of control when important decisions are being made by someone else," she says of the typical employment situation. "Do you feel better when you're driving the car or when you're a passenger? Entrepreneurs jump out of their skins sitting in the passenger seat."

Brenda Schiedel agrees. "The biggest difference between me and an employee is that I have control. Whether I make the right decisions or the wrong decisions, I'm in control of my destiny, whereas so many employees feel out of control. They see things that are wrong in their company, but they're powerless to make changes."

"Risk won't kill me," says Tracey De Leeuw. While she believes wholeheartedly that she will succeed as long as she continues along the path she has laid out, this is not blind faith. She is absolutely unflinching in her consideration of the worst-case scenario.

"Yes, it would be tough to recover if the company I was building died, but then I could certainly consult for other companies. The worst case is fine because I'm not in this to make a million dollars. I'm in it to make it happen. By the year 2000, I believe our sales will be a billion dollars, but that's completely dependent on whether the customer wants to buy. I can master an Excel spreadsheet, but I can't make the customer buy."

What is risk? It's a ghost crouched in the corner of a dark room. "If you put ten women in a room, you'll get ten different definitions of risk," says Susan Steinberg, a Toronto career transition consultant. Loosely defined, risk is the surrender of certainty. How much certainty one needs in one's life is very personal. You either like the idea that your survival depends on your own efforts, or you don't.

The fear of risk is what prevents women from becoming entrepreneurs and what prevents entrepreneurs from making the big decisions necessary to propel the business forward. Risk realized is failure, but the definition of failure varies from woman to woman.

Grace White, the president of CanJam Trading Ltd., a Halifax-based international distributor of frozen foods with sales in excess of $13.5 million, sees her risks as both personal and financial. "If I failed, I would lose my personal earnings, my future earnings, and my investment in the company," she says. On the personal side, she risks losing her self-confidence and even her sense of self. She mitigates risks by soaking up knowledge, keeping overhead at a minimum, capitalizing on her strengths, and delegating her weaknesses to others.

Leaving a senior position at Bell Canada was a difficult decision for Marnie Walker. "I was well paid, and it was a safety net. It took me about six months to stop worrying about going bankrupt. Then I realized that I would have to work for three years as an employee to make what I was earning in six months as my own boss. Mind you, I was reinvesting the money in the company."

What follows is a menu of the risks entrepreneurs choose to face:

Losing your shirt
You will be stripped of everything you own if the business doesn't succeed.

Losing your edge
Competitors will copy or improve what makes your business different or unique. Customers will change their minds about what they want in your product or service.

Losing sight of the bigger picture
Changing regulatory laws, including environmental laws, close down your business overnight. Cultures, laws, and customs in new markets turn what is a winning formula in your home market into a dud.

Losing your talent
Your best people leave.

Losing your grip
You can't get out of bed one morning.

Many women struggle with perfectionism, and the risk of not achieving this supernatural standard is eventually too much to bear. "But if you only did 50 percent of what you wanted to achieve, would it not still be amazing?" asks Steinberg. "It's very hard to overcome the fear of stepping outside your comfort zone into the unknown, because you know you may not do as well as you want to do.

"Ask yourself, how far am I willing to go?" she advises. "Don't compare yourself with others. You don't have to go all the way. It's okay just to put your toe in the water."

A 1993 study of the sex differences in risktaking[5] suggests that women are more risk averse than men because of lower self-confidence. "They [females] cannot seem to maintain confidence without explicit positive feedback; without such feedback they tend to assume they are not doing well." This trait, says the study's author, makes it harder for females to undertake potentially risky ventures. "In contrast," the author adds with the faintest tinge of irony, "males tend to maintain confidence in themselves *despite* feedback."

Successful entrepreneurial women have acknowledged and used this fear rather than succumbing to it. "Fear is why so many entrepreneurs are successful," says Brenda Schiedel. "Because they're afraid, they work hard. There's a big difference between spending someone else's money and spending your own. You become more cautious, and you gather more information. Everyone says entrepreneurs are risktakers, but they're actually more careful than anyone I know. It's their own money on the line — their future and their job."

Andrina Lever, past-president of Women Entrepreneurs of Canada, agrees that most women entrepreneurs don't see themselves as risktakers. "They are, but in a controlled way. I know it sounds like an oxymoron, but they won't bet the family farm." She finds that rather than risk losing what they have, they will not break through and grow their company to the next size. "They had to work too hard to get to where they are, so they won't risk losing it. Whereas a man might go the whole crap shoot."

One of Lever's business partners call this the *cash or flash syndrome*: as soon as a man in business gets successful, he goes for the flash — big car, big desk, big office — whereas a woman will put the money back into the company.

Of course, the perception of risk is a very personal one. Some women view bank debt as an untenable risk. "Entrepreneurship is about taking risk, and a lot of people don't have the gumption it takes," says Bonnie Bickel. "I started young when I had nothing to lose."

As president of B. B. Bargoons, a fabric and home decorating retailer, Bickel reached a peak at twenty-two stores, has experienced two bankruptcies during the past sixteen years, and went through a failed partnership with Molson. Today she is content with two stores and sales of $5 million. At the age of fifty-one, she finds her appetite for risk has been fully slaked. "Now I can sleep through earthquakes, partly because my life is not on the line," she says.

As a mentor at Step Ahead, a networking and support group for women entrepreneurs in Toronto, she has discovered that fear of failure and risk is what holds entrepreneurs back. Many of her protégées are loath to owe their banks a dime because of the fear of being out of control. She's learned that it's hard to grow with that kind of attitude.

Experience takes a lot of that fear away. "Almost nothing terrifies me now — not in terms of real terror, of being paralyzed," says Wanda Dorosz. "And in my business there have been huge financial risks, great turmoil in terms of people, great anxiety and change. You can't be in the financial community and not encounter deception, politics, and major blunders."

Delores Lawrence has a spit-in-the-face-of-risk solution: "Go with your idea and sign your life away. If banks see you putting all that you have into your dream, then they'll give you the money, and you'll have to give it your all. You'll be more successful if you risk everything. Keeping a nest egg just in case your business fails will feed its failure."

Many women are responsible for the welfare of children, and putting them at risk jars their maternal instincts. "I'm doing this for us," says Elizabeth Scott of her two boys, eleven and thirteen. "For our life, to make it better." A single parent who receives no child support, has no assets, and began her newspaper while on unemployment insurance, Scott has nothing to lose and everything to lose. "We struggle. Kids need a lot of things, and I'm not always able to provide them."

Risk is almost always intrinsic to a new idea or never-tested solution to a problem. Says Dorosz, "The challenges increase as you continue to push the envelope. Making intelligent decisions on the basis of fewer and fewer facts is always fraught with terror. In a high-growth environment you can't wait until you have all the facts.

"There is a saying that I love: there are three types of people, those who make things happen, those who watch things happen, and those who wonder what happened. I say it in jest, but it couldn't be more true. If you're going to wait for all the facts, it's already passed you by."

Dorosz recalls the president of a huge multinational who lost a major market-share position in the space of five years. The reason: his management team moved too cautiously. They always met their goals, but no more. The risk-free approach proved to be the riskiest of all.

Companies grow in lurches and in nonlinear ways, she finds, and the stress of managing the growth is really the tension of creation. "The challenge of being part of that movement is really significant, particularly when you don't know what your own limits are — intellectually and in terms of stamina."

Knowing what is possible and what is impossible to control is important to ease the terror of risk. "I have no confidence that I control or even manage my company's destiny ten years out," she says. "I don't think it's possible, even if you had a grocery store on the corner. This world is morphing every six months."

"The challenge for me is not corporate finance or even negotiating; it's truly understanding that you have to make judgments that have consequences, *without* all the facts. That by definition means that you must have the emotional equipment to handle the consequences if you're wrong."

Roz Usheroff believes in blind faith and optimism. "Forget what other people are doing and do your best. If something messes up, don't get emotional about it and don't give up." Every night she follows the advice of one of her first bosses at Harry Rosen. "When I go home at night, I make a point of thinking of one new thing that has contributed to my success — a big leap or a little leap — it doesn't matter."

"Beliefs are just that, beliefs, that's all they are," says Giselle Briden, president of the Magellan Group. "I set out to get rid of all the beliefs that were holding me back. We can choose our beliefs, but sometimes we cling to old beliefs from tribes we no longer belong to. I thought I was too young, that no one would take me seriously, that because I didn't have a degree I was missing something that everyone else had. I thought that because I was brought up poor I would always be poor. As long as my actions reflected those beliefs, I would never try to do things."

BARBARA'S STORY

Barbara Mowat's move from a teacher to an entrepreneur was sudden, risky, and — as it turns out — the best decision she could have possibly made.

One day in 1986, as she stood in the Safeway supermarket lineup in Abbotsford, British Columbia, Mowat happened to notice the cover of *Ladies' Home Journal,* which listed an article about three U.S. women with successful home-based businesses. She bought the magazine, went home, tracked down one of the women in the article and phoned her, barely containing her growing excitement. She knew, absolutely, that home-based businesses were the way of the future.

Today, at age forty-four, Mowat is the president of two companies: *Home Business Report,* a national magazine on home-based businesses; and Impact Communications, a company that produces trade shows in British Columbia, Alberta, and Ontario and develops training programs to help microbusinesses gain access to the global market-place. Her blue-chip client list includes Microsoft, Bank of Montreal, the Yellow Pages, and Royal Bank of Canada. Revenues exceed $1 million. She has five full-time employees and fifteen contract workers. In 1993, she won the Woman Entrepreneur of the Year Award for her impact on the B.C. economy.

For the unknown world of entrepreneurship, Mowat traded a secure position as a senior faculty member at the University of British Columbia and Douglas College, teaching courses in career and lifestyle planning, earning $68,000 a year, and enjoying three months off every summer.

"I was going through the same process as my students, reevaluating where I was after fifteen years as a teacher," she says. "I realized that I was a closet entrepreneur." And the time was ripe: her three children were grown, she was tired of commuting, and she wanted to put her own advice into action.

These were the arguments for starting her own business. The argument *against* was also compelling. Her husband's construction company had failed in the recession, and they had no savings. What's more, since her credit rating was attached to her husband's, she couldn't get a loan.

Mowat's business is a success because she had the right idea at the right time, and because she slaved to make her business a success, brick by brick, client by client. Her thirst for success is at least as strong as her aversion to failure and even mediocrity, both whetted razor sharp in childhood.

Her early years as the youngest of five children were marked by poverty. Her father was a bootlegger, employed in menial jobs all his life. Her mother ran a boardinghouse with forty-seven boarders, and Mowat's home often resonated with the noise of drinking and fighting.

When her father lost his job in a paper mill, he found employment in the city dump. "I remember feeling embarrassed by this dirty man, coming home at the end of the day with salvaged trash, which he would store on the verandah," she says. Now, she looks back and realizes that he was collecting copper wire from discarded machinery and appliances, selling it for $40 a pound.

An avid reader who loved stories about the triumph of the underdog — "I loved it when Betty got Archie" — Mowat was determined to escape from the wrong side of the tracks through education. She was the only child in her family to complete university.

Her business is teaching small business owners how to succeed. "I can teach people to be good business managers, but entrepreneurialism is an innate quality," she says. "We probably all start off with entrepreneurial skills, but they get knocked out of us."

Mowat regularly sees people who have received a large severance package and are considering franchise opportunities as investments rather than businesses. "They think that if they invest their money, they'll get a successful business. It's simply not true. You have to start with your own interests first, and you have to have certain qualities to succeed."

For Mowat, an entrepreneur is someone who can intuitively see an opportunity, can live with risk, and has the drive to get ahead. In addition to these intrinsic qualities are skills such as the mastery of the technical aspects of a specific business, the marketing aspects, and the financial management. She advises her students to determine very early their strengths and weaknesses, "then sell your skills and take care of your weaknesses."

FINDING GOOD PEOPLE

We all have days when we wish we worked with a bunch of computers.

— Brenda Schiedel

Delegation is a struggle for me, but I've worked hard to do that well. Practically speaking, I am a good delegator, but I hang on to the worrying.

— Elizabeth Stewart

There is one large, compelling reason for having good people in your business. You can't do everything well. However, finding, managing, and trusting employees is one of the entrepreneur's greatest sources of stress, and a huge consumer of time.

Manfred Kets de Vries, a psychoanalyst, once wrote that the biggest burden a growing company faces is having a full-blooded entrepreneur as its owner. He's referring to the crucial step many entrepreneurs struggle with: letting go. In the early days, the entrepreneur usually does everything — from accounting to cleaning the washroom. As the company grows, she has to begin shedding responsibilities, passing them on to those who can perform them better or more economically. While attention to detail and tight control is a virtue when a business is beginning, an inability to let go and delegate routine and tactical activities can cripple a growing organization and alienate good employees.

One study showed that successful women entrepreneurs commonly delegate activities such as training new employees, handling customer complaints, answering the phone, and ordering and receiving supplies.[6] Delegating these tasks frees up time for the entrepreneur to concentrate on higher-level management tasks. In this study, two-thirds of female entrepreneurs did tasks they could have delegated because they wanted to maintain a tight control over their businesses. Their companies had low profits.

Dorothy Millman, president of DMS Intelecom, a company that manages telephone sales and service activities for other companies, uses these criteria for assessing whether an activity should be delegated:

- Is this activity a strength or a weakness of yours? If it is a weakness, it should be delegated.
- What are you earning? Does it make sense to pay yourself this amount to do this activity? If you're overcharging your company, find a more economical way to get it done.

Second, there is a strange truth that delegation becomes harder the more pressured you become. In her role as a consultant to entrepreneurs, Babs Sullivan finds that overworked entrepreneurs are less likely to delegate. When an entrepreneur is caught in the spiral of too many fires and not enough sleep, it seems easier to just deal with them herself rather than tell someone else how to do it.

For Nancy Adamo, owner of Hockley Valley Resort in Ontario, learning to delegate was a do-or-die proposition. When she left teaching more than two decades ago, she opened a small catering business. She loved it because she was in control of everything, from food preparation to delivery. Ten years ago, when she took over Hockley Valley Resort, she was suddenly immersed in a business employing 250 people in an industry she knew very little about — skiing, golf, and hotel management.

She realized quickly that she couldn't be on top of everything and everyone. "I had to learn to let go, trust others to do the job, let them make the decisions. The advantages are unbelievable," she said. She no longer spends sixteen hours a day working six days a week because she learned to delegate.

Part and parcel of effective delegation is good people management, and this is the Achilles heel of many entrepreneurs. Tracey De Leeuw, president of ManGlobe International Exchange, constantly struggles with keeping her people focused on the same vision and working well together. Her business provides Internet services to other organizations, and requires employees to apply their technical expertise to a new business concept in a new marketplace. She is the first to admit that people management is her weakness.

"I wish they could all be as happy in their jobs as I am, because I know what an extremely fulfilling experience that is. I feel as if I'm failing in that inspiration. I don't understand politics and power as a motivator, and that's blindsided me. And often people don't have the confidence they should have. I know they can do it, but they don't. I'm surprised when they can't find it within themselves."

LISA'S STORY

It was bad enough when the two biggest tutoring competitors moved aggressively into the private tutoring niche market that Lisa Jacobson had discovered and dominated. She found a new, untouched niche — tutoring well-off students on their summer holidays. But then she discovered that half of her employees were stealing from her.

Jacobson started New York-based Stanford Coaching in 1988. Her company, with sales of more than $2 million, provides one-on-one private tutoring for SAT exams and other "test prep" subjects. In the fifties, Stanley Kaplan had created a demand for a service that helped students prepare for college entrance exams. Then the Princeton

Review came into the market, and for decades the two companies dominated the market for tutoring in a classroom setting. The industry has grown as competition for acceptance to Ivy League colleges has soared.

Jacobson's niche was the individual tutoring session in the privacy of a student's home. Her target market is young, academically accomplished people from affluent homes. With a stable of about sixty tutors, Stanford Coaching's revenues are the spread between the hourly rate she charges the student's parents and the hourly fee she pays the tutor.

With hourly fees of up to $200 an hour, the total bill for SAT preparation ranges between $2,500 and $5,000. The full menu of test preps can run up a bill of $10,000. Price resistance seems to be virtually nonexistent in this industry. Many of her clients have just finished paying $100,000 for their child's private school education and are facing another $100,000 in college fees, so what's another $5,000 to ensure their child gets into one of the best colleges in the country?

But clients and tutors were cutting their own private deals — the tutors got a little more, and the clients paid a little less. A disgruntled employee let that slip during an emotional exchange with Jacobson about another matter. Shocked and disbelieving, she hired an undercover investigator to identify the guilty employees. They turned out to be her most highly paid and trusted employees. Jacobson sued them, successfully, although she did not recoup all the money she had lost. "When I realized how much money they had taken, it was really horrible."

Jacobson, with the resiliency that typifies successful entrepreneurs, views negative events as new opportunities — quite an ability, given that she subsequently lost half of her tutors and the students who were with them. "It was very tough," she says. "But the stealing forced me to change the way we deal with the tutors, to set much stricter and clearer guidelines to curtail theft. I wouldn't have looked at this area if the problems hadn't surfaced."

Jacobson took the novel step of engaging her competitors in a discussion about their experiences with theft, and a couple of them admitted it was a problem. "One said that every two years he sued the most egregious ones. That cost him $40,000, and he probably got back $20,000. For two years people stop and then they start again and he sues again."

Being prepared to sue is necessary, says Jacobson, because employees have to know that you mean what you're saying and that you'll enforce it. "But that's not my main focus. We tell them up front, and we have them sign non-compete contracts." There are misconceptions about the impotence of non-compete contracts, says Jacobson. "If an employee takes a customer directly from you, then the contract is enforceable. If they take a referral of a direct customer, it's a little trickier." The contract has to have a fair time duration so that employees aren't restricted from making a living for years on end, and it has to apply to a specific geographic area.

Since 1993, Jacobson has read many books on employee theft. "The thing that sticks with me is that out of a hundred people, ten will never steal from you — you could leave an open cash box in front of them and they just wouldn't. Ten will always steal, and the remaining eighty ... it just depends. If you put the cash box in front of them, they might. In my case, you have a parent asking my tutors if they'd like to make $20 an hour more than they're making. So the cash box is right in front of them."

Jacobson tries to hire people with integrity, a quality she thinks is apparent in the way they answer questions and conduct their life. But even then, she worries. "When it comes to money, people twist integrity."

To help prevent future problems, Jacobson hired a human resources manager. "She says to them, *Here's what you have to do. If you don't do it, we're going to tell you about it. If it happens more than once, you can't stay here.* We warn them that once they sign the contract, they will be sued if there is cause." The clients also sign a contract, but it is not in Jacobson's interests to sue a client, however big the breach.

Jacobson leaves no doubt in employees' minds about her expectations, but she always works hard to make them feel part of the company. For her employees, bringing them together is something everyone enjoys. "They're all communicators, and they love meeting one another. Where else would they meet people like themselves except here? We pay attention to them and care about them, but what I've learned is that some women have a tendency to be too nice and too pleasing."

Still, she seems to be sympathetic to her employees' feelings. "If you're an employee and you've never been an employer, you see things from where you sit, which is totally justified. Unless they tell me, I can't imagine what it's like to wear their shoes. I've been a tutor, but I've never been a tutor for my company."

As for the employee theft, Jacobson is philosophical. "People ask me if I felt betrayed. At first I did, but what I learned is that their decision to embezzle really has nothing to do with me. It's the same thing I learned in acting: if I'm not blonde enough for a part, it's really nothing to do with me. You have to keep moving on, keep your vision and do the right thing."

Yes, Jacobson was an actor, or trying to become one, for five years in New York. While she was trying to get auditions and roles, she supported herself by tutoring math instead of waitressing and doing temp work. Her students consistently did well on the math section of the SAT. Word spread, and her business grew. But her dreams centered on acting.

"I'm dark with dark eyes and curly hair, so I was always cast as a Lebanese terrorist or the Brooklyn motorcycle girl. My girlfriend was always the smart, funny, beautiful blonde. I would get called for auditions but I wasn't 'this' enough or 'that' enough. I look ethnic, but when I auditioned for a Woody Allen movie, he said I didn't look Jewish enough, and I'm Jewish! They would say, *You're fantastic, but I don't know if people in Ohio will buy that you're American.* Or, *I don't know, we need a tall, beautiful woman. You're not quite attractive enough.* Or people would say, *You should dye your hair and eyebrows blond and get breast implants.* So I said to myself, *There's something wrong here.*"

Jacobson tried to run her search for acting roles like a business, which was impossible because the decisions were out of her control. She created marketing materials about herself and sent them off to 500 decision makers at a time because she sensed it was a numbers game. "You just have to cross the right desk at the right time." So she went from door to door, all of them firmly closed. "I got acting out of my system and learned so much about rejection."

"At any rate, I was much happier tutoring the kids, although I didn't admit this to myself at the time." She would teach math to math-haters, and they would leave loving it and getting A's instead of F's. "It was totally satis-fying. With the work I put in, I could control the reward that came out."

By this time she was charging $75 a hour to sixty students and tutor-ing 80 to 100 hours a week. "My students would say they wished I did French and physics and English SAT, and the business started brewing in my head." After emergency surgery in 1987 to have a disc removed from her neck, she lay in bed and came to some decisions about her life. "I decided I didn't want to be an actor anyway. I'm not really great at it. What I'm great at is business. I said to myself, *Why not start a business where I go out and find the best tutors in Manhattan?*" And she did.

OBSERVATIONS ON EMPLOYEES FROM WOMEN ENTREPRENEURS

Don't expect that employees will dispel your feelings of isolation

Marnie Walker, president of Student Express, feels isolated in her $2-million company despite overseeing a bustling head office and a fleet of drivers. "Some of my work no one can do but me," she says. "If I don't know what to do or if I have a problem, no one can give me an answer. You have to work them through yourself. There's nowhere to go for the solution."

Don't hire in your own image

Ellie Rubin believes that entrepreneurs tend to hire people who are like them. "I'm attracted to people who have lots of ideas, and of course this is not what you want in someone who is going to be your vice president of operations." Instead of hiring in her own image, she looks for people who complement her, people who can follow through on her creative ideas.

With the same strategy, Brenda Schiedel has taken her personal nemesis — detail — out of her job and delegated it. She spends her time exploiting her strengths: setting the strategic direction of the company, coaching employees, and developing a customer base.

Delegate hiring and people management if it is not your strength

Melodie Stewart, president of Pro-Net Business Connections, dislikes hiring people because she likes everyone. "I'll give anyone a chance because somebody gave me a chance once. I shouldn't hire people."

Pro-Net's current administrative assistant is the third in the company's first seven months of life. Stewart's first hire was a girlfriend of a friend in Stewart's motorcycle club. It didn't work out. The next hire was a woman she met at a networking meeting. "She had the most humongous chest I've ever seen, and that's all she cared about," says Stewart. The third hire was referred to Stewart from a trusted business associate. This time it worked.

Recognize that your human resource needs will change as your company grows

When Schiedel's company generated $300,000 a year in revenues, her tenured employees handled their jobs well. They were used to the pace. They knew who did what and what their role in the total mix was. As the company grew, their jobs and time pressures grew. Three people, each with over fifteen years' tenure, balked.

"They were still okay when we hit $3 million, but when we doubled that, they couldn't handle it. They couldn't see the future or the potential; all they could see was that they had too much work. And no matter what we did in terms of training, it just didn't work."

One finally quit, openly admitting a dislike for the new work environment. One was offered a different job in the company but chose to leave. The third was dismissed.

Schiedel installed a new management structure, including a chief financial officer. She wanted someone with manufacturing experience, strong financial skills, and an ability to see beyond the numbers to the potential of the company. "And he had to be a good fit with me." Luck smiled on her. She remembered someone who had the qualities and characteristics she was looking for, phoned him, and they hit it off.

She was also in desperate need of a director of sales and marketing. The incumbent never left his office, never met with customers. "Plus he was computer illiterate and refused to learn. All of his salespeople were using computers for order entry and recording sales calls, and he didn't even know where the button was to turn the computer on."

Her wish list here was a computer-literate, enthusiastic someone who would go out and work with the salespeople. And equally important, she wanted someone who wouldn't compete with the chief financial officer — "that kind of thing can rip a company apart." She found him. "My director of sales and marketing is fifty-five and my CFO is thirty-three, so there's no competition. They absolutely work in sync. The director doesn't want my job. He wants to be the very best director of sales and marketing and triple our sales over the next four to five years."

Recognize that people management and motivation will consume a large part of your time

Even women entrepreneurs who have delegated the human resources function spend a large part of their day dealing with employee issues. A third of Schiedel's time is consumed in this way. "I think I take personal problems into consideration more than a male-run business would. If I know that Sally from customer service is really having problems at home with her kids, and her work is only at 85 percent, I will coach her along to get her back to 100 percent. Sometimes that means things like arranging counseling for her kids, but in the long run it achieves my goal of getting Sally to work at the 100 percent level. Because I do that for my staff, I know that when I need them, they give 110, 120, 130 percent. I don't just jump on them and say, *Get your act together*. I try to help them. I think it's the best way to manage people."

SEXUAL DISCRIMINATION AND GENDER ADVANTAGE

Stop obeying men. Give them the benefit of the doubt and treat them as your peers.

— Marnie Walker

I figure if my legs can get me the appointment, then my brains can make them write me a cheque.

— Melodie Stewart

Women entrepreneurs in many industries have both the blessing and the curse of being anomalies. Being female is a blessing when it distinguishes you from the competition and moves the media spotlight onto your company. It's a curse when your abilities are perceived to be less or to lie elsewhere.

Some women entrepreneurs have never bumped up against special treatment because of gender. It's a non-issue to Mary Connolly, who recently closed a successful consulting company to search for an equity position in a fast-growing company. "I've always gotten exactly what I want out of life, and I've never felt that I have been discriminated against because I was female. But I don't look for it either. I think a lot of women expect it. They're waiting to hit the glass ceiling, for someone to slight them, to be passed over, and they have that attitude. I'm not saying that it doesn't happen. I'm saying that when you anticipate it, you increase the likelihood of it happening."

Most women believe that their gender does affect the playing field, more positively than not.

Giselle Briden feels that being female is a strategic advantage in business because she can easily exceed the typical expectations of men. "When I walk into a business meeting or presentation, I know that the vast majority of people in the room are going to be men. The reaction that goes through men's minds is *Oh, it's a woman!* I'm not knocking men. It's a cultural attitude that in most cases they're not even aware of. Their expectations are low. They're not expecting something awesome, and you can turn around and be as strong and powerful and dynamic as a man. If you were standing side by side with a man and were equally talented, you would be astounding because you're female, and it makes you more noticeable."

Wanda Dorosz believes that trying to be one of the boys is a mistake.

"People in business are far more interested in the fact that you're different," she says. To her, capitalizing on being female is all about playing to your strengths.

Sexual Interest

Melodie Stewart has been on the receiving end of a great deal of sexual interest over the years, and has learned to defuse it or use it. "I know a lot about men and how they think. We'd be kidding ourselves if we didn't think they weren't looking at us. But people who know me know they won't get away with sexually harassing me. I command respect because I give it." A born salesperson, Stewart reads body language for a living. If she senses someone is "going down the wrong road," she corrects it through humor before it gets to a point where a rebuff is required and the deal is compromised.

"A lot of men have said to me, *Melodie, if you and a guy were selling the exact same product at the same price, I would buy from you because you are a beautiful young lady and you can make me laugh.* That's what it's all about. Knowing, trusting, and liking the person you're dealing with. Part of that is the package that I come in. It's also my personality, but if you're not too bad to look at, what's the problem with that?"

Says Stewart of her partner, Kim Doherty, "She's a knockout too. It wouldn't matter which one of us it was, if we get an appointment, we're going to sign someone. It may not be right, but that's the way it is." Doherty is single but doesn't broadcast the fact after being phoned by a male television viewer smitten by her on a television talk show.

Sexual Prejudice

While it is possible to smoothly manage sexual interest, sexual prejudice is more volatile, with the capacity to create a sudden crater in the playing field. Paula Jubinville, an expert on developing sound financing proposals, was told by a banker that what she submitted wasn't good enough. Then he asked her out to dinner. And she's had investors hesitate or refuse to invest in a woman's business out of a fear that the owner will become pregnant and lose her interest in the business.

Marnie Walker's father told her that she had her brother's brains, a troubling compliment since it implied an ability that was not rightfully hers while suggesting profound disappointment in the son. Later, when Walker was working at Bell Canada, she overheard a boss say to someone about her: *She's not like a woman — she really understands.*

"I quickly realized that it didn't matter what I did. As a female employee, I wouldn't get to the table for years," says Walker. "I had taken a subordinate role in my marriage and in my career. I wasn't being myself. I was being what girls 'should be' even though it was offensive to me. Had I been male, my life would have been much easier. Once I realized I had my own cards, even though they weren't face cards, I could play my hand and be effective."

"Being female works for you and against you," says Janet Sinclair, who is a partner in a bed-and-breakfast and also works as an interior designer. "In catering, it's assumed you cook better, and in residential design, people find me less threatening because design is very intimate, very psychological. When I'm working with construction trades on a restaurant, it's harder because the men are saying to themselves, *You can't do this — you have ovaries.* I love to prove them wrong. I use a lot of humor. It helps me get away with things, and the trades think designers are all flaky anyway. When I earn their respect, they go, *Wow, she's a woman and she's good!*"

Gender Advantage

In Ellie Rubin's experience, her sex is an advantage in the fast-growing high-technology industry — not just because she is an anomaly, but because she can behave differently from her male peers.

"My ego is not caught up in how technologically savvy I am," she says. "So I can walk into a room and not have to show off at all. In fact, I'm much happier saying, *Tell me everything because you are an expert.* I can easily say, *I don't understand,* and all of a sudden, these guys who are fighting over who's got the bigger megabyte can just settle down and explain."

Rubin is ready to play any boardroom game. She's found that it's possible to become a real catalyst and a leader in a meeting even from a starting position of underdog, which Rubin defines as a female without an engineering degree in a roomful of technophiles.

"I have rarely found that gender gets in my way," she says. "But I've worked very hard to make sure I'm politic enough to walk into a room and sense if there's going to be trouble — if they don't like women or if one guy has a problem with women in authority. In that case, I'm going to play a completely different person."

Her solution is to minimize any need for the man to show authority. "If you're too nice, there's almost nothing someone can do to you. I just very quietly prove that I am smart, and that I'm smart in a different way than they are so that we can *all* be smart." In other meetings she might act the complete opposite — if she thinks it will help her goal.

Rubin's goal is closing the deal. "I'll give them credit for ideas even if they're mine. Who cares? The whole point is deal making. If that's going to make the deal, then I'll say, *Great idea, love it. Can I take your idea now and do it?* Then we're all happy."

It's not that Rubin is egoless — she is the first to admit her ego is a hefty one. But making her ego's care and feeding a top priority would be dangerous. "It just doesn't work to take a stance where you're saying, *I am a woman and I'll show you how great I am because it really bugs me that you assume maybe I'm not so great.*"

Rubin finds she is acutely aware of the undercurrents and innuendos in a meeting. "I've walked into meetings where I can tell it's going to be a disaster, that I'm going to hate this person and they're going to hate me. So I'll just say to myself, *By the end of the meeting I'm going to get two names from this person or I'm going to get them to agree to this or that.* If I accomplish nothing else, it doesn't matter."

For Tracey De Leeuw, being female is a plus. "I get their attention for an extra thirty seconds and that matters big time. You have just one chance to make a first impression and grab their interest." She also finds that being female affects her perspective on the business. "Because ManGlobe is my baby, I'm not going to let anything bad happen to it. If it needs me at any time of the day or night, I'll take care of it.

"I don't bond with men in business the same way men bond with each other. Most of the men I work with are a lot older. My relationship tends to be more like a little sister, child, or grandchild, more nurturing — not with everybody but with some."

WANDA'S STORY

Wanda Dorosz is a co-founder and controlling shareholder of Quorum Funding Corp., a venture capital firm, and president of Quorum Growth Inc., an investment fund specializing in high-tech companies. Venture capital companies take an equity position in promising young companies with the aim of selling their interest when the company has met their high expectations of it.

As the only female CEO in the high-stakes Canadian venture capital industry, Dorosz might be expected to be as cold and calculated as the criteria used to buy and sell equity positions. But she's not. Her office is filled with color and drama — the walls are covered with oil paintings and limited edition prints, and every horizontal surface save her desk is crammed with the mementos of her international travels. Only her desk is austere and barren, with a few file folders stacked neatly in one corner.

Dorosz's hemlines are shorter than the conservative dictates of the financial community, and her suits shape rather than drape. When she talks, it's not about financial ratios but of companies and trends as though they were living things. That a steel spine, a prerequisite for flourishing in such a risky business, exists beneath the sheer blouse and jewelry can be disconcerting.

"We're not deal junkies, we're company builders," says Dorosz. A team of Quorum people will work together on improving the company's performance, with each team member bringing a different skill to bear on the company. "We come together as a mosaic of ability," she says.

Dorosz's contribution is the "softer" skills. She works with the CEOs of her investee companies to help them obtain peak performance. "It's a difficult and necessary art. If you don't truly stretch yourself, by definition you can't ever beat the average."

Her definition of average is based on a friend's study of the real return on equity and real estate over the last two centuries. After taking out anomalies like war, depression, deflation, and hyperflation, he found that real returns on property were 2.5 percent and real returns on equity were 5 percent.

"So if you accomplish 30 percent or 50 percent growth, think of what that means. You're way over on the edge of the bell curve. This is absolutely about training for the Olympics, sustainable winning. Everything goes with it: nutrition, family, spirituality, all those things that can take you to the edge. Having ability isn't enough. Being at the right place at the right time isn't enough. Being in the slipstream isn't enough. I spend a lot of time working with individual entrepreneurs and sharing their mental and emotional rigors. It's not my ideas that help — they always have the answers. It's the listening."

Dorosz is a lawyer by profession with a background in the humanities. "I was trained as an art historian and minored in music history. I have a deep passion for ancient man and archeology and history, and I use that every single day of my life."

She works every night of the week, having dinner with each CEO of her investee companies to talk about what's working and what's not. These meetings are part of the Olympic training she refers to.

For example, one CEO had been the controlling shareholder for fifteen years. He sought venture capital because he wanted to grow, and the time came to become a public company. "But as we got closer to the closing date, I could see something was wrong. He said to me, *I'm terrified that this is going to change me. It's going to be too formal. There will be board meetings and memos.* So I told him we would hold a board meeting — just the two of us — at an Italian restaurant in North Toronto. One time I'd buy; the next time he'd buy. It doesn't have to be formal. As long as he brings the stuff that matters, the financials, the two of us could have a board meeting anywhere.

"Six months later, he graduated to accepting the board and ultimately became the chairman of a public company. If we had done the formal thing to start, it would have been a big mistake."

CHAPTER 4

... And the Ecstasy

FINDING YOUR LIFE

Don't compromise yourself. You are all you've got.

— Janis Joplin

Advice to women entrepreneurs, courtesy of Brenda Schiedel:

- Create a good relationship with your bank.
- Have your business plan in place: know where you want to go and how you're going to get there. Figure out what dollars you need to generate results.
- Be prepared to work long and hard.
- Be prepared to make trade-offs in your life. You can't do it all yourself. You have to decide what's important in your life and know that you're not going to be able to do every little thing that you want to do.
- Your business drives your life. If you love your business, you'll love your life.

NATALIE'S STORY

Natalie Rostad-Desjarlais's education ended with Grade 8 when she left home at the age of fourteen. Her mother, a Cree Indian, was an alcoholic. Her father, a white trucker, was rarely home. When there, he abused his wife and children, and sexually abused Rostad's older sister, who became a drug addict.

"I had no self-esteem. I had no belief in anything greater than myself," she recalls. "My family moved around a lot. There was racism even within our own family. When my father was abusive to my mother, he would always say that it was normal for her to be an alcoholic because she's Indian.

"I remember thinking that this was as good as it gets, and it wasn't very good. But when you get out and walk your own path, you start discovering different things — families that can laugh together, families that can grow together. People who have their own homes and businesses. I began to believe that I could be one of those people."

Alone on the streets, Rostad lied about her age, got a job as a waitress, and soon after met the father of her daughter, Jennifer, now fourteen. "It was the classic situation of leaving one abusive situation to go into another. I stuck with him for eight years. Leaving him was the most powerful thing I've ever done for me and my daughter."

Although employed, welfare had to help her out at the end of every month. Rostad felt frantic all the time, trying to make ends meet. Getting back with her abusive spouse was beginning to look like the best alternative in a hopeless life. "When you don't have faith in yourself, every thought is desperate. Every direction you turn seems to have a dead end. That was the way I lived. I was starting to think about crime, about desperate measures. I hadn't stolen, but I had borrowed without asking. Then the rocks spoke to me."

Rostad is referring to an incident in 1990 that she interprets as divine intervention. A storm had washed away part of the road, exposing stones normally hidden beneath the surface. As she walked by, a piece of white quartz caught her eye, and she picked it up and took it home. She pointed out to several people that the stone looked like a horse, but nobody could see it. When she painted an eye on it, it *was* a horse.

Rostad was so compelled by the emotional experience of coaxing a horse from a rock that she drove her Mustang to the ditch the next day and filled her trunk with rocks. "I didn't know why I brought them home or what was on my mind," she says. "I knew I needed to be creative, and I knew that I'd never felt like this before in my life. It was like a baptism. It was seven years ago, and it feels like yesterday. When I'm feeling a little negative, I try and remember that day."

Rostad showed her painted rocks to the teacher of a life skills course she was taking. The teacher exclaimed over her talent and asked her to display her rocks at a local art show. Rostad agreed, and was the star of the show, selling every rock but one, which she saved for her mother.

"It was overwhelming. I had never had that kind of experience before. I came out of there floating ten feet off the floor. I was selling the rocks for $40 or $50, and I felt rich, rich beyond belief. It wasn't the money that made me rich, it was the acceptance that people showed." She figured if people would give $50 for something that she created, then she was on her way. She could get a home, a horse, a decent car. "I started thinking about things that I could achieve. If I could bring a rock to life and make a person appreciate that rock, then I could pretty much do anything."

For Rostad, her art is a story of her life. "What makes the rocks beautiful is the trauma that made them what they are. I learned that you are shaped by your journey. I used to feel sorry for myself, and there's nothing more damaging. When I finally allowed myself to look at the bad things that happened in my family, I got strength from it. It started opening doors and revealing the true me, and I started to discover that I had potential, that the bad things that happened weren't my story.

"All my life I've been ostracized and picked on because of my heritage. When I'm talking with children about my work, I talk about how geodes represent us. We're all children of the earth on the outside — it doesn't matter the color — and inside there is beauty in each of us." Her company, which sells her work, is aptly named From Beneath the Surface.

She became engaged in late 1996. It took her nine years to overcome her dread of male power and allow a man to put a ring on her finger. "I just couldn't trust them. I absolutely hated them. All the pain that I've ever seen and experienced in my life was due to men, and I needed to confront that."

Her life continued to blossom until her mother's husband killed himself. Rostad's mother blamed her for his death. She had stopped drinking to take care of Rostad's daughter, but when Rostad took her daughter back, her mother started drinking again and left her husband, which precipitated his suicide.

For several months Rostad was so depressed she couldn't paint. "Then one day I was sitting there, looking at this big, big rock. It became wolves, touching noses. They showed me that communication was the key to my healing."

They did more than that. Her neighbor, who displayed flower arrangements at a Winnipeg hotel, offered to show Rostad's wolves with her displays. The wolves caught the attention of Susan Scott, a well-to-do Winnipeg woman who owned significant properties. She was so affected by Rostad's work that she donated a valuable downtown property to the aboriginal population and flew to Toronto with some friends to give support to a show of Rostad's work, organized by Charlie Coffey of the Royal Bank.

Among Scott's friends was Linda Lundstrom, a Canadian women's clothing designer. She asked Rostad to design the artwork for a coat, which became the top seller for the year. The year following, Rostad designed the artwork for another coat and it topped the sales of the previous year's coat. In 1996, Lundstrom bought three designs from Rostad, including one by her sister, Cheryl Desjarlais.

Rostad's business both saved and created her. "Life can't get better. It's magic. Every day I say thank you about a hundred times because I can't believe it."

ELIZABETH'S STORY

Elizabeth Scott is the owner of *Woman,* a quarterly newsmagazine. Her first issue hit the stands in the fall of 1996. The newsmagazine covers topics relating to finance and business, health and wellness, arts and creativity, parenting, single motherhood, women and their successes. Scott is adamant that the tone will never be fluffy or glamorous.

At thirty-eight years old, Scott and her children are truly starting over. She was married to a lawyer who in 1986 sold his practice and threw himself into writing what he assumed would be a bestseller. They lived in France for a year and then returned to Midland, Ontario, to live in the cottage of Scott's parents. The bestseller never materialized, and the marriage fell apart.

In Midland, Scott worked at a newspaper for less than a year, earning $7 an hour. It was grueling work, but she learned a lot about newspaper production. Finally she quit. "The pay was crummy and the work was unorganized and stressful — the editor would start writing his editorial at eleven o'clock on production night."

Increasingly uncomfortable as a single parent in a family-centered community, Scott moved to Toronto and got a job working in a law office earning double the money. But paltry sums doubled are still paltry.

Then one day, the unhappiness of her failed marriage and her dislike of her job combined to stop her in her tracks. She found that she literally could not type another letter. She took some time off and went into therapy, and through this process found the courage and desire to take control of her life.

In September of 1995 when the law firm announced that it would be laying off staff, Scott asked to be included. She had heard about the federal Self-Employment Assistance program (SEA) where, in order to qualify for entrepreneurial training, a person had to be on unemployment insurance and have a viable business idea.

She thought about what would be meaningful to her, something with the potential to grow and provide for her and her sons. She also wanted to build on her work experience, which included book publishing, newspaper production, some freelance writing successes, and a B.A. in English.

"Having seen for myself what women go through during the legal process of separation, including all the responsibilities with the kids, I certainly feel for women and children. I saw the information gap, that there was nothing speaking to the very real needs that women have. Glossy fashion magazines talk peripherally about issues but don't really give hard information. So I decided to try to fill that gap."

She was accepted into the SEA program and began to create a business plan. It took her thirteen weeks to do her market research — how the paper should be formatted and which organizations would want to advertise in it.

"I went through all the planning stage in terms of thinking about and assessing costs. For example, if I go with a certain format, how much is it going to cost to produce? I had to figure out how I was going to make money. My plan gave me a way of tracking what's important, and where I should be focusing my energy on a day-to-day basis."

Revenues were difficult to forecast, so Scott lowballed them and overestimated her expenses. "That way, if you do more, it's a bonus." Reality has proven to be rosier than her forecasts, which planned for a loss on her first issue. In fact, she sold three times more advertising than she expected, kept her costs to the bone, and made a small profit. A graphic artist was willing to design the paper for free to gain the experience, and writers also provided articles pro bono, leaving her with printing as the only significant cost.

Rather than pursue bank financing, Scott financed her first issue with advertising revenues, which she attracted by cold calling companies and presenting her business plan. "I can't tell you how impressed people were with my business plan. Every step of the way, advertisers would go, *Wow, you did that*? It helped them believe in me."

Selling advertising — an initially terrifying prospect — was easier when she spoke to female decision makers. "They immediately recognized the need for *Woman*. I faxed information to a woman at the Bank of Montreal, and she phoned back and said, *We'd like the back cover*, and that was it. The men I spoke to wanted to wait a few issues and see if I was still around. Men don't see that there's not a lot of information getting out to women. They can't relate to our situation because it's so different."

Scott didn't approach the banks for financing because of her poor credit rating. Her marriage had left her with huge debts, which she chose to pay off rather than declare personal bankruptcy. She had no assets, no car, nothing to give as collateral. "I really have worked from the ground up in building this."

If the paper fails, Scott is prepared to cross that bridge. "If I thought about failure every day, then I wouldn't be where I am. I don't think about failing because that's not the reality. The reality is that I've got a lot of support. I'm getting phone calls for ad rates, and people want to subscribe. Things are just getting better.

"But if things don't work out, I'll get a job. I've learned so much in the last year, and that would show on my résumé. I can say, *Here's my magazine. It's my baby — the format, everything.* And an employer can look at that and say, *If she can do that, what else can she do?* I can never fail, because I've done it."

AUTONOMY

What's great about having your own company is you create the social norms. You create real work, not make-work. I don't want anyone to write me a memo. I just want the information, clear and simple.

— Marnie Walker

I want to be a strong role model for my son.

— Trish Haddad

There's a myth about entrepreneurship and autonomy. It's something to the effect that when you have your own business, you call the shots and are answerable to no one. You're a kind of Wild West, gun-slinging Annie Oakley.

It's not true. Entrepreneurs have lots of bosses that they have to pay attention to: customers, suppliers, employees, government officials, family members, and if they go public, shareholders. If anything, you're more beholden to these groups than you would be as an employee because it's *your* company on the line.

But if your definition of autonomy is a gentler one, where you want the ability to cut out for an afternoon to watch your child's little league baseball game, or greater control over what you choose to focus on at work, or clear responsibility for your efforts, then entrepreneurship does mean greater autonomy.

TRISH'S STORY

Since May of 1995, Trish Haddad, thirty-eight, has owned the resale clothing store called Bean Sprout. She returned to the retail business after seven years in public relations and fundraising.

Her work as an employee wasn't conducive to being a single parent. Haddad often had to work late during the week and on weekends with committees. The divorced parent of a son aged nine, Haddad would leave her job at 5:30 every day to pick up her son at his after-school program. "When you're the boss with a staff, and they're all working late and you have to leave, it's very uncomfortable."

Now, if worse came to worse, Haddad will put a note on the door to her store that says, *My child is sick.* "He can walk to school, and he can walk over to the store after school if he wants. I have control over my life again. I'm even able to fit exercise in before I open the store."

While her life is more balanced, she still feels a void. "I always thought I would be married, and I haven't given up on having more children. That part of my life is not completely fulfilled. But I do have a lot going for me." As well, there are days when she wishes she could be home with her son. "It would be nice to have a reliable staff person, but I'll have to be doing a lot better before I can do that."

When Haddad was laid off from her job — to her silent relief — she did intensive market research to identify the best location for her store. She put together a business plan, which forced her to walk through each step of her business. To do her market research, she went to Statistics Canada for data on children's clothing sales and how many pieces of clothing she needed per square foot. She obtained literature from a used clothing franchise, which gave some rough measures of gross sales, and visited resale shops to see how many staff were on the floor, the store's square footage, and the number and kind of items they were selling.

Since there were long-established resale shops in the area, Haddad knew there was receptivity to the resale concept, but since none of these shops offered children's clothes, she wasn't positive that her store would succeed. So she researched the average income and number of children in the area and conducted a telephone poll of 300 people. "I confirmed that people had the money to spend and the children to spend it on. Plus, people always want clothes for their kids, especially in this neighborhood. It's not poor people who buy secondhand."

Detailed research is important, she says. "I think a lot of people are in a kind of dreamland when it comes to running a business. One man I met talked about all the bells and whistles of his business but didn't see the reality of it. He was going to run a little Brown Betty tearoom. He had visualized what the place would look like and who the customers would be. But when it came to a location, for example, he didn't have a clue. And location is the most important thing."

Today her annual sales exceed $100,000 and her monthly draw is less than what she earned as an employee. She runs the store by herself, except on Thursdays, when a part-time employee fills in for her; the store is closed on Sundays. Often there will be lineups of customers to buy clothing or ask questions. "It's so busy now that I'm looking into getting additional help," she says. "Since I'm there alone, I have to put a little sign on the door that says *Back in Five Minutes* just to go to the wash-room. There's always someone in my store now. It's like a real business.

"I need two people in the shop all day, but I can't afford it, and yet I know I'd get more clothing out the door. Growing too fast is a nice problem to have. Still, it's a bit of a worry — how to handle it all."

Her success, she says, depends on her will and desire to do it. "You have to be highly organized to be able to juggle a number of things at once and put them in priority and identify what they all are. There are a million things to do at once. You have to have guts ... and money. I could have done with a lot more money."

To finance her business, she remortgaged her house and got a new venture loan for $7,000. A new-venture loan, no longer available, matched the amount of money available to the entrepreneur and repayment in the first year was interest only.

"But it was like asking for a million," groans Haddad. "My bank rep wanted a lot of detail. I had to go over my marketing and promotion plan with him a million times, and he tried to talk me down to $5,000. I wanted to get a line of credit for the bad months, but he wouldn't give it to me. Other than that, he was pretty good. He was impressed with my business plan."

One month, it rained endlessly and traffic through her store dried up. "Things got a little tight financially, but that's the nature of retail. The store goes silent and you think, *Oh my God, it's over.* I didn't stay on top of my bank balance — you need to monitor it daily. I was able to go to my family for a bridge loan, but that's something I don't want to do ever again."

That month her bank representative called, concerned, and asked for a net worth statement. "It's a ridiculous request, for the $6,000 I had left on the loan," she says. "I pretty much made the statement up. I have friends who own the Second Cup on the corner, and they got a $250,000 loan like nothing. I suppose the small businesses are a risk, but I'm not. I'm not one of those people who would declare bankruptcy. I would pay back the debt no matter how I had to get the money."

Haddad is not a stranger to entrepreneurship. At twenty-one, she started her first business, one of the first resale clothing stores for women in Canada at the time, and operated it for five years. "I didn't really know what I was doing," she recalls. "And I didn't do very well financially." She married in 1985, and divorced in 1988 when she was pregnant with her son. With her portion of the proceeds from the matrimonial home, she bought a house with her sister. Later, in May of 1996, her sister left, and Haddad bought her interest in the house.

She fell in love with her rental space the first time she saw it — lead glass windows and a perfect display window. On either side of her store are high-end children's stores, which underscores the low prices of Haddad's inventory.

The only problem was, the landlord wouldn't rent it to her. "It was vacant for years, but the landlord just felt he hadn't found the right business. It was a strange space because there's another 2500 square feet behind me behind a partition and he keeps his junk in it. He wanted to rent the whole space, but it wasn't feasible for me. I just kept at him until I got it."

Haddad is proud of her store. "It's not damp, like a lot of stores, and it smells nice. Unlike other resale stores where you're almost knocked over by the amount of stuff, mine is organized like a real store. The clothing is all clean, and I am very picky. I have one whole room dedicated to a play area for kids. It's not the best business decision at $22 a square foot, but the mothers love it."

She also pays a window dresser $90 every month to design her store window. "It makes such a difference. The shop looks professional, which means you can get more money for the things. The window's lit up at night. Half the people don't know it's resale until they see the prices."

In the children's resale clothing business, mothers are the customers — stay-at-home moms during the week and working moms on Saturdays. Haddad works hard to keep her customers coming back. "They can talk freely, breast-feed their babies, and change diapers. There are cookies for the kids, and they can run around. It's totally conducive to women being comfortable and finding nice things to dress their kids in. It's a real little community, where everybody knows everybody."

At the end of her first year, Haddad was 20 percent over her projections. "I don't know whether I was way off or just had a better thing going than I thought," she says.

Other than money, the only other problem she wrestles with is advertising. She finds its impact hard to gauge. Recently, she bought advertising space in a local paper and included a coupon to measure its effectiveness. No one came in with the coupon. "But on the other hand, I advertise in *City Parent* magazine every month, and people mention it all the time. So I know that's working."

The cost of setting up her business was approximately $16,000. She bought most of her equipment secondhand and started collecting inventory on consignment months before the store opened. "I put an ad in the local paper, which didn't do much good. Most of it I got from friends of friends. I went all over the city and picked it up, and gave people handwritten receipts. When I got my space, I put a huge sign on the door saying to call for pickup. I washed it all and put it in the shop."

Haddad's loan payments are $150 a month. The $40,000 equity line, in fact a second mortgage on her home, is maxed out at $40,000. "I only pay the interest on that. I expect I'll never pay it off until I sell the house. When my sister left, my business plan sort of shot out the window." In order to stay in the house, Haddad had to increase her monthly draw, but her business revenues, so far, are supporting her increased needs.

"I have thought about expanding, but I'm not ready. It would be too much work. I don't want a huge business. My accountant told me I had to double my sales when I told him about taking over the house payments. It threw me for a loop. I will take risks, but if I take too big a risk, I'm in trouble. I don't have anyone to fall back on.

"I would like more things for myself though," she sighs. "I don't buy as many clothes as I used to. But in 1995 we went to Nova Scotia for a week, and I drive a nice car. I work hard, and I don't mind working hard. So far so good, I pay my mortgage and all my bills. I've done well.

"My son thinks I'm cool," says Haddad. "But sometimes he gets frustrated. He wants to come home for lunch or leave school at 3:30 like some of his buddies do instead of at a quarter to six. I try to explain that it would be the same with any job I had, and I have to work. I think he's proud. I advertise in the school newspaper, and I hear him telling his friends that we own Bean Sprout. Tonight when I was putting him to sleep and I said, *I'm so tired,* he said, *Oh Mom, that's how you feel when you run a big business."*

BALANCING WORK AND FAMILY

If it's okay to take time off if you have a heart attack, why not take it off before that?

— Babs Sullivan

The two major barriers experienced by women in starting or operating a business are: the difficulty in obtaining financing and the difficulty in balancing work and family responsibilities.

— Federal Business Development Bank[1]

I've had to give up needlework, pottery, painting — all the things I used to do for enjoyment. Someday I'll go back to those things, but at this stage in my life I haven't got time. Period.

— Brenda Schiedel

Some well-meaning person, somewhere, invented the standard of balance, built on detailed research of those things that provoke feelings of guilt and inadequacy in working women everywhere. Balance is not about conforming to what doctors, children, spouses, and friends think you should be doing. It is about achieving those things you want to do in life. If you define that as a sixty-hour work week, with three hours of exercise and three evening meals with your children, then so be it.

It has been suggested that women often choose entrepreneurship because they are dissatisfied with their careers and because they want to meet both their career needs and the needs of their children.[2]

Suggest that entrepreneurship is the perfect way to balance family and work to Joanne Thomas Yacatto, president of Women and Money Inc., and she laughs and laughs. "If women are looking for more time to spend with their families, why in hell would they ever start their own business? Because exactly the opposite happens. You end up having to put ten times more effort into your business than you would have to in a corporate job."

When Yacatto started her own business, she believed in the myth of balance. "I wanted to be an involved mother and be able to work from home, and you know what? Reality set in. You can choose to have that balance in your life, but there is a tremendous financial price tag attached to it."

This obligation to balance work and family is the main reason women's businesses are a lot smaller than the male equivalent, she says. They don't seem to grow their businesses past a certain stage, because they sacrifice growth to maintain their connection with their family.

And so balance is a competitive disadvantage that many women drag into their businesses on day one. They juggle more and make more compromises across all aspects of their life. "It's a huge stress point," says Eva Klein, a psychologist. "You get good at something only when you're a maniac at it. The more you scatter yourself, the less effective you can be."

"There isn't a year that goes by that something's not out of balance," says Schiedel. "The important thing is that you recognize it. What am I doing about it? How long is it going to be out of balance? And then let your children know what's going on. They only notice what affects them: *Mom wasn't home four evenings in a row this week.* But if you go to them and say, *I have a really busy three weeks coming up. It will only last for three weeks and then I'm out of the woods,* you'll get a lot more cooperation at home."

Schiedel disappears from sight during hectic times at her company, and her family knows that this is part of owning a business. "You can't always be where you want to be at the right time. There has to be some give and take. If my children want the privileges that go along with having a mother in my position, they have to help and cooperate. Everyone knows how to cook; everyone knows how to clean; everyone knows how to do laundry. And I'm not afraid to hire help. Having someone else cut the grass might give you two free hours you haven't got right now."

Working hard is essential, but not all the time. "It's not how much you work. It's really what your brain has the capacity to do," says Babs Sullivan of the Strategic Coach. "You need the mental wherewithal to deal with rapid change, to look at your market in a different way and grasp an opportunity that you haven't seen before."

When fatigue makes a permanent perch on your shoulders, you lose that ability to see new opportunities. Situations become a crisis when they're simply something that must be dealt with. If you're constantly having to respond to crises and demands and difficulties without help, it depletes the strengths you need to excel in business.

Free time is a competitive necessity because it rejuvenates, adds a fresh perspective, and enables the mind to move out of automatic pilot and into more creative planes. Amazingly, the Strategic Coach recommends that entrepreneurs should work toward a goal of 200 free days a year. "Our clients are ambitious, they want big futures and big results, so they don't have a problem with motivation," says Sullivan. "They just need to get rejuvenated so they have greater energy and mental capacity. You don't tell them how to use free time — they use it and have breakthroughs."

She finds that entrepreneurs buy into the value of free time on a conceptual level but in practice are afraid to take the plunge. "Emotionally, they feel they can't take free time because they can't leave their client base or because their business is unique and the concept of free time doesn't apply. But once they try it, they become convinced they can't do without it."

To those who resist the importance of free time, Sullivan simply shrugs and waits. "The pain just isn't great enough yet. Some people like to avoid pain: they see it coming, and they make the change. Others wait till they have to. If it's okay to take time off if you have a heart attack, why not take it off before that?"

Some women entrepreneurs complain that their free time is consumed by responsibilities at home. Delegate, advises Sullivan. "You have to have somebody else doing the housework so that you can focus on the important things, like your relationships with your children. You really have to have a team in place, at work and at home."

SARAH'S STORY

I'm a single mom and an entrepreneur. If it were just me, I'd get rid of three staff and work the store myself, but I need to be available to Zoe. I have no formal education. I didn't get into a major corporation where I could follow a path. My mother had me believe that I was never going to have difficulties, that I would marry and be supported. But it didn't happen. The whole white picket fence thing didn't happen.

— Sarah Band

Sarah Band is the owner of Bianco Plus, a kitchen store that sells household goods from ironing boards to candlesticks. She has been in the retail business since 1983. She is forty-eight years old, and a single parent of a seven-year-old girl. The girl's father is not a part of her life, but he pays for her private school education.

When Band failed to get the marks necessary to be accepted into the agriculture program at the University of Guelph, her mother expected her to go to work. She went down to the local bank and was hired as a teller, where she worked for a year and a half. Then for almost a decade, her life took random twists and turns. She went to England and taught children to ride horses. She earned a Cordon Bleu degree, became active in politics, worked as an executive recruiter, and then finally opened her first retail store, which sold Italian giftware and tableware. She closed it when her rent increased 50 percent, and in 1989 opened Bianco Plus in a less expensive location.

Band's mother is the entrepreneurial role model in the family. "My mother is enormously successful. She's the president of a flour milling business and paper box manufacturer, left to her by her father. She's seventy-six and won't let go." Band's father disdains entrepreneurial businesses, but her relationship with him is huge and comforting.

Band has always been one to speak her mind, publicly. She has expressed her outrage at the public's treatment of retailers by writing to the *Globe and Mail*. As president of the Empire Club, a long-standing speaking club in Toronto whose membership is predominately business-men, Band announced her out-of-wedlock pregnancy to the membership in a speech by noting there would be one new member by year's end.

Her weekday begins with taking Zoe to school. Bianco Plus opens at half past ten, so she has a couple of hours each morning to do household tasks and volunteer work. When she needs help, her dad is available, and a nanny takes care of Zoe for the remainder of the day.

According to a 1996 study on women entrepreneurs in Canada,[3] close to half of women-led firms are in retail. "When they did those stress charts about moving, divorce, and death, they forgot to include retail," Band laughs. Her stress comes from living daily with the inse-curity of her business, the constant pressures from curmudgeonly customers, impatient banks, and cautious suppliers.

"Retail is tenuous. The mood of customers is not a good one. People are hanging onto their dollars, keeping their money for repairs, summer camps for the kids, and breaks from life. And the customer thinks the retailer is ripping them off. Christmas was good, but it's not enough to carry us through the year. Three months from now, I have no idea what will happen.

"At Christmas, a lady came in and bought twenty glass dessert plates. She returned them, a week later, in a plastic bag. She told me they didn't wash well in the dishwasher," says Band through gritted teeth. "I look at the Wal-Marts and Price Clubs, who can afford to eat questionable returns, like a washed, ruined sweater with a tag that says Dry Clean Only. I can't afford it."

A customer who borrowed some planters from Band's store for the weekend "to see if her husband would like them" returned them on Monday. "Then a friend of mine in the floral business told me that she had been hired by the customer to fill the planters with flowers for a Saturday night party."

In addition to customers from hell, the bank is also a source of frustration for Band. "From the bank's perspective, inventory doesn't count for anything. I'm not into the bank for substantial amounts — only around $10,000 — but the second you're over your bank line, they're on the phone to you. Once a year I give them sales projections I would love to see happen."

Band stays in the retail business because "90 percent of customers are great" and she loves her store. "It's never tiring," she says. "Last Christmas I worked twenty-three days straight. I'm exhilarated by the ring of the cash register, by helping people make the right decision."

She is constantly searching for new ways to entice customers into the store: "Will a promotion cost me to no avail? How should I change the storefront window? Do I buy ten or two of something? These are decisions for which there is no formula."

Not only is there no one to give her the answer, but sometimes Band thinks the answers are serendipitous. One fall, her business took a huge turn upward. "I have no idea why. Here's one story: I've always carried tea towels. I had ten dozen tea towels come in — the same ones I always carry — and I decided to mark them up 50 cents. I saw some old clothes pegs at an antique shop, so I bought them and strung a clothesline across the window and hung the tea towels up. At the end of two weeks, I had sold eight dozen tea towels. That supply of tea towels usually lasts me three or four months. And they were gone inside of two weeks. So you have no idea what brings people in."

Women who want to own a retail store should go and work for an existing store for six to nine months, Band advises. "Keep your mouth closed, learn as much as you possibly can, learn who their suppliers are, what sort of customer base they have, and go from there. I didn't do that, and I regret it to this day."

Band bought the name of a store in Montreal for $30,000, expecting to receive their expertise too. When she got nothing but the name, she renamed her store with her own name. "They tried to sue me, but I closed my eyes and shut my ears and they went away."

Prepare for start-up costs of two months' rent up front, the cost of a lawyer for the rental agreement, a $1,000 deposit for electricity and telephone, costs for staff, signage, store fixtures, cash registers, lighting, leasehold improvements, inventory, a mailing list, mailings to notify people you're open, and postage. "And you can't go in with minimal inventory, or no one comes in," warns Band.

It took three years before her first store was profitable. "It takes so long because you're reinvesting in inventory. I couldn't call up my supplier in Italy and say, *By the way, could you ship me over two crystal candlesticks?* I've had to have fairly extensive inventory, which ties up money."

Today her inventory is all on the shelf and she orders from local distributors. "When it's gone, it's gone until the next time I order."

Building a rapport with suppliers can reap big dividends. "They can get you two of something or four of something or rush something for you, or give you an 8 or 10 percent reduction, or forget the freight charges. The old-time reps are marvelous because they come in and nurture you along. They want you to do well because it means they'll do well. The others have too many lives; they're trying to make fast money, and they don't try to help you."

Band's store is unique — her inventory and her presence make it so. Here's a typical exchange between Band and a customer: A man picks up a green bowl and says, *I like this.* She tells him it doesn't make sense to buy just one green bowl. *Push, push, push!* he says, laughing. She folds her arms, leans back, and says, *So, you've invited your girlfriend to dinner, and you've got one green bowl. You're going to serve her the green bowl, and you get what, a white bowl?* The man agrees, *Okay, okay, give me two green bowls.* When a customer asks her what credit cards she accepts, she answers, *Visa, MasterCard, dinner dates, and diamonds.*

Band has no intention of encouraging a retail career for her daughter. "Retail stinks. You get beaten up by your bank, and by your suppliers who cancel delivery of your inventory, and by governments who are onto you about what you're doing and how you're doing it, and by your landlord who wants to increase your rent. People in general assume that shopkeepers aren't educated. They think your abilities are limited, and they treat you in a patronizing way. I won't let that get to me. I'm just as good as anyone else. Some may have a little bit more money or brains, but in the end we're all the same."

To succeed in retail, Band recommends finding a niche market and then investing all your time and energy in it to keep the wolves from the door. When Band started in retail, there were two kitchen stores in all of Toronto. Now there are twenty-two.

MONEY

Average annual earnings of self-employed women were $18,400 in 1993. This compares with $25,900 for female paid workers and $33,400 for self-employed men.

— Statistics Canada, Spring 1996

You drive yourself so hard in the beginning because you're driving an idea. But keep your eye on profitability. I bought my house three times as a result of mistakes.

— Dorothy Millman

If your ambition is to become a millionaire, you're better off with a lottery ticket than your own business. A 1991 Canadian study[4] found that entrepreneurial women typically work a fifty- to seventy-hour week for less than $30,000 a year. You can beat the odds, however, and Marcella Abugov describes how.

MARCELLA'S STORY

I have more energy than the law allows.

— Marcella Abugov

Marcella Abugov, forty-six, is president of what she affectionately calls a mom-and-pop store. A Touch Of Gold is a twenty-year-old retail jewelry store in Halifax with sales in excess of $1 million a year and a bottom line that is "quite wonderful."

A Touch of Gold sells two kinds of jewelry: expensive and very expensive — gold jewelry, diamonds, Rolex watches, and the like.

Abugov has another store in another part of town called the Vault. Ten years old, it sells only "fun" things like sterling silver, Anne Klein watches, "things that women will say *Yes, I'll take it*, without having to bring in their husbands like they do when it's a diamond."

At 450 square feet, A Touch of Gold is very small, so small in fact that Abugov believes she may have the highest sales per square foot in her industry. Unlike many of her competitors, she has always shunned giftware and other merchandise, which eat up space, to focus solely on jewelry.

Every year has been profitable, rain or shine, recession or not. Sales have gone straight up, except for one year when sales remained constant out of nominal respect for a recession.

"I've always said that to make some real money in a small business, you have to do many jobs," says Abugov. She does the work of three people: buyer, chief financial officer, and manager of four employees. Her husband, an award-winning jewelry designer, also manages the advertising, works with customers, and generally troubleshoots wherever he is needed. "We could pay someone else $30,000 to do our advertising, but my husband would only go over what someone else did anyhow," she shrugs. "To make serious money, you have to work really hard."

Abugov emigrated from Belize in Central America to Canada when she was nineteen years old. "I didn't have a formal education, but I have a lot of common sense," she says. "To be a successful entrepreneur, you don't have to have ten degrees."

But you do have to have talent for the business you choose. Abugov has an extraordinary eye for jewelry design. "I thought that everybody had it, and that everything you bought sold for you. It's always been that way for me, but five years ago it came to me that not everybody can buy. I realized that there is such a thing as a good buyer."

A Touch of Gold prospers in an industry teeming with cutthroat competition and big players. There are three reasons for this mom-and-pop success: sheer hard work, customer service, and a unique product offering.

Sheer hard work

Abugov and her husband work hard, Monday to Saturday, at levels that competitors cannot hope to match. Abugov's husband is the workaholic, and she nearly became one too, trying to help him.

"I didn't know what I was dealing with until eight years ago I read a book about workaholics and I said, *Oh my gosh, Honey, they wrote a book on you.* He is a perfectionist, very hard on himself." Abugov tries to follow the maxim "Strive for excellence, avoid perfection," but her husband has yet to accept her philosophy. "He'll work from 7:30 in the morning to eleven o'clock at night and then take paperwork home. He says, *I can't just come down right away,* and I say, *Pick up a magazine.* Then I'll see him with the *Financial Times.* He tries, but work takes over.

"He's relentless in his effort, his striving for excellence. I don't have as much of a desire. I want to get better and do wonderful things, but I don't have to be the best in the world or in the country." Over the last three years, Abugov has gradually removed herself from behind the counter to do more paperwork and attend jewelry shows. "I think I have a balance."

Customer service

"We're wonderful behind the counter and we take exquisite care of customers," she says. If a customer can't come down to the store to pick up a piece of jewelry, her husband, David, will drop it off, even on a Saturday night. On one occasion, when American tourists asked where they could buy sweaters, David drove them downtown to the appropriate store, then took them to a pastry shop for tea. "It's little things like that that keep you in the ballpark," she says.

It also helps that she loves what she does. "There's nothing else I'd rather do than help my customer look wonderful with the right pair of earrings. I say, *If you look good, I look better. I get ten of your friends wanting to buy from me.*"

She likens her store atmosphere to the old-fashioned corner drugstore, where people from all income levels drop in and visit, and Abugov knows all their names. "In my store, you can look for two hours and not buy. I tell the staff I don't care who it is. If it's the guy who washes floors for a living, his ten dollars are just as important to him as anybody's. And with our luck, he'll win the lottery and he'll remember us."

"I tell them the story of the man who came into my store when I first started. He had no teeth and was looking at gold chains. I showed him one for $140, and he asked to see something in the thousand-dollar range. My first husband panicked because we had been robbed the week before, and this guy was scraggly. Anyway, I just took over. I showed the man a necklace and he bought it, paying cash. I always say, you never know."

The Bank of Nova Scotia owns her mall and a couple of years ago audited all the stores from a customer-service perspective. They had people shop all the stores in jeans and three-piece suits. A Touch of Gold won for the way customers were treated, regardless of what they wore.

Abugov's passion for customer service trickles into unusual territory. When an emotionally ill and financially destitute woman — and regular visitor to A Touch of Gold — was hospitalized, Abugov brought her cigarettes and baby powder and a few dollars to tide her over. "All the people who work in my store treat everyone with the same respect, buying customers or not," she says. "Sometimes if they're acting up in the store, it can be embarrassing because other customers might think you've upset them. But all this is part of retail, and you have to care. A lot of people are lonely and just want someone to talk to."

Take little old Mrs. Reynolds. "She's so cute, and she loves my husband, because he kisses her. When I got back from a vacation we took with another couple, she asked me if we swapped partners. I said, *Mrs. Reynolds, you're bad.* And she said, *If I can't be bad at age eighty-five, when can I be bad?*"

Unique product offering

"If I'm just like everyone else, why would you buy from me?" is Abugov's philosophy. She uses her intuition and experience to buy the beautiful and unusual. "I figure there's enough 'ordinary' around." Added to Abugov's talent for picking beautiful inventory is her husband's design talent, which contributes approximately 30 percent of the company's revenues.

An American from San Francisco bought three pairs of earrings from Abugov one afternoon. ("I love earrings and lipstick," says Abugov. "I would go out naked as long as I had my earrings and lipstick.") Abugov pointed out to the customer that two pairs came from San Francisco. "I know," said the customer. "But I've never gone into a store before and found this concentration of wonderful things. So I don't care *where* they come from."

Fifteen years ago when few Canadian businesses went to the New York jewelry shows, Abugov was going. Now Canadian businesses are flooding such shows. "All of a sudden they realized they had to have wonderful things and learn about customer service," says Abugov of her competition. "They think these are new ideas and they're not. They're something they should have always been doing."

Good people

Abugov isn't interest in hiring crackerjack salespeople with a hard, fast sales pitch and heady track record. "I'm in business for the long term. If you pair an item with your customer and you've done your job, you and the customer both win. If I win all the time, I won't have any customers. If the customer wins all the time, I'll be out of business. We must both win."

For her, the sign of a good salesperson is low returns and exchanges, particularly in December when a huge percentage of the yearly sales are realized. Her mantra to employees is that lazy people give themselves more work. "If you're lazy and you just want to shovel it out, then you'll have to work ten times harder later on dealing with gift exchanges." She works with customers to find out who the present is for: What does she do? Is she a nurse? Is she athletic? Is she glamorous? Is she tall, short, long hair, short hair? Are her features delicate? Does she like tiny jewelry?

"The man may love a certain thing, but that doesn't mean that *she's* going to love it. If he gets a positive reaction, he'll come back to you. There's no point in saying, *If she doesn't like it, sir, you can exchange it after Christmas* because you want him to have just as good an experience as the person getting the gift. And you cut down on the work after Christmas."

Abugov believes that the reason so many retail businesses fail is, quite simply, the owner. "A lot of people think it's a quick way to get into business." While it is impossible to decide to be a doctor tomorrow, anyone can open a retail store. "It's easy to say, I'll open a store ... I like marbles, so I'll go sell marbles." To succeed you have to be passionate about your product and service (which implies knowledge), capable of managing all aspects of the business, and know that there is a market need that you can fill.

In the early days of her own business, she lent $15,000 to a man who had lost his job in the travel industry. He needed the money to start his own travel agency. "In the back of my mind I was thinking, *Gee, do we need another travel agency? I don't think so.* But it was what he knew, the only thing he thought he could do.

"I'm sure he did some parts of it very well, but there were lots of other parts that he wasn't able to do, so it didn't work for him. He struggled for a couple of years. Maybe he should have been a consultant rather than try to run the day-to-day retail operation of a travel agency. He just thought, *I'll have a travel agency and it will work.*"

Abugov always wanted to be a merchant. She was born in Central America, the result of a short-lived romance, and raised by her aunt and uncle. "I didn't meet my American father until I was twenty-six because I was a little accident that happened to him in Central America. He was a well-to-do young fellow just floating through the country." Her mother left Belize shortly after giving birth to Abugov, to find a job so that she could send money back to her family. After a few years, she disappeared. Abugov defends her. "The story goes that she had a nervous breakdown after she had me, because it wasn't a nice thing in those days to have a child out of wedlock. She deserves a lot of credit: at least she had me."

The aunt and uncle were proud people who taught Abugov that she should work hard, not complain, and not ask anyone for anything. To this day, she has trouble sending unsatisfactory soup back when she's in a restaurant.

And her entrepreneurial spirit was always waiting just under the surface of everything she did, ready to seize an opportunity. When living in Belize, the Christian Social Council was selling goods received from the States to raise money for the poor. Abugov bought some goods and resold them for a profit. "Well, my aunt thought I was going straight to hell," she recalls. "How could you buy something from the church and then sell it? She was mortified. But, to my way of thinking, I saw a good item for a good price and recognized it."

She married when she finished high school, which was common in Belize, and came to Canada with her first husband, who had an engineering scholarship. For several years, she earned money taking care of children, doing bookkeeping in a bank, buying and selling old newspapers and furniture, and selling Tupperware and Avon products. Every week, a portion of her earnings went back to Belize to her aunt and uncle.

"I don't have any resentment toward anyone. Do you know what I have today and how much I have to be thankful for? Whatever happened to me in the past contributed to what is happening today. I don't go backward."

Her husband's CIDA scholarship required that they return to Belize on his graduation to work for ten years. But when they returned, the teaching job awaiting him had nothing to do with his chemical engineering education. For a year, Abugov bought silver, leather, and clothing in Guatemala and sold it in Belize. Then, frustrated with her life, she said to her husband, "Look, they've broken their end of the bargain. You are not using what you learned in university, so let's immigrate to Canada. He was a quiet man, a good soul, not a go-getter. I filled out all the forms, and we came back in 1975."

Back in Canada, her husband couldn't find work. "He's brilliant, hardworking, and honest, but he couldn't sell himself. So it was hard for him to find a job. We ran out of money, and I'm at home with two little ones." They couldn't receive social assistance because they hadn't been in the country long enough. But in their darkest hour, the phone rang with a job offer in Halifax.

They found the cheapest apartment available, in the roughest part of town, and stayed there for two years. "It was all we could afford. We slept on the floor until we could buy a mattress from the bargain basement at Sears. We found a Formica table all burned in the middle and two chairs in the garbage — that was our table and chairs. We never went into debt. I don't like the pressure of paying for something that I don't have the money for now, and that's part of my business philosophy too."

Abugov got a job at a bank and continued to send money home to Belize. Then, in 1976, she heard from her father, and a year later met him in California with her children. This was a pivotal event in her life.

"When we were on the boardwalk, I saw all this gorgeous jewelry, soapstone and coral and silver, at really inexpensive prices. I had been selling costume jewelry in Fredericton and knew I could sell this real stuff." She tracked down the wholesaler and pored over the catalogue. Her father encouraged her to order some. "I said, *No, it's too much,* and he said, *How much is too much?* I said, *$1,033.95,* and he said, *Order it. I'll pay for it.*

"He paid for it in February 1977 and in December 1977 I gave him back $2,000 from the proceeds of selling the jewelry in people's homes. It wasn't a loan, but I didn't want to take anything."

Soon after, Abugov's marriage broke up. Her husband moved back to Belize, became a teacher, and eventually remarried.

Abugov's business grew enough that she could afford a small retail space downtown for $225 a month. Then she moved into a mall and met David, her second husband, soon after. In 1982 they were married.

She empathizes with people who are starting out in retail today because most of them must finance large start-up costs. Her beginnings had very little fixed costs, as she began selling at home parties, motivated in part by her fear of debt. In the past five years, Abugov has begun to relax a bit. "I've said to myself that we can stay at the Four Seasons in Toronto and the Plaza in New York and not worry. I can eat those absolutely wonderful meals. That's my passion — to have a wonderful meal and a great bottle of wine."

Abugov once read that in life, we strive for two things: to make it and to enjoy it. But only a very few achieve the latter. "I always said that I'll be one of those very few. Because a lot of people don't know when to quit."

Her husband has talked to her about expanding the Vault concept with additional stores, and other people have approached her with equity offers. "I could do it, but I've had twenty years of retail. I've done it, I've loved it, but I want a life now. I don't want to make more money. I've been blessed, and I don't want more than I have already. Sometimes I think I have too much."

When her husband gave her a new car as a present, she had to work hard to pretend she was excited. "The car I had was five years old. It was spotless, worked well. I said, *What do I want with a new car?* He said, *It has airbags.* So I had to say yes."

Abugov summarizes the reason for her success like this: "Necessity is the mother of invention. I was responsible for my aunt and uncle, for my kids. My first husband was not strong as a provider. Because of the way I started my life, I always tried to make sure that I was never at the mercy of anybody else, ever again.

"Bad things that happen to you give you that way of thinking. It's very difficult for someone else who hasn't experienced these things to behave like I do. They don't understand what you're talking about. It's like trying to explain to someone that it hurts when you have a baby. They believe you, but they don't have a clue what you're talking about. Until it happens to them, they just don't know."

Abugov won't read articles that are written about her stores. She finds it embarrassing. "I like to feel as ordinary and grounded as possible. When I'm behind the counter, if someone comes in and thinks I work there, that's better."

"I don't need power because I know in my mind if I want to learn to fly a plane tomorrow, I can. But you know what? I don't want to learn how to fly a plane. I know that anything I set my sights on, I'm capable of doing. But I only need so much. We made some investments in real estate and did very well. But after two projects, I said to myself, *I don't do this for a living. I don't know what I'm doing. I made some money, that's it. That's enough already.*"

AVOIDING THE ALTERNATIVE

No one wants a sixty-year-old hairdresser.

— Claire Cobourn

Sometimes, there simply isn't any other choice. But sometimes the only choice left turns out to be the best.

CLAIRE'S STORY

Claire Cobourn is in her early sixties. In 1994 she opened her door for business under the shingle of Comfort Care, a company that provides in-home care for the elderly, ill, or disabled in Toronto.

Cobourn was an employee for her entire working life, and her last four years of employment were sharply punctuated by two terminations. JDS Investments, a property developer, went bankrupt in 1993, shortly after Cobourn was laid off as executive assistant to the president. Three and a half years earlier, she had been laid off after working thirteen years in a similar position, again because of the company's difficult financial situation.

"I got a week for each year I'd been there, and I was fortunate that I got that much. It was a blessing that I wasn't there when they locked the doors. Someone was watching over me. I was already on another path."

Suddenly unemployed, Cobourn was worried about her future. Retirement was not an option. Not only was Cobourn not interested, she couldn't afford it. "I was creeping up on sixty years old and it was very difficult because of my age and the lack of security. I thought, *What am I going to do? Where do I go from here?* I had this ominous feeling that no one would hire me in the capacity I had been working, and it was a fact."

Despite an exhaustive job search, she received no job offers and finally gave up. "One day I realized I was being lied to, and I couldn't do it anymore. Even though employers claim they don't discriminate because of age, they do."

The man with whom she lives suggested that this was the best thing that ever happened to her. *Just pull up your socks and do something different,* he advised. *Don't be hurt anymore. Make your own decisions.*

Cobourn is no stranger to making her own path in life. When her marriage ended years ago, she raised her two children by herself. Her son is a surgeon and her daughter, a public relations manager. "I did fine," she says of her life as a single mother. "I became bullheaded and strong and perhaps a little better.

"Before I made a decision to — what's the buzzword? — embark on a new career or change my path or whatever, I did lots of research. I went to research libraries and self-help centers and whatever was available and used whatever resources were there — including people I knew who had gone through the same thing. I knew that nobody in hairdressing or banking or any of the typical female jobs wants someone who's sixty years old, despite the fact that you can do it and have the interest. You're just not "with it" anymore. I decided on the health care industry because in my research I found a bigger demand there than anywhere. I figured that if they need people so badly, they're not going to turn me down."

After receiving her aide's certificate and apprenticing in a nursing home, Cobourn's interest in being an employee plummeted. "My goodness, the wage scale in nursing homes is next door to starvation. I couldn't support myself. People were getting $7.50 an hour. This was very disheartening — after I'd gone to school to find out that I couldn't make a living at it. Then my companion said, *Why should you work for someone else?"*

Cobourn applied to the federal government's Self-Employment Assistance program, which offered applicants an opportunity to get business training while receiving unemployment insurance. She was accepted, developed the idea of Comfort Care, and tested it with market research, which entailed:

- getting the brochures of competitors, which listed their services and rates charged;
- accessing the local library, daily print media, and government departments to learn more about the aging population, their health problems and issues; and
- visiting a number of retirement facilities, nursing homes, and medical practitioners to assess their level of interest in referring clients.

Cobourn subsequently won an Enterprise Award in 1995 in recognition of her business accomplishments as a student in the SEA program.

"I'm the company," she says. "I don't have a big business. At any one time, I have half a dozen clients on the go. My business is small. I report my income and manage to keep the wolf from the door."

Cobourn isn't interested in building the company into a large agency. "I don't have great aspirations. I want to carry on the way I am, partly because I'm sixty-one and in another four years I don't intend to work anymore."

Start-up costs were minimal and Cobourn refused to dip into her savings. "I just decided I was going to learn to do without, do things a different way. Living is very expensive, but I'm thrifty. I don't enjoy shopping. Most women like buying things, but I don't. I'm very independent. I can stretch a dime into a dollar very easily. I had to do it when I was a single mother with a mortgage. I learned, and those lessons never leave you."

Cobourn set up a home office, upgraded her computer, prepared brochures and business cards, and changed the insurance on her car. She incurred some advertising expenses, which she regretted since they failed to generate business.

"So I approached people I know. I went to my local drugstore, which I've dealt with for thirty-some years, and asked the owner if he would be kind enough to put my little brochure and business card in his store. I got my first client through the drugstore. Networking with other people is the best way to accomplish anything — meet friends, find people to fill in for me when I need them. I just ask people I know."

Cobourn is usually busy during the week taking care of one of her clients. She has a network of other caregivers, which she matches with a client's needs for a fee. If it's a long-term job, she always takes the first few days herself before giving it to another caregiver.

"These are all elderly people, and most of them are senile. Lots of them have Alzheimer's and various other conditions. I learn about the family and their needs and the idiosyncrasies of the client before I send someone in."

She prides herself on the extra care and attention she takes, which she believes distinguishes her service from the impersonality of the large agencies. "I always do everything a little more than I need to. If I'm making a cake, I put a little pinch of something extra; if I'm cleaning the garage, I'll shampoo the floor — that kind of thing," she says.

This "little extra" carries over into her work. "I looked after an elderly woman for several months who was suffering from congenital heart failure, and she ultimately did pass away. But I became very close to the family. We still see one another."

The sad side of her business is when she loses a client to death or to a nursing home when more expert care is required. "I get close to them. People say that you can't get close to your clients, but I do it. I take them by the heart. And it hurts when someone's gone. But I've never lost a client because of my failing."

She believes that being female is an advantage in her business. "The elderly trust me. I have the compassion that a man might not. It's a woman's field. Maybe I'm wrong. I don't know men who do it."

Cobourn's income is half of what she earned as an executive secretary. "I don't know how I do it," she says. "The transition from having a paycheque come in every two weeks to having a cheque arrive *whenever* has been very hard. I have never gotten used to that."

She and her companion split living expenses, including groceries and the maintenance costs of her house, his cottage, and their mobile home in Myrtle Beach. Her thriftiness allows them to escape to their mobile home 100 days a year.

"I used to worry when I first started the business," she recalls. "They impressed on us at the SEA program that this is going to be a seven-day thing — you're never going to have a minute to rest. They really hammered it into us: *This is really going to be tough. The first year will tell the tale,* and on and on. So at first I thought I should be busy every day all day, but it really wasn't necessary. Maybe I'm just lucky that it's working, I don't know. I do work very hard at it, at making it a success.

"This is the biggest risk I've ever taken in my life. Sometimes I make a comfortable living and sometimes I don't. I own my home, so perhaps I have a cushion that young people don't. I own my car and I'm debt-free, so I can accept a little less. I don't have money in the bank to fall back on, but I'm not so sure the money is the big thing. I am so content and happy. Everyone says I'm not the same person I was. For years I sat behind a desk and played at being someone's right-hand person, and I never smiled. But now I laugh and go places and talk about my work.

"It just worked out. My life is so good, I can't believe it."

CHAPTER 5

STARTING UP A BUSINESS

KNOWING YOUR STRENGTHS

Your strengths are the heart of your company. They are what differentiates your company from other companies, allowing it to survive and grow. You focus on those strengths in your work, and delegate other activities.

MARY'S STORY

Mary Connolly's strength is seeing a company's pluses and minuses from forty miles up, and then being able to reorganize or fine-tune as necessary. Forty-seven years old and a chartered accountant, Connolly has been self-employed since 1986, consulting to a wide range of industries in general management and systems areas. Her story is not about the company she built but about the company she searched for and found.

Connolly has done well financially and professionally all her life. Married to a senior partner at a major public accounting firm, she has never found money a problem, and her own business has done well even through recessions.

"I've been a generalist all my life," she says. "I've always been in demand because I can do so many things." She contrasts her success with her peers, other chartered accountants, who often have a hard time getting work and go through protracted negotiations about their fees. "The demand isn't for financial statements. There's a ton of people who can do that stuff. Luckily it's not my love." Her love is helping clients improve parts of their companies by organizing systems and people and making sure that activities are in line with overall corporate objectives. Her consulting job required operations analysis as well as a lot of hand-holding and psychology.

Ten years in the analysis and hand-holding business was enough. "It was time for me to do something different, to make a change," she says. She briefly considered growing her business, but "the problem with that is that you then have to do things you don't really want to do, like managing people."

As a consultant, she was always an outsider. "You can't control what an organization does. You can recommend and review, tell them the alternatives. But you're not the decision maker. For a while that's okay, and then it starts to get frustrating. There isn't the same challenge that there is if you're part of the organization. I don't want a job; I want an experience."

She closed the company in September 1996 and began her search for one that needed her expertise and equity and that promised high returns. "For me, the reward is twofold. One is psychological/emotional — being part of what's happening when it's happening. The other one is financial — expecting at the end of the road that the dollar signs will be bigger than if I had continued consulting and putting money into RRSPs and investments."

To assist her in a search for a company to invest in, Connolly joined the Business Centurions, an organization that helps individuals find equity or employment opportunities in small- to medium-size enterprises.

Through her mentor, Ralph McLeod, Business Centurions gave Connolly advice and concrete leads. Initially, McLeod would call her to check on her progress. "At first it was serious, but it became a joke," says Connolly, who is a highly motivated woman. "I'd often have four appointments in one day."

Connolly added these contacts to an already extensive network that she developed as a consultant, plus referrals through her husband. Her objective: to find the deals and then sift through them to find one good idea backed by good people who can communicate effectively and want her active participation as well as her money.

"It would have been a lot tougher if I weren't connected. It's like being an independent consultant — I know people who are very good who get minimal amounts of work because they're not connected. It's making calls and pounding the pavement and finding out who knows who. You go and talk to people who you think will be a total waste of time and it turns out not to be at all, because they know somebody who knows somebody who knows somebody who has a company looking for somebody. That's the best way to find a deal."

Connolly built relationships with brokers and has taken advantage of a free provincial program called Opportunities Ontario, which helps people sell businesses whose value isn't high enough to attract traditional brokers.

It took Connolly half a year to find her ideal business venture, an apparel manufacturer that needed an infusion of capital and new ideas. "It was a constant reaching out. At times it was tiring but I didn't get discouraged because I knew it was going to happen."

She didn't consider businesses without a business plan. "A business plan should lay out the vision of the company, their market, their competitors, officers — that kind of stuff. But a plan also shows an awareness. You look at some business plans, and honestly, those people are out to lunch."

For example, Connolly considered the business plan for a personal and home security company. The owners were two engineers who had excellent credentials. But she couldn't get past the fact that the two engineers were reinventing technology that already existed. "That's stupid. You don't need to do that," she says. "Instead of using existing technology, they wanted to reinvent the whole thing and put some huge bay stations at a huge cost across the country when we already have cellular phone stations."

She finds that a lot of people have pie-in-the-sky ideas. "Sometimes if you say it fast, it doesn't sound too bad, but once you start to analyze it, it doesn't make any sense at all. Or the ideas are really good and they've got the whole thing worked out but the principals have no credibility in the marketplace. Or they're control freaks and there's no way they would allow someone else to work with them.

"I'm not a control freak, but I don't want to play second fiddle. I'm prepared to accept that I'll probably end up with a minority interest and won't call the shots, but I can't work with someone who treats me like a second-class citizen."

Once Connolly did find a promising business plan, but she lost interest when she met its owner. "He seemed on the surface to be a really nice guy who said all the right things as long as he was giving a monologue. This was a bright guy with a good business idea, but he didn't seem capable of opening up — no feedback, no humor, nothing. I got the feeling that he wanted my money and practiced his monologue to get it."

SETTING GOALS AND OBJECTIVES

I wanted my own business so that I could create an environment that would be personally fulfilling. I didn't say this to the bank.

— Marnie Walker

Many women start their own businesses with inappropriate goals. Some goals, like self-actualization, aren't quantifiable and make bankers leery. Others, like controlling your own destiny and making millions overnight, are just plain naive.

Want to win

Gamesmen are the best leaders of companies, according to Wanda Dorosz, Quorum president. "They're the people with the mindset that says, *When I'm on the playing field, I'm on to win.* But when the game is over, it's over, and you go on to the next game. And you know that one game is not a season."

Eva Klein, a clinical psychologist, finds that women aren't taught to enjoy winning to the same extent that men are. Sports teaches a comfort with competition, with winning and losing, but the participants are more often than not males.

According to Klein, "Some women feel that winning isn't nice, or that saying that they want to win or succeed isn't nice. But you have to be competitive to make it. Part of it is personal competition, doing the best you can. Part of it is actually wanting to win and enjoying the sheer thrill of winning."

Layered on top of women's thin apprenticeship in competitiveness is often a dangerous lack of self-confidence. "To succeed, it really helps to feel there are no barriers rather than to think that you have to overcome barriers," says Klein. "It makes you feel less of a victim and that you can do anything you want."

Many of the cooperative attributes ascribed to women do not work well in the entrepreneurial world: such qualities are better suited to a corporate environment that rewards team skills and common goals and shuns even the most brilliant lone rangers. In an entrepreneurial environment, the reverse is true. What's needed is a strong ego, and the will to win.

Describe your dream in the language of money

Goals can differ immensely from entrepreneur to entrepreneur. One entrepreneur may want her own business so that she can be in control of her life, while another may seek entrepreneurialism to remove herself from the control of another, like an employer.

These goals, however, are not what banks and investors want or need to hear. They want pro forma projections, repayment schedules, market research, collateral, proof of experience, anything and everything that reduces the risk to them and heightens the probability of business success.

Social scientists have tried for more than a decade to differentiate the motives between men and women entrepreneurs. Studies have shown that entrepreneurs, both male and female, attach a great deal of importance to their independence and their achievements, and are risktakers.[1] On the whole, social scientists are willing to allow that women and men entrepreneurs' goals are similar, with some differences in attitudes to risk, self-confidence and the role of the business in the entrepreneur's overall life.

One 1987 study suggests that women are less concerned with making money and often choose entrepreneurship because of career dissatisfaction and as a means of better balancing the demand of work and family.[2] In the early 1990s, Rena Blatt, an Ontario social scientist, analyzed survey data to determine whether men and women have different ambitions. She found that men frequently expressed the goal of making money, whereas women frequently expressed the desire to run their own businesses. These nonfinancial goals may actually keep women's businesses small.

MARY'S STORY

There's nothing like having no money to make you really functional.

— Mary Fote

Babies, weddings, dead bodies, fashion models, and corporate annual reports. These seemingly incongruous things all have one thing in common: Mary Fote. For most of her career, Fote has managed her business on sheer talent alone. Only recently has she learned to establish objectives and methodically pursue them.

As a photographer who specialized in each of these areas, Fote is now president of a multimedia design company called the Medea Group. "It's really simple," she says of the best approach to running a business. "Never, never, never *not* deliver. If clients don't pay me, my kids don't eat. It's that simple. I'll stay up all night to fix a job when it's screwed up, but clients don't see that part of it. There are never any excuses — never, ever. I may drive them crazy, or they may not like me, but I get the job done, and it's always beautiful."

Fote was one of those smart kids who did abysmally in school. She is dyslexic, crackling with energy and good-natured waywardness, and her laughter has the velocity and impact of machine gun fire. Of her time in an all-girls private school, she cheerfully recalls, "They had mental abuse down to a science. Either you fit or they would pound you until you fit. Their mission in life was to make me fit into that square hole, and my mission in life was to torture them as much as possible and get out of there. We both did a good job, but it meant I didn't get an education."

After squeaking through high school, she was accepted into nursing at the University of New Mexico, where she managed one semester before calling it quits. Her alarmed parents begged her to stay in school. Fote flipped through the course books, saw a photography class that looked mildly interesting, enrolled, and found it fascinating. Returning home to upstate New York, Fote got a job as a waitress, acquired a 35mm camera, and began developing film in a closet. A man on her street who owned a passport portrait studio allowed her to use his darkroom in return for her cleaning services.

Then one day she was out driving and came upon a garage burning. She took a picture of a fireman silhouetted against the flames and sold it to a local newspaper for $5. Thus her career as a "shooter" began.

Her next contract was with the Lackawanna police department in 1972 to photograph accidents and murder victims. "The cops would come by late at night and bang on my door and wake me up to take pictures," she says. At the same time, she bought the phone and address lists of women who had just given birth. "I'd phone them up, go and take pictures of their babies in the house, and then sell them prints." Her business further expanded into photographing children's hockey teams at arenas, and weddings.

"I had this baby/team/dead body/wedding picture business and I started writing things down in a ledger and delivering prints and paying suppliers and running around and trying to collect $5 and $3 and $2 from people," says Fote. "And I've been doing the same damn thing ever since, in one form or another."

Married at nineteen, Fote had her first child when she was twenty-two. Two years later, she was operating a sizable wedding photography business from her house, with three employees, divorced, with no child support. "I was working out of my living room, and my daughter was always in the middle of it all the time. I'd be in the bathroom-darkroom while she was watching *Sesame Street* and she'd get up and bang on the door — *Let me in!* — I was terrified we'd die of chemical poisoning. I would hang film in there, and when it's drying and tacky you can't open the door, and so I'd have her pee in a bucket in the living room."

Then boredom set in. "If I hadn't been bored, I'd be rich, but when I get bored I need to change things." Her interest strayed to fashion photography, so she took an eighteen-month course in pattern design and then applied to a week-long photography workshop run by a famous photographer, Bill Hayward.

"The class was loaded with New York photographers, and I walk in with this bride stuff in my portfolio," she says with a laugh. She was accepted, and for ten days didn't sleep, so great was her excitement at learning, at having real equipment, and a teacher who knew what she wanted to learn. At the end of the course, Hayward took Fote out for a sandwich and told her she had real talent and should get a job as a photographer's assistant. "I didn't know anything. I didn't know what a boom stand was. Everything I did was by figuring it out, reading and listening and observing."

Her teacher gave her his phone number, and Fote would call him frequently with what-should-I-do questions, delighted with the novel experience of having someone who wanted to help her. She approached all the big advertising and commercial photographers in Buffalo, "but this was 1980 — like, forget it. Photography was and is very male. Then there were zero women. No one would give me a job. They were like, no, *nada*, forget it." She was offered jobs as bookkeeper or receptionist, but a job as photographic assistant was out of the question.

Hayward suggested she put together a portfolio. She made up pretend jobs, put them all together, then walked into a department store with her new portfolio and introduced herself to the art director in charge of fashion photography. "She gave me my first job, taking pictures of shoes for a bill stuffer. I'll never forget her."

The art director asked how much she charged. Fote gave her price as $100. A silence. The art director suggested she charge more, and they agreed on $300.

The next hurdle was Fote's studio. She didn't have one. "The art director wanted to come down to my studio, so I said, *Well, my studio's pretty busy. How about if I shoot it here?* She said that would be wonderful. I went out and got a loan for $3,000 — my father had to co-sign it — and I ordered equipment and had it delivered to the department store. I spent a week shooting the shoes, and she loved it. She gave me more work, and that's how I started out being a fashion photographer."

When Fote saw her photographs in the newspaper, she was dismayed. "The black-and-white photos looked like shit. I called the paper because I was so upset. They told me to talk to Jack in the press room. Jack turned out to be an old cigar-chomping guy. As far as he was concerned, I was just another pain in the ass. He said, *Goddammit, if you want to know how this works, get down here, but we don't run nuthin' till midnight.* I said, *That's perfect because I can get one of my brothers to sleep over and look after my daughter.* I was relentless." She spent eight months working with Jack, and in return he taught her printing.

"My motivation was to find out why my pictures looked like shit in the newspaper. In order to fix that, I had to learn the printing business. I had to learn ink copy and all the interim film processes." She realized she needed to learn how to control contrast. Fote took a three-week class with Ansel Adams to study compression technology.

"I applied it to the fashion photography business — and wham! — I got newspaper production that astounded everybody." Armed with this competitive advantage, Fote traveled to Rochester, Cleveland, Columbus, and Pittsburgh with the guarantee that if she didn't give the newspaper the best reproductions they'd ever seen, she wouldn't charge a cent.

"It was a no-brainer," she says. "I would go down to the printer and find out what kind of presses they were running, how much ink they were putting in, and what kind of plates they were using. Then I would tailor my photographs to what they needed. It made them look like heroes. That's how I started my fashion photography business."

All this time, she was struggling with managing her business. "I'm an artist. I didn't have business skills. To me, you get cheques and you write cheques; you feed your kids and you buy equipment. And that's about it. I never thought about it. Whatever happened I always ended up making money. I didn't get financing from banks because who would look at you? I was this *girl,* and everybody was waiting for me to get a real job. I wasn't going to be viable; I was a nut case. Whenever I went in to talk to somebody, they'd look at me as if I were pink or purple, or try to feel me up. I'd say, *What's a business plan?* I had no idea."

"The competition was freaked out by me. I came in and took all the fashion photography business out of the whole town. Being a woman didn't matter, I'd slap my stuff down on the desk and they'd look at it and go *Wow.* The only time I felt being a woman was an issue was with any kind of business stuff — bankers, whatever." To this day, clients still think her male assistant is the photographer.

As her fashion photography business spread, Fote learned the art of not sleeping. "My baseline of sleep was four or five hours. You have to will yourself to do it, and I was a lot younger then. Today I can do four hours a night for a couple of days, and then I really crash. I definitely don't have the energy I had, but I still burn everyone else up."

The next challenge was finding models and makeup artists. "I was picking up girls in malls, I was so desperate," she says. Then a revelation hit her when she was in Toronto. While looking in the Yellow Pages for a restaurant someone had recommended, she stumbled on pages and pages of modeling agencies. She phoned one at random and asked if they would send models to Buffalo. The agent replied, "Oh my God, can you come in today?"

The big shocker came when Fote worked in Buffalo. "The clients were thrilled, the prices were reasonable, and I paid the bill. The agency called me and said, *You gave us a cheque in American funds.* I got my first lesson in what the exchange rate really means. It became my competitive advantage, and it still is to this day."

Fote started pulling whole crews out of Toronto — models, makeup artists, set builders. Still without a studio, she specialized in location photography. "I was the only person insane enough to pack all these people together and all the clothes and stylists and move everything to these locations to shoot." In 1982, she didn't even notice that there was a recession.

Then the idea dawned on her to shoot in Toronto, thereby avoiding paying for hotels and transportation for the models and crews. But customs became a problem when Fote tried to take clothes across the border for the purpose of shooting pictures. "Customs didn't know what slot to fit it in. So I took a customs broker course to figure out what the hell they were talking about. I had an employee take every U.S. customs broker out to lunch to figure out how to get the boxes into Canada for a month and then returned to the States. Once we figured it out, we started shipping tons of stuff to Toronto."

Fote moved to Toronto in 1983 and continued to work for her U.S. clients, amassing fifteen employees at one point to meet the demand. She didn't pursue Canadian clients because there wasn't a large market for her predominantly catalogue business.

She still had no idea of how to manage a full-blown production company. She knew how to take care of customers and meet their needs creatively, but managing employees was a mystery. The result was high turnover.

"I've never been an employee. It's a disadvantage because you have no idea what people *do* with employees. Except for the last two years, I've been a difficult employer because I had no idea of how to deal with people. It's like asking someone who's blind to describe the color red. You have no idea about reviewing employees' performance, or job descriptions, or what the average person's workload is in a normal situation, no idea about structures around what people do all day long. I figured it out by being brutally honest with people and having them slice and dice me up. My employees have to be people who don't need a lot of structure. It's just totally alien to my nature.

"I should have hired an office manager but I didn't even know what that was," she recalls. It wasn't until the late eighties that someone turned her on to the fact that there were books about management. But despite her ignorance, her revenues grew to $1 million, without the help of a credit line or an organizational structure.

"I learn by doing. It's the worst way, the hardest way. You make horrible mistakes. For example, I had no idea that I should have had a relationship with a banker, lines of credit, and somebody to manage the cash flow and look at the tax situation. My accountant just handed stuff back to me, and I said okay."

Then the trouble began. In the space of eighteen months, her U.S. client base, small and mid-size retailers, was bought up by large retailers, and by 1986 Fote didn't have a business anymore.

"I decided against shooting fashion in Canada because there's no money in it. Then someone said, *Why don't you do annual reports?*"

When she found out how much companies paid for that service, Fote was sold. And it sounded much easier than fashion photography. "If I had to go up to Yellowknife to shoot a gold mine, I wouldn't have to take six whining girls with me who didn't eat spinach, and make sure they didn't get drunk at night. It would be just me and an assistant."

But there she was with a portfolio of fashion photography, which hardly demonstrated a capability to do annual reports. So she called Ashland Chemical's director of marketing. "I said, *Can I come down for two weeks and shoot your annual report free?* He said, *What's the catch?* and I said, *There is no catch.* So I went and shot Ashland Chemical. After the first week, the guy was thrilled. I said, *What if I go and shoot the plant in Ohio and corporate headquarters and everything else?* It was as if he'd won the lottery. So basically I spent the whole three weeks shooting every division in the place and assembled a perfect annual report. Then I went to people I knew at Bethlehem Steel and shot their steel mill and made a whole bunch of prints." And so an annual report portfolio grew.

Clever? No, says Fote. Necessity. "There's no choice when there's no cheque and no work. I never planned anything — I mean I'm doing it now, but back then it was ... *strategy? What's a strategy?* My strategy was if the cheques stop coming in, you do something about it. A friend of mine says I should be a general in an army. When the waves hit, I do something."

Fote got work, lots of it. "There weren't many people shooting annuals at that time, and because I'm a woman, the suits were in shock half the time so they were cooperative. I had tremendous location experience, so what the hell's the difference between shooting girls or going down a mine — it makes no difference to me. It's all the same stuff."

In fact, she loved working in the mines: "The people were fabulous. The fact that you were suffering there with them meant that they killed themselves for you." But the travel and accommodation were often uncomfortable. Once when she was flown into a hydroelectric project in Sundance, Manitoba — flown in because there were no roads — she was bemused by the enthusiasm of the employees until she realized that they had mistaken her for a stripper from Winnipeg who was staying in the next room of a particularly tacky motel.

By 1989, with two recessions under her belt, Fote could smell another one coming. "When you hear the cab drivers talking about stock markets, you know you're in trouble, that the world is going to end fast." In 1990, her fears came true. "Corporations were printing annual reports on toilet paper if possible; I'm pregnant; the business is draining away; and I am in deep shit. I got blindsided again — by getting pregnant. I had to shift my business away from annuals, but how could I do it when I was pregnant?"

She hurt her back and was immobilized for three months. Then her marriage failed. "I had an infant on my hands, and my business was going under. Sales were down to $150,000 a year. I just tanked."

A disability policy purchased in 1983 kept her going, but her biggest problem was that she couldn't do photography lying on her back. When she finally returned to work, she had to lie on the floor for several hours a day. She would plunk herself down in the middle of a set and look at Polaroids, directing things from the floor.

By 1992, Fote still had not found a way to resuscitate her dying business. Competition for the annual report business was ferocious, and even worse, she was bored again. "I had had six years of annual reports, and I had seen it, been there, done that. I'd been to every place in

Canada — the North Pole, living on airplanes. Places in northern Alberta. At least with models we were going to nice places."

Then she read about a program called Step Up for entrepreneurial women. "I had no idea I was an entrepreneur. I figured maybe if I asked them, they'd say I was one. So I called and they suggested I send in something that explained what I did. I did and they called me and asked me if I'd like to be a protégée. I said great, this is cool, someone's actually going to help me. Suddenly I'm in this group with all these women who have businesses. And they all have kids, the same problems that I have, and I think, *Oh my God, I'm not alone.* It was amazing, a revelation."

One evening she made a presentation of her annual report business to Step Up members. "They were suitably impressed — I have a lot of big suit clients. After the presentation, someone came up and asked if I would do a brochure for her. I agreed, knowing enough graphic designers. So I put a team together and did the job. She was thrilled, and that's what started the advertising side of my business. I knew everybody. I knew all the best graphic designers in town from working with them. I could talk to the customers and figure out what they wanted. And I'm a good mom, so I'm know how to get everybody on my team to be nice to each other. *No, no, no, you cannot rewrite the writer's words* — that type of thing."

The Medea Group takes words and turns them into visual images, multimedia, and print. Revenues for 1996 were approximately $1 million, and Fote expects 1997 revenues to increase by 50 percent. She has six employees and a partner who owns 20 percent of her business and is a professional financial manager. He writes business plans, articulates their strategy, and manages cash flow. He puts specific goals with time lines in front of Fote.

"I still work like a dog all the time. I'm too stupid to do it any other way. But I really feel that for the first time in my life I have my shit together and we're going to drive this thing big time. I know exactly what I'm lousy at, and I know exactly what to get rid of. And I know exactly what I'm really good at, and that's all I'm doing now."

THE BUSINESS PLAN

I'm confident that I'll get financing. I can't not feel confident, because then I wouldn't get it. This is where your plan comes in.

— Dianna Rhodes

In a business plan, you have to figure out how you're going to make money.

— Elizabeth Scott

To be successful, you have to do something different. I don't always see things the way others see them. If you just re-create what others are doing, you're managing, not creating and building. Your solution should demonstrate that you're not like the rest.

— Marnie Walker

Research indicates that four factors differentiate the successful woman entrepreneur from the unsuccessful one:[3]

- the amount of time spent planning the start-up of the business: more is better;
- the extent to which professional advisers were used during the planning period: more is better;
- how many business-related courses or how much reading the entrepreneur undertook before launching her business: more is better; and
- level of income expectations: less is better.

As past-president of the Canadian Association of Women Executives and Entrepreneurs, Dianna Rhodes has witnessed firsthand the root cause for the downfall of many businesses: the absence of a business plan. *"These businesses don't have goals, and they don't have anything to measure against what they're doing and what they should be doing."*

Many women aren't as proficient with business plans as they might be, she finds, despite the fact that there are plenty of resources around: library books, college and university courses, and specific instruction in disk or text format from all of the major banks in Canada.

"I think we as women have to be a little smarter in the way we do our presentations to banks," she concludes. "And maybe a little broader thinking about the way our businesses could grow. Women's businesses tend not to be quite so big as they could be."

Generally a business plan is composed of:

- an executive summary, setting out in three or four paragraphs a description of the business, the required investment, and the anticipated returns;
- a detailed business description;
- a marketing plan;
- details of the operation, including suppliers and production processes;
- a description of the management and legal structure, including outside professional advisers like accountants and lawyers;
- financial data like cash flow projections;
- a short conclusion; and
- appendices.

Obviously, this is not something you can whip up in an afternoon. After laboring over your plan, what do you do with it?

Banks and other stakeholders in your business adore business plans

"Whether you like it or not, your business plan is what is going to get you into the bank," says Rhodes. "It has to be good and you have to be able to explain it precisely. You can get some professional help developing it, but it still has to contain your thoughts about what you're going to do, and where you're going to take the company."

But if you create a business plan solely to sell a bank on giving you a credit line, you're missing out on additional important benefits.

You'll know your business better

"The exercise of doing a business plan, much as I hate it myself, is good because you're forced to think through every aspect of your business," says Rhodes. "By the time you've explained it to the financial institutions, you absolutely know what you're going to do, inside out. And you'll have a better understanding of the financial side."

When it's finished, Elizabeth Stewart suggests reading it aloud, one sentence at a time. "Then get someone who's mad at you to read your plan."

You can gauge your progress

Keep your business plan in front of you as you work so that you can see if you're achieving your goals, and why you are or aren't. "It keeps you on track in your mission and your market and product, and makes life easier," says Rhodes.

Stewart suggests starting the process of defining your goals by completing this sentence: *In order to retire from active participation in my company by age sixty and have a retirement income of X, I must ...* "People should go into a new business venture thinking about when and how they are going to leave it. Is it something that will cease to exist when you retire or is it something you can sell?"

She believes that your business goals should encompass your personal goals. "Don't be driven by a revenue goal that prevents the achievement of other goals, like enjoying your children. You don't want to be trapped in a business that is running you."

You'll be comforted by it

A good business plan provides emotional support. "Everyone hits a time when her cash flow is absolutely zilch and the bills are coming in like crazy and people are calling you to collect. Your instinct is to not answer the phone and give excuses," says Rhodes. "But if you've got your plan and it's current, you can keep your perspective. You know there's always someone who won't pay you on time or that your production sometimes falls behind. You learn to pick up the phone immediately and call your bank and suppliers to say, *Look, this week is going to be a problem.* They're reasonable. Banks would rather know what's happening than have to phone you to find out.

"One side of me is overly optimistic, assuming that unforeseen difficulties will sort themselves out, so I've had to deal with that tendency to be like an ostrich. But a carefully devised business plan that's sensitive to the ups and downs of a particular company can reassure you."

Not all entrepreneurs begin with a business plan. Carol Denman, the president of a court reporting company with sales of $2 million, has never had one. Creating one is hard, she says, if a person has never had a business. But when she needed $15,000 to buy a new computer, she had to say *something* to her bank. "My business plan was that I could handle, say, five discoveries a day five days a week. I left the bank laughing hysterically, thinking, *As if that would ever happen.* But it did. Now that I know what I'm doing, I think business plans are valuable."

Helen Sinclair, once the chief executive of the lobby group for Canadian chartered banks, is now an entrepreneur. As head of the Canadian Bankers Association, Sinclair used to spent a lot of time talking to entrepreneurs about their business plans and how essential they are.

"Banks say *focus, focus, focus,* which can translate into a very timid attitude toward sales and listening to the market and being flexible. It's not that I think the advice is ill-intentioned or wrong, but let's say you go into a new business with a business plan and do everything the banks tell you to do. You end up with a set mind, and then if the marketplace shows that you didn't get it quite right, and you stubbornly dig in your heels and refuse to move, you're in trouble."

Delores Lawrence's first business plan was a couple of pages with a "kindergarten cash flow," created at her kitchen table with no real understanding of business concepts. For Lawrence, it had no value, since it didn't affect her banks' sweeping search for every piece of collateral they can get their hands on. Now with a multimillion-dollar business, she uses a sophisticated business plan not to get capital but to educate each new account manager about her business.

TRACEY'S STORY

When Tracey de Leeuw tried to show her 1,800-page business plan to Nick Curry, a strategic planner for Great West Life in Winnipeg, he laughed and asked for a forty-page summary. She cut it down, and when he finished reading it, he told her enthusiastically, *You have to do this.*

It took de Leeuw four months of frenzied inspiration to write those 1,800 pages. She needed the extra space because she was describing a novel business concept to herself as much as to her prospective readers — a service that helps other companies sell goods and services over the Internet.

Tracey's concept is the ManGlobe International Exchange (www.manglobe.com), an electronic shopping mall that sells everything from shoes to spray-on hair. The idea first evolved when she read about a bookstore that had taken its business onto the Internet.

Intrigued, she set out to see if she could sell her products that way. De Leeuw took 350 training videos and posted them on a variety of news groups relating to business, education, software, training, and entrepreneurship. The test was a success, and she also ran smack-dab into the problems that come with Internet sales.

One mistake was using a 1-800 number with no time restrictions for calling. "The Internet is global and operates twenty-four hours a day, and most people log on at 5 p.m. and end at 4 a.m.," she groans. "The phone rang every hour, all through the night, and that spelled doom for the next couple of weeks."

Then she couldn't find a bank that would accept credit card numbers relayed over the Net. It was 1992, and banks, who had only the barest glimmer of understanding about the Net, wouldn't provide a merchant Visa account for her business. She was forced to ask clients to send a cheque before receiving the goods, which decreased her chances of making sales. And finally, the Internet makes it easy for people to request information. Without standard replies set up, De Leeuw found herself typing her fingers to the bone.

But to her delight, these problems had *nothing* to do with technology and *everything* to do with selling goods in a virtual marketplace.

"There's this huge trend toward global marketing of products, and there's this wild technology that allows you to do it almost free twenty-four hours a day. People were constantly complaining about not getting the true value of their technology. Here, all of a sudden, for a buck an hour, people can reduce their costs of sales, customer service, research, collaborative development, and sales automation."

De Leeuw was out on a boat with a friend in December when she had an epiphany. "I was jumping around and words were pouring out of my mouth, and for the next four months, day in day out, I sat on my couch and wrote and wrote my plan. First I assembled the information part of the plan, then I built the financial part based on what the opportunities were." She could estimate the costs of running a business and the start-up costs for getting her service to the marketplace; when it came to estimating the revenues, she was staggered. "The revenue numbers were just so huge, so big that I knew there was room for error — a lot of it — and it would still be viable."

De Leeuw's epiphany was simply this: in order for companies to do business on the Internet, they need a series of services in place to support them. They need people to answer customer queries, in many languages. They need a facility for processing financial transactions. They need an order taking and shipping process. Her idea was to pull together established partners — banks to help with the financial transactions, distribution companies to help with movement of products from one place to another, brokers to help goods cross customs efficiently — who together could serve a global market, in all languages, in all currencies, electronically. De Leeuw decided that only a skeletal staff would work inside ManGlobe, with the bulk of staff in local regions the world over.

Her business plan called for bringing in partners whose expertise complemented one another so that they could provide a turnkey solution for businesses interested in getting on the Internet. They could sell their goods internationally without having to deviate from their core competence, which might be manufacturing or retail, and wouldn't include ManGlobe's offerings, like exporting, brokerage, even running a multilingual call center twenty-four hours a day, seven days a week.

ManGlobe provides management services like credit card authentication and settlement and credit card merchant services; it builds and hosts Web sites ("host" means the site resides on ManGlobe's computer); it secures and tracks the purchase order process and settles with the distribution companies and banks; it operates a 1-800 call center for membership registration so that customers don't have to send credit card information over the Internet (the call center operates in multiple languages) and to answer post-sale questions and returns. If a client doesn't have a site, ManGlobe will create one for them for $3,500.

ManGlobe's revenues are a percentage of the transaction. "Clients don't have to pay to stay with us; they just pay when they use us. It's very much like when a merchant pays Visa a merchant fee, except that we throw in these other services and charge 5 percent to a maximum of $10."

The philosophy that her company wouldn't earn a dime until its customers earned substantially more is based on De Leeuw's ten-to-one rule. "Things have to be ten times better for your customer than they are for you. It's better for the customer because we don't make our money until after the sale is done."

De Leeuw believes this fee structure is also critical for businesses leery of investing heavily in an unknown sales channel. "If you ask people to pay for something that they're not familiar with, you have to educate them on it, then you have to withstand their comparison of you to others and answer their questions — it's a much longer process," she says.

Despite its girth and weight, De Leeuw's business plan was invaluable in its clear outline of where she wanted to go and how she was going to get there. "You have to attach financial projections for banks and financiers. What *you* need to know from an operational level is what is it going to cost to deliver the basics. Everything above that is gravy — more money to invest in the intangibles like marketing."

De Leeuw figured that she needed $2.4 million to get her concept off the ground. "It didn't all have to be cash because we needed bank services, telecommunication services, distribution, and things like human resources and expertise," she says. "So I pitched investors on half cash, half in kind."

The first organization De Leeuw approached was the Manitoba government. "I figured if I was going to go after these big partners, I'd have to have someone big behind me, so I went to them to get R&D money." They told her that they would grant her $500,000 if she could raise a comparable amount.

De Leeuw ended up raising $1.2 million in cash and $1.2 million in in-kind contributions. "I just went for corporate investors," she says. "I got $500,000 from the province, and then I went to the federal government, and they contributed through a sponsorship for human resources training and computers. And then I had to borrow at the eleventh hour from the Business Development Bank of Canada because Royal Bank took so long to close."

ManGlobe's partners include the Royal Bank of Canada and

Manitoba Telephone systems, as well as other financial investors. Finding the partners and building her virtual company took a year, and by early 1997, ManGlobe was starting to generate revenues. Eaton's, Ontario Hydro, and Bata were using De Leeuw's electronic shopping mall, and the federal government was using it to sell statistics.

De Leeuw acknowledges that despite a well laid out plan and a carefully articulated goal, she learned by the seat of her pants. "It's amazing when you're on a mission what you learn. You figure out what you have to know and you made a gazillion mistakes. Hindsight is twenty-twenty. I could have done a whole bunch of things better, but every lesson taught me for the next time.

"For example, when I started this, I honestly believed that a large corporation's employees were empowered to make decisions. That was a fatal error, and had I known that, I would have kept my old job for an extra couple of years while I beat the pavement on this thing. Everything was always going to happen *tomorrow*. To the banks and Manitoba Tel, tomorrow means *in six months*. I didn't know that then, and I would be making commitments to pay back debts in short periods of time and having those things screwed over. But ultimately I kept things out of the Completely Fatal Zone."

Surprisingly, De Leeuw's background is bereft of sophisticated information technology training. After completing high school, she had two children, who are ten and twelve now. She worked in her father's real estate company until her marriage ended. Since the computer industry was booming, she joined a computer assembler as a sales rep and learned on the job.

She moved on after a year and a half to another software company. The market was depressed, and De Leeuw found that customers who needed software couldn't really afford it. So she looked for a new product to market and identified a line of contact management and integrated accounting software. Soon afterward, she decided to start her own company.

"I had my kids in day care, and since there was no child support, we basically starved. I was like every other single mom," says De Leeuw. Her husband is now paying child support and relations are amicable.

"My husband was a football player, and he played for a bunch of different teams. He went through the transition from stardom to normalcy, and it got the best of him for a couple of years. But now he's bounced back. He's a fireman and lives two streets over, thank God. I'm able to travel since he takes the girls half the time. Because we live so close, the girls feel they have the best of both worlds right now."

De Leeuw's original business, Fundamentals Group, dealt solely in real estate agent contact management software, and she worked out of her house. After two years, she hired an executive assistant and expanded her offering to more generic sales contact management software.

In the process of helping some clients who were trying to reduce their telecommunications costs, De Leeuw stumbled on the Internet, and so began her journey to creating ManGlobe. The journey included pawning her car to meet payroll in 1995 when she was winding Fundamentals down and allowing her credit rating to be "beaten to death." She still doesn't have a car, "but other than that, I'm happy with my life."

Her goal is to reduce her ownership interest to 20 percent through the sale of equity to her partners, after which she will take ManGlobe public through an IPO. Ultimately, her vision is to have offices in twenty countries around the world.

Real and prospective competitors are large and well capitalized, but rather than fear them she welcomes them. "Competition is the only way the industry will actually develop. I'm selling a solution, but if customers can't figure out what the problem is, then my service doesn't appear to be a solution. AT&T and IBM and MCI and all the big guns are saying, *Hey, this is a real industry and we have some real solutions.* That's fine. I don't think any one person is going to have the perfect answer. We have a good solid answer for a business that wants to check out the Net but can't necessarily justify a business case for it yet."

Her advice to other entrepreneurs is *Don't start unless you plan to finish.* "People start with dreams and optimism but not always reality. You have to look very closely and as pessimistically as possible at the worst-case scenario and ask yourself, *Can I live with that?* People don't realize how hard it really is, that you have to live on less than $20,000 a year and you have to work eighty hours a week, and you don't get to go out to the bars on Friday nights with your friends because you have to work all day Saturday. Take a good hard look at what you're getting yourself into, and decide whether you're prepared to deal with the absolute worst scenario."

So far, she hasn't met a hill she couldn't climb. "But some of them have been very, very steep, and I needed all the ropes and pulleys I could grab to get over them. It's been very intense for the past three years, and lately I'm feeling tired. But usually, no matter how big the mountains are in that particular day, I'm reenergized at the end of the day from getting over the mountain."

MARKETING

I should have researched more about my market and figured out where I really wanted to go with my company. I've gone through two years of major struggling about that. I should have done more research on marketing in the beginning.

— Louisa Nedkoff

Most companies fail because of a lack of market knowledge.

— Audrey Vrooman

Elizabeth Stewart of Elizabeth Stewart Associates, a Toronto-based company selling marketing support services, is a regular instructor at the University of Toronto's entrepreneurial program for women. In this role, she often sees women who are considering entrepreneurship and shouldn't. What they lack principally is an understanding of marketing. They may have a unique product idea, but they haven't figured out whether anybody wants it.

"That comes from being inside an organization where work is always delivered to you," she says. "You have no idea where it comes from. In the corporate environment, sales and marketing is *over there,* and processing is *over here,* and administration is *over here.*"

Stewart finds that women underprice their goods and services. "We're scared because we constantly compare ourselves to perfection and fall short, whereas men compare themselves to each other and are happy with *just as good* or *better.*"

If trying to be superwomen isn't bad enough, Stewart also notices that women scrimp with money in areas "that will save their lives." For example, many women realize late in the game that they have to bring in professional help, that they can no longer be the controller and the president. Their fear is with taking on substantial additional overhead. "But you must," says Stewart.

"We're cautious spenders and cautious company builders. We pile money into our companies and take very low salaries in the early years, which probably accounts for the high survival rate of women-owned businesses. It's a scary trade-off between *Can I afford to do this?* and *Can I afford not to?*"

Stewart's explanation for this is women's source of funds. Their companies are financed with *love money* — their savings, and whatever they could beg or borrow from their friends and family. "So the money has a different personality. It's sweat money, yours or your mother's or whoever's." It's a different kind of risk, in that they can't walk away from their commitment. The risk attached to failing with it is a more profoundly dangerous risk than the risk associated with bank money.

A woman's transition from the corporate world to entrepreneurship is often hampered by her traditional position as an employee. Women are massed in staff positions — human resources and administration — and have little experience with production, distribution, and marketing.

"If you've always been in human resources, you might decide to set up a consulting company dealing with payroll issues. But there may not be the market for it. How much do you understand about what clients need and do? You have to know if there's a need and how you're going to get it out there in the market. You have to have more than a focus on your product. You can't tell people about your grass; you have to tell them about your lawn."

She advises women who are uncomfortable marketing to find a partner or associate who can do that. "I don't believe that you can change people at their core. It would be absurd to say that if you're not a gregarious, outgoing person, you're going to have turn around and become that in the next month. I'm one of the shyest persons on the planet. But you can do it if you have a passion for your business — you throw up with fear and then you go on."

The marketing plan is a central, yet often absent, part of the overall business plan. According to Stewart, 87 percent of business owners have no plans, 10 percent have one in their heads and make ten times as much as those with no plan; and 3 percent have a written plan and make ten times as much again. Bank of Nova Scotia's Audrey Vrooman finds that inadequate business plans typically lack competitive information and market research. This is a dangerous flaw, she says, since most companies fail because of a lack of market knowledge.

The marketing plan articulates the needs of your market and how you will meet those needs through your unique selling position, be it price, the nature of the product, customer service, or delivery. It should address a period of time that is real to you: one month is preferable to ten years. And it should be revisited regularly — monthly if possible, "because that's how fast you learn and how fast things change," says Stewart. Every client success should be added to the plan, because in Stewart's experience, case histories are the number-one marketing tool of any entrepreneur.

Stewart recalls a woman who came up with an idea for an audiotape cum tour guide for people visiting historic sites in Ontario. She had done a great deal of research into the costs and sources of the product. But Stewart stopped her in her tracks with the question, *How many people would want your product?* It turns out that the answer was *not enough.* Her target market was people who like sightseeing independently, who like listening to tapes, and who would be doing so in a quiet car. Stewart suggested that a more salable product might be one directed to the noisy kids in the back seat of the car.

Stewart is skeptical about the value of media and print advertising, especially in a start-up situation. "It's a numbers game and expensive," she says. "Instead, think of ways to get to your market without advertising." Alternatives include press releases, public speaking engagements, networking, and cold calls.

On another occasion, she received a call from a woman who manufactured high-end women's clothing. The woman had just printed 30,000 color catalogues of her clothing and wanted Stewart's advice on where to send them. "There's an old saying that if you don't know where you're going, any road will get you there," says Stewart. "You have to know your goals. And then you have to have a plan of action for achieving them. You can't say, *I'm going to be the dominant supplier of X through effective promotion.* You have to define what effective promotion is. And stay focused on your core market. If you neglect it for new markets, smarter, younger, tougher competitors will take your market share."

Market research, which uses surveys and focus groups to help determine what your marketplace wants, is often seen as the domain of only large companies. But even a start-up entrepreneur can obtain some independent corroboration of the usefulness of her product or services. Use other people's research, says Stewart. Use the library, stories on your marketplace, and competitor's strategies and how they worked or failed. Use the Internet to get information. Focus groups, made up of friends of your friends (not friends or family), can help you with pricing your product and service.

ELIZABETH'S STORY

I'm a hyperactive person. I like lots of variety and I like to learn. The day you don't learn something is the day you might as well pull the coffin cover over your head.

— Elizabeth Stewart

Elizabeth Stewart is in her late forties and has been self-employed since 1989. Previously, she worked in a marketing and sales capacity for an American insurance company for six years, helping them set up a Canadian subsidiary. "Then they fired me," says Stewart. There was a change in management, and she didn't get along with the new people and didn't agree with the changes they were making.

Her severance package included the services of an outplacement firm. At that time, they had very little experience with women in senior management positions. "They were nice people, but they weren't a great deal of help," she says. "I hadn't a clue what I wanted to do."

Before she worked for the insurance company, Stewart had worked extensively in the office furniture and equipment industry. She had maintained contact with many designers, and she began to think about professional firms and how poor they are at marketing their services.

She did all the research that she now advises her clients to do. Her conclusions screamed, *don't do this* because 1) your target market is frequently start-up companies that can't afford you; and 2) one of the reasons professional services companies are no good at marketing is that they don't respect it and don't think they need it.

"So the whole idea was goofy," concludes Stewart. I thought, *Oh dear, I've wasted several months trying to figure out what to do.* So I literally went and sat on a mountaintop. I have dear friends who live in the mountains, and I went there and thought about what I would do next. When I returned to Toronto, there were several telephone messages saying, *I hear you're starting a business helping professional firms market. Would you come and talk to me?* I thought, *Well, some-one wants my help.* I proved that my market research was wrong."

Her first years were a struggle, not only because she was trying to sell a solution to a group that didn't realize there was a problem, but also because North America was in the midst of a recession.

In the early years, she targeted the architectural design industry because she knew the industry and their needs. She soon found that clients wanted more direct and simple help, like writing marketing letters. She also soon learned that her target market was too small, especially since she couldn't service competing firms. And so she moved into other professional services firms with similar characteristics and problems — accounting, legal, and architectural.

"I was pigheaded. I kept going and suffering and wondering how I was going to pay the rent. But it got better. My clients' competition was heating up, and they realized they had to do something about it."

Since 1996, her business has boomed. What's been keeping her awake at night these days is how to stay small but still manage the work volume, and how to fund her retirement.

"I'm looking at the personal issues related to how I want to live. It's an issue of concern for all women. It's *women* who are the poor in this coun-try. Someone once said that every woman in Canada is only one paycheque away from poverty, and it's often someone else's paycheque. I joke that if I don't control my own destiny, I'll end up living in a cardboard box under the Bathurst Street bridge. All of us need to look at this pattern in our society, including fourteen-year-old girls."

Stewart is long divorced and has no children, yet she has a large family of close friends, as well as four brothers and sisters and their children. Because of this strong support network, she never feels isolated, and her network helps her emotionally manage the risks of being an entrepreneur.

"I was raised dirt poor on a farm in Saskatchewan, and there is a little piece of Scarlett O'Hara in me that says, *I will never go hungry again.* There's an enormous survival instinct that comes out of that experience. In some ways the risk is not as terrifying as it would be if I'd never been there before. My way of working and forming connections is grounded in that experience — we help and support one another as a group."

Going back into the corporate world as an employee is not an alternative. "I've spent a lot of time in the corporate world managing large groups of people, and getting involved in the nonwork agendas. A friend of mine spends 85 percent of her time managing her boss. I'm not prepared to go that way again."

As an entrepreneur, Stewart has her highs and lows, both emotionally and financially, but the difference is that they're her responsibility, and she controls her next step. "Even though my work load is based on someone else's demand, it's not based on somebody else's agenda." By agenda, she means the unique corporate experience of working hard on a project only to see another issue kill it, be it a practical problem or politics. "Then everything gets filed and you feel out of control."

One of Stewart's managers during her previous employment noted Stewart's style in a performance appraisal. *Elizabeth,* he said, *you are a superior manager but a terrible employee.* Her focus was her division, and her manner of achieving her goals entrepreneurial. "My attention, caring, and time was spent managing *down* versus managing *up*." To her, taking care of her bosses' concerns and expectations got in the way of getting work done.

She relies heavily on networking and speaking engagements to secure new clients. "People who don't have a network are going to have a tough time, God bless them. Getting out of your box and becoming part of the action in the rest of the world is a big challenge."

CHAPTER 6

SUCCESS

Success is hard work. It's getting up and doing the hardest thing you have to do first thing in the morning, facing up and taking responsibility.

— Carol Denman

To be successful, you need confidence, determination, and staying power. Be resolved not to get discouraged. Have your own opinion, and if you know it's a good idea, stand behind it.

— Delores Lawrence

I never wanted to earn money at the expense of anybody, or to be controlled by an outside force, not even a cigarette. I don't ever want to be poor again, and I don't ever want to wonder where my next meal is going to come from.

— Marcella Abugov

WHAT SUCCESS IS

For Angela de Martigny, success means sales of $500,000 and being able to pay her bills and take a two-week vacation. For Melodie Stewart, it means not having to eat Kraft dinner anymore. And for Wendy Banting, success is still being in business.

Just as true peace of mind may be achieved only after great personal struggle, success is sweetest when it is built on the rubble of failure. "The key ingredient for success as an entrepreneur is a ton of self-esteem," says Paula Jubinville. "You have experience failure and learn that the world doesn't end when that happens."

Men understand this. Says Marnie Walker, "They're raised on sports that teach them if they miss the ball, it's okay, there are two more chances to hit the ball. Girls are taught that if they trip on the rope, they go to the back of the line. If a man hits it out of the park once a season, he's a hero; women think failure is the end of the world. Instead of moving on, we wallow in it."

For many successful women entrepreneurs, admitting their success is more difficult than talking about their failures. Women's definitions of success are always changing to keep it just out of reach; some women are worried about appearing arrogant, others don't want to risk jinxing their journey.

Owning an $8 million company is a considerable feat, yet Schiedel still doesn't consider herself a success. Now she wants to triple sales by the year 2001. "I sometimes wonder if at age twenty-five I had written down what success meant for me then, if I would be there now. I don't particularly feel that I'm a success. I can't remember what I thought about things back then, but then I can't remember what I thought last year."

Wanda Dorosz deflects the question as to whether she views herself as a success. "The question is a trap because it's a little like asking a man if he's stopped beating his wife yet. If you say yes, you're a monster; if you say no, you're a monster. I have accomplished enough that I am buoyed by it. When I look at what I want to accomplish ... (she whistles) there's a long way to go."

Says Carol Denman, "My fear of failure gets less and less every day. I was afraid that I would fail and look stupid. When you're fairly successful, you have the nagging feeling that you haven't thought this through somewhere; something's going to blow up, and it'll all fall apart. You risk so much, personally and financially. You don't want to have spent all that time for nothing."

Sometimes she has to give herself a mental shaking. She tells herself, *You did win an award. Your name's still on the door. Your profits are great. Your children love you, and you're still married ... hmmm, maybe you* do *know what you're doing.*

"Success can only be measured in hindsight at the end of it all — when you're eighty years old and look back and ask, *What did I do?*" says Tracey De Leeuw. "I set goals every day. I'm proud of my achievements, but a whole bunch of achievements in a row doesn't always spell success. So I'm going to reserve judgment on that."

Success must be measured, and the best way to do that is in cold hard cash, says Andrina Lever. "Women don't look at the bottom line closely enough. They are too relationship oriented. Be realistic — it's not a cakewalk. You better love what you do because you're going to spend many long lonely hours doing it. And when the times get tough, unless you love what you do, you're not going to get through them."

Here is the story of a woman who recognizes her success.

SUZANNE'S STORY

I see myself as a success. We do very well — a lot of profit. It's like a dream. The recessions, which were so hard on other companies, didn't affect us. We just do better and better.

— Suzanne Leclair

This is a story about a stay-at-home mom, who, after ten years of taking care of her children, decided to open her own trucking company. It's also a story about an employee from hell, and a bred-in-the-bone entrepreneur. Suzanne Leclair, president of Les Fourgons Transit, the largest truck box manufacturer in Canada, is all these things.

In her first year of business, 1978, Suzanne Leclair generated approximately $600,000 in revenues; by 1996, they had reached $15 million. "I couldn't join a big company because I had no education," she says. "Having my own company was my dream."

One day, Leclair decided to go back to work. She answered an ad for a secretary and got the job. Then she asked her boss if she could be a salesperson.

"I said, you pay a very handsome salary to the men and they play golf and ski. They don't always work like I will do, and they can't do the paperwork. You will save so much because I won't golf or ski and you won't have to pay a secretary to do the paperwork." It was an offer her boss couldn't refuse.

The next offer she made, her boss did refuse. She offered to buy the company. "He was upset. He said, *You work for a good company. Why are you saying this?* and I said, *Because I want to buy this business.*" He declined her offer.

She parted ways with her employer, rented a building, and started her own business. She and her husband took out a mortgage on the house and obtained some personal loans. She had no business accounts — "nobody believed I could succeed. Now of course the banks believe in me. I don't have debts. Everything is paid for."

Fifty-two years old, Leclair, who is on the board of directors of the National Bank of Canada, is a staunch defender of banks and their financing policies. "Sixty percent of businesses don't last longer than five years, so we can understand why it's difficult to get loans."

As a bank director, she sees a lot of business plans. "Some people just dream. They think they will have a million dollars after a year, and everybody will do their job, and they will just sit. If you want to succeed, you have to work very hard to make it happen. It doesn't come just like that. People say, *If I'm successful.* You can't say *if*, you have to say, *I'll do it.* You have to be very positive."

Leclair wanted to be an entrepreneur since she was a child. Moreover, she was enthralled with trucking. "I loved trucks and I thought it would be a good industry because they're needed every-where, always, to carry everything. Everyone in my family was an entre-preneur, so I think it was in my blood." The idea of taking over her father's furrier business never entered her mind. "I like to be indepen-dent — to say, *Nobody helped me.* I didn't want his business because I didn't want people to say it had been handed to me."

The one flaw in Leclair's plans was having to build a business from scratch. Her goal had been to buy a business. "When you buy, everything is there — your staff, your machinery, everything. It was tough to build it from the ground up. For starters, where do you buy the machinery?"

Her competitors supplied her with the answers. "I visited all the competitors, every one, and I told them I'd like to start my own business. Everyone laughed. They thought I was a joke. So they gave me everything, really everything. They opened their books and showed me the numbers. They thought I would walk out the door and forget everything because I'm a woman and I'd never succeed. You can learn so much through your competitors."

When her company was three months old, Leclair had more contracts than she could easily handle, despite a brutal daily work schedule that went from 6 a.m. to 8 p.m. She was the boss, the foreman, the salesperson, the shipper, the buyer, and didn't sleep much in the early years.

"I used to take on too much. I always promised the shortest delivery time. And when you promise, you have to deliver." Keeping her promises was a constant pressure. "A couple of men might not show up for work, or your truck might be late, but you told your customer you would deliver the truck today, and somehow you do it. I promise and I deliver. That's very important. So many businesses are not strong in the market because they don't keep their promises.

"When I get customers, I never lose them. I tell them that I understand you can buy somewhere else, but I'm the best so I know they'll come back. I have the best product and the best service."

Today her market share in Quebec is 75 percent. When her competitors wised up and shut up, Leclair turned to her customers for advice. They tell her, *If you can do this, we will buy it.* "I contact my customers all the time and go and see their trucks. I figure maybe I can do *that*, *that* might be good, and *that* and *that* and *that*. Between the customer and what we do here, we learn, and we always progress."

As a final *coup de grâce*, Leclair bought her old boss's business in 1989 when it went into receivership.

"When I started my own business, I made a lot of sacrifices. I worked long hours and didn't see my husband and my kids as often as I would have liked. Now I do everything I want. I help take care of my grand-children and see my kids often. I think anything is possible."

Leclair's husband is in charge of the company's finances, and her two sons have responsibility for production and sales. The four family members own the company, and Leclair is the major shareholder. "My sons love the business. They eat the business. They have helped me a lot. If I were alone, maybe I would be dead because that's a lot of work. You can't work fifteen or eighteen hours a day all your life."

Today, Leclair's job is steering the company. "My family is so busy they can't see the big picture. I am both detail oriented and big picture oriented. I talk with the family before I make a major decision so they know exactly what's happening and can give their opinions. We discuss everything because I think that's fair, but one person has to make the decision in the end. Sometimes, if there's not too much money involved, I'll say, *Okay, if you would like to try that, maybe it'll be a mistake, but you have to learn.* But when it's a big decision, I make it. And I won't take big risks. I do things because I believe I can do it."

In 1996 Leclair purchased some large manufacturing machinery, and in 1997 the company began making its own parts. While Leclair wants her company to grow, she wants to do so little by little. That way, she can maintain a firm grip on her competitive advantage: design. "I'm always the first one, and the competition copies me. That's fine." Her focus is on the Canadian market, as there is still a great deal of market share opportunity.

Some of her conservatism is based on taking her company public for four years, and then taking it private again. In 1990 she bought back all the outstanding shares. The share price was very low at $1.10, in sharp contrast to a book value of $2.75. Because so many of the shares were held by employees, she added a premium of $.25 to the book value "so that nobody would complain and say I took advantage." Leclair was also relieved to be rid of the cost and time involved in being a public company. She was spending approximately $125,000 a year for the privilege of being public, plus attending regular board meetings and presenting financial statements quarterly.

Leclair is interviewed constantly by the media about her success. Her message is that women can and should be as successful as anyone. "Some men like to have the best salary, the best position, the best everything, so we have to teach them why we are as good. Many husbands wouldn't like it if their wives had a higher salary than they did. And there are still people who say that I'm taking a job from a man, but they don't say anything about how many jobs I've created."

Leclair knows that, as a woman, she manages her businesses differently. The difference lies in the way she treats her eighty-five employees; the proof is that there is no union. "I am like a mother. I know my employees' names. We have a Christmas party for the employees' kids with gifts and a Santa Claus. If employees have problems, they can talk to me. We loan them money at no interest. They like to work here. It's like a large family.

"We tell employees to be proud of what they do. It's important to be able to say, *I did a good job*. We tell staff often that if the customer is happy, they keep their jobs. Even the guy who sweeps the floor, I tell him he's important to the company. I *thank* my employees when they do a good job. They don't feel like numbers; they feel they're an important part of the business."

Today Leclair has four grandchildren who take up a lot of her time. "I am like a queen. This is what I wished for and what I want to do. Sometimes I don't work a full day because I'm busy with other things. I can take a day to do something else. I can go on vacation. I really do what I want to do. As long as I have the health to work, I will. I'm lucky to do as I want."

GROWING YOUR BUSINESS

Women have to understand that it's a whole new ball game once you start to get into the multimillion-dollar businesses. It changes because you can't do everything. You have to look at your own strengths and weaknesses and see where you need to employ people. You have to relinquish and delegate a lot.

— Dianna Rhodes

On all levels, in every business, you have to remember that your customer is smarter than they were yesterday. I'm a sponge. I look for opportunities to learn wherever I am. I observe other people's businesses and what's going on in the world around me. We talk about continuous learning as if it were a new model, but it's always been true for successful entrepreneurs.

— Elizabeth Stewart

The entrepreneur who starts his own business generally does so because he is a difficult employee. He does not take kindly to suggestions or orders from other people and aspires most of all to run his own shop.... His idiosyncrasies do not hurt anybody so long as his business is small, but once the business gets larger, requiring the support and active cooperation of more people, he is at risk if he does not change his approach.

— Manfred Kets de Vries

Don't automatically say no to a crazy idea. Sometimes those crazy ideas can result in a very, very successful business.

— Dorothy Millman

A 1991 study[1] showed that the size of a business is the single biggest predictor of an entrepreneur's income. An obvious point, but a critical one for women entrepreneurs. Why? Because their businesses are generally smaller than men's. They are smaller for several reasons:

- Women gravitate to the service sector, where growth is heavily dependent on the capabilities of the owner-manager. Here, small companies are common and profit margins are narrower than in other industry sectors.

- A significant number of women start businesses with no related experience and no managerial experience.
- There are few role models to encourage ambitious growth objectives.
- A woman's double shift of family and work responsibilities and her desire for a balanced life may make it more difficult to grow her business.
- Women have lower expectations. As the 1990 Quebec study on women owner-managers states: "They started in business with very little (money, managerial experience, personnel) and they are used to that situation."[2]

In part, the relatively small size of women's business is due to the relative youth of women-owned businesses. Only 39 percent of women-owned businesses have been in business ten years or more compared to 59 percent for businesses owned by men.[3]

The implications of smallness are huge. Staying small centralizes decision-making power exclusively with the owner and personalizes the company according to the owner's wishes. It allows the owner to maintain control and independence, but often at the expense of growth. In a snake-eating-its-tail cycle, the smallness constrains financing options and the recruitment of talented employees, and prevents growth.

"There are enormous advantages to growing," says Nancy Adamo. "When I was in the catering business, I had to wear many different hats, and it was difficult. It meant that if something happened to me, what would happen to the business? It was always a huge concern."

Dorothy Millman is president of DMS Intelecom, a public company that provides telemarketing services to companies. Her business started in her home when Millman decided she didn't want to sacrifice the experience of raising her children for a fourteen-hour day as an employee. The hardest decision she ever made was moving her growing business out of her home into 2,400 square feet of commercial space. "I didn't want to change," she says. "I didn't want to leave my kids. But you have to identify the need for change because no one else is going to do that for you. And if you don't, it will come and hit you over the head."

Often, growth requires the injection of new equity and new management skills. There may come a time when you determine that the best solution is an equity partner. The job of Keith Pugsley of the Ontario Ministry of Economic Development, Trade and Tourism is to make potential equity investors aware of Ontario manufacturing or high-technology businesses looking for equity. He suggests that you consider the following issues when selling or seeking a capital injection.

Price

Don't price your company high with the intention of negotiating down to the amount you really want. In Pugsley's experience, many prospective investors dismiss the opportunity at first glance because of the price. He suggests that your price be one that you would be willing to pay if you were in the investor's position.

Location

If your business is not in a major city, it is more difficult to find investors.

The right investor

Imagine the ideal investor for your business. What type of background would that person have?

Appearance

Potential investors or buyers are affected by the appearance of the business, just as they are when they purchase a home.

Financial statements

Maintain up-to-date financial statements. Last year's statement is not sufficient.

Business plan

Pugsley finds that investors are always interested in business plans, but few firms have them — nor can they speak persuasively about the company's direction.

Timing

Companies seeking equity typically have a deadline because they need the capital for a specific reason. Therefore, the search for equity should be well planned and with a realistic view of the time it takes to identify the right equity partner.

Exports

Exporting is an essential part of many businesses, says Pugsley. If you're not exporting, the value of your business will be negatively affected.

Partnership

All partners in your company should be in agreement with the search for equity. Any buy-sell options should be exercised or refused before soliciting an investor or purchaser.

Internal search

Have you exhausted your own leads for an investor or buyer before undertaking a broader search? A competitor, supplier, employee, or friend could be the right match.

CAROL'S STORY

Very often when you want to make a change and move in a different direction, there are a lot of people who are just waiting to see you fall on your face so they can say, I told you so.

— Carol Denman

When her business was ten years old, Carol Denman, president of Atchison & Denman Court Reporting, became disenchanted. She was unhappy, ready to sell the business and do something else.

Then during a conference she was riveted by a woman who spoke eloquently on the importance of relationship-based marketing. After the session, she told the woman about her problem, how she just couldn't seem to move her business ahead.

"Your problem," said the woman, "is that you're driving a little red sports car with the pedal to the metal but you've got a load of cement in the trunk. You're trying to get somewhere, and everyone else is trying to put the brakes on. You have to do something about that." "How do I?" Denman asked. "The last time I looked, your name was still on the door," said the woman. "So you can pretty well do what you like."

So Denman went back to her company and listed the difficulties she was facing. Hers was the first company to offer transcriptions on disk; now there was competition. Her software needed upgrading; she needed new equipment; and she needed new approaches to marketing. She wanted to aggressively pursue new niches in the market, such as a contract with the tax court of Canada for all of Ontario.

Her people resisted. Many of them had worked with Denman since the beginning and were happy with the status quo. They didn't want change.

"For a long time I treated everyone as equals and tried to run the business as if it were one big happy family. Women like to have consensus, whether it's in their business life or personal life, but it's really hard to work by consensus and also be a leader. I discovered that reaching consensus is less important than simply getting the job done."

Change — painful change — was resisted for a year before her employees acknowledged that change was inevitable, regardless of whether they liked it or not.

"Working for me was very lucrative, but I had reporters saying, *I don't want to go to court. I left a court job to come and work freelance for you.* But this is the nineties, and you can't pick and choose like that."

Denman hired new freelancers to do the tax court work. But the old guard began to complain: *Gee, I don't have any work this week. Tax court is starting to look good to me.* At the same time, they continued to complain about her decision to take on this new business. "My answer was that it's huge volume and it's right across the street. Yes, the margins are small, but it looks good on our client list. You get really frustrated if you have to listen to people complain. I've been running this business for ten years. I know where I'm going, and I certainly know what I'm doing."

The pressure mounted on Denman to do something about her relationship with those who worked for her. "I was suddenly struck with the realization that I had become the mother hen and the reporters were all my chicks." Over the years, Denman had retained reporters who were easy to get along with. "I was very chummy with everybody — too chummy." A reporter called her from the Bahamas to ask if she could advance him $3,000 because he'd lost at the tables. Her office manager stole from her, using the company's Grand and Toy card to buy school supplies, writing company cheques for personal purchases, and dipping into petty cash.

The lesson for Denman was that you always have to be on your guard. "Not only do people think you're really nice, they think you're really stupid. My mother always said, *I hope you don't get tough.* I tell her, *Well, Mom, I'm not tough, but business is tough and sometimes you have to be too.*

"That's when I realized that they didn't see me as the boss. They saw me as a soft touch, as needing them. And of course I kept telling them how much I needed them and how wonderful they were, and I gave them big bonuses. I was trying to make them all happy. Big mistake.

"I felt guilty because I was so successful. I had a great desire to help people out. I had reporters coming in here and saying, *Oh! my Visa bill* or *My kids need new shoes,* and I'd say, *No problem. Here's a cheque.* As I sit here now, I can't believe I did that, but hey, I'm still here."

The "new regime" put each reporter in competition with the others for the best jobs. It was a thunderbolt for most of them. "They thought they had all the power and they could moan and groan and change things if they stood fast," says Denman.

Resistance swelled again when Denman streamlined office procedures. For years, her freelance reporters could submit their invoices at any time and be paid immediately. People would drift in and out of the office, and it became more difficult to respond promptly as the business grew. So Denman changed it. On Wednesdays, if reporters submitted their invoices by noon, they could have their cheques by three o'clock.

"I had huge complaints about this," says Denman. "They said, *Why do we have to wait three hours?* and *Why do we have to hang around the office?* I told them they could send it in by courier, fax it in, mail it in. The three hours gives us the opportunity to have our accounting run the cheques and be able to check them over. People thought it was outrageous. My answer was: *Imagine having to wait thirty days.*"

Finally, Denman realized that some people can't change. "It was very difficult for me. Most of them had worked with me for a long time, and they had this entitlement attitude: *Carol, we've helped you get to where you are and now you owe us.* Well, I don't owe them anything. I paid them for every job they did."

Denman hired an office manager who runs the business with an iron fist. "It really helped me because every time I'd go to do something outside the system — like trying to get a reporter a cheque early — Sharon would come in and say, *Carol, this is really counterproductive.* I had to let go of the nice guy role.

"Sharon also interviews new reporters and makes hiring recommendations. Because she's twenty-nine and I'm forty-seven, she has a better rapport with the younger people, and she knows how to pick the sharp ones. I was always picking the older experienced ones who didn't want to change. That is the most interesting phenomenon — you go through trying to change everyone, and then you give up and hire new people who think they've walked into heaven."

The old guard is gone. Today there is a new company culture and revenues of approximately $2 million a year. Each of Denman's reporters wants to be the one with the best skills, attitude, equipment, and clientele. They want companies to phone and request them by name. "They also see that I don't have to do this to make a living," says Denman. "It's not as if I've mortgaged my house and am living hand-to-mouth. I will continue to do this as long as I enjoy it, not because of the money.

"But the process was very painful. I'd go home at night and have a couple of glasses of wine and a big weep. I lost somebody with whom I'd worked for a long time and shared some good times with. In the early days, we used to stay up all night to get a transcript out and sleep on mattresses on the floor. It was all very dramatic, but it's not that way anymore."

When Denman started her business, she was new to entrepreneurship. She had just remarried, and her new blended family consisted of four children. "I wanted to control my destiny. I was making good money working for the Supreme Court as a stenographer, and I had seniority, but the hours weren't conducive to looking after children." When one of the children had to go into the hospital for treatment, someone in management told her that she would have to make a choice between her work and her kids. "And I thought, *I don't need this.* I didn't like the travel, and I knew I could make enough money on my own." She was right.

Although Denman sees the opportunity to franchise her business into different markets, she hasn't pursued it. "I say, wait a minute, what is this about? Is it about being big or is it about the bottom line? So the way I grow my business is to have as little real estate and as few people as possible and to have all of us make as much money as possible."

Denman has learned two key rules for keeping her clients happy. The first is always to err on the side of generosity. "I tell my reporters that if someone wants to make a deal with you — faster or cheaper — and you think you're giving something away, do it. Just let me know about it. But don't do it the other way. Don't say you can't do it. Go with whatever makes the client happy." This approach gives reporters the power to give added value to clients, be it an extra transcription disk or an extra hard copy or an extra hour charged at normal rates rather than overtime rates. "I think that if a reporter is willing to take a cut to make a client happy, I'll take the cut too and I'm happy to do it. And it's come back to me so many times."

The second rule is about repairing errors. "When you screw up, you have to make up for it so well that the client never remembers the error." When a mistake happens, Denman immediately goes into damage control and looks for ways to turn it into a good experience for the client.

"It can be as simple as we've overbooked and there is only my office to conduct an examination. I go right to the client and say, *I overbooked. It's my mistake. You don't have to pay for the room, and I'm not going to charge you for the transcript.* Once you've done that, they don't care if they take the examination in a phone booth. It has worked so well for me. I tell my people, if you screw up, don't hide it, face up to it and let's see if we can make the best of it."

Denman is less generous in her attitude toward debt. From the get go, she has always maintained a very disciplined approach to avoiding debt. Her recent expansion into mediation and arbitration meant that she paid $100,000 cash for construction.

"I've never taken a whole lot of money from the company. There's lots of money in there for contingencies, and the furniture and leasehold improvements are all paid for."

Her exit strategy is to look at a five-year plan and be bought out by an employee out of the profits over some extended period. If someone made her an offer, she would consider it.

DIANNA'S STORY

After a career in senior corporate life in England, Dianna Rhodes decided in 1992, at the age of forty-eight, to become an entrepreneur. "Quite often a stage in life will open up new opportunities. For me, it was time to get out. I changed my life totally. My marriage had ended, and I left my job. I went through a complete life change — not a new chapter in my life, a new *book*."

She came to Canada, and during the recession of 1991 began a jewelry business in Toronto.

"In my business, the recession has never gone away," she says. Her market is the businesswoman who accessorizes with precious metal jewelry that has good design and value. But in the nineties, Rhodes's customers have changed their purchasing behavior. "We're not high on people's grocery list," she says wryly. "I used to do some magnificent large pieces with diamonds, but now everyone has scaled down. People still buy diamonds for weddings and special anniversaries, but they don't wear the size of jewelry that was popular in the eighties."

Rhodes exports because the Canadian market just isn't big enough for a manufacturer of high-quality precious metals jewelry. "There are only 30 million people here. Half of them are women, and of them only 2 to 3 million buy jewelry. So we have to go over the border."

Canada is an excellent export base because of its proximity to the huge market in the United States and Asia. For example, California's population alone approximates that of Canada's. As well, financiers and investors are attracted by companies that export.

Rhodes, who began her push into the U.S. market in 1994, finds that many women entrepreneurs don't think past the borders of their own city, never mind Canada. Women in the service industry often assume that their businesses aren't good export candidates, but Rhodes's business activities in the Pacific Rim suggest otherwise.

According to 1996 Statistics Canada data, companies that export are among the most profitable in Canada. In businesses with less than $5 million in sales, seven of the top ten industries were service companies.[4]

For six years, Rhodes managed her business by subcontracting her manufacturing and hiring employees on a contract or part-time basis. But beginning in 1997, Rhodes's business will be transformed, from a company with sales of under $1 million to one with fifteen full-time employees and targeted sales of $3 to $4 million.

"So here I am starting all over again," she smiles. "I'm putting together a completely different new company, one that is a high-technology jewelry manufacturer, a first for Canada, and with only two comparable competitors in the United States. Right now I'm focused on putting a lot of money in place to get this going."

Without her new technology and a financial commitment to a factory, Rhodes knew she would never achieve her financial ambitions, which is a nest egg that will maintain a comfortable lifestyle when she retires.

"When you're small, you can't do anything," she says flatly. "You can't have a company that's interesting; you can't make enough money; you can't borrow enough. There is a point where you are just too small."

She shrugs her shoulders at the notion of risk. "The worst thing that could happen is that I could go bankrupt spectacularly," she says. "On the other hand, I could end up very rich. Reality is probably somewhere in the middle."

For the past two years, Rhodes has been working with Research and Development Canada to find a manufacturing method that can deliver lightweight jewelry in 18-carat and 14-carat gold and platinum. Because the jewelry is lighter, it is more comfortable and can be priced more moderately. "And it's real, with a value and a quality that you would be proud to pass on." The other benefit derives from the fact that an aging population is developing allergies to costume jewelry, increasing the need for good quality, affordable gold jewelry.

Rhodes traveled all over the world to find a commercially viable manufacturing method and found it in Israel and Italy. While in Italy, she met a factory production manager who was experienced with the technology. Today he is her factory manager in Toronto.

Rhodes is calm about this huge push forward in her business. "I would have liked all this to have happened ten years ago, but all the bits of my working life are coming together into this. I have manufacturing experience; I know about production, sales, and marketing; I know about catalogues and mail order. All these things are important to what I'm doing today. The travel I've done is also coming into play. I started out in Canada only knowing one person, and I pushed myself and networked. Today I have a huge network here and in the U.S. and Asia. I didn't have that ten years ago. I feel that this is the right time."

Just to make sure, Rhodes retained a business psychologist over a three-month period to help her assess her strengths and weaknesses. "I wanted to know that if I was going to take on a debt of millions, I was capable of succeeding." She also put together a personal plan. "I knew that I'd be working every hour that God sends, and I have to know that I can deal with the pressure and disappointments. When you're in your twenties and thirties, you don't think twice. But when you get older, you have to make sure that you're capable of doing it."

She wants to have a factory in England and develop manufacturing joint-venture partners in Indonesia, Malaysia, and Inner Mongolia. To achieve her global ambitions, she is building a team that will share in the success of the company.

"My strengths are that I'm well organized; I can see the big picture; and I'm very creative. I'm not a detail person; I hate the financial side; and I need somebody who keeps me on track because I have a million ideas a day. I'm a risktaker, but I need a steadying influence."

Because she can easily get sidetracked, Rhodes hired a marketing manager who can stand up to her in a nice way and say, *Hang on a minute, this doesn't make sense.* "She is everything I'm not, and I'm everything she's not. We make a fantastic team."

ANDRINA'S STORY

Andrina Lever, like many of her entrepreneurial peers, leads a life that would exhaust most people. She is the president of Women Entrepreneurs of Canada and has four business ventures: Lever Enterprises, which advises to companies across a range of issues; Expansion International Advisory Inc., through which Andrina and two other women consult for companies looking to expand internationally; a partnership in the U.K. called JIT International Limited, which delivers training programs for women entrepreneurs in former Eastern European countries; and incongruously, a partnership with a good friend in a balloon and special events company in Australia. "It started out as a bit of a joke, but it's profitable and a lot of fun," she says. Total sales are approximately $1 million.

This is a woman who truly views the world as both her backyard and her market. She's a lawyer by training who lived overseas for twenty years before returning to Canada.

Lever has developed strong market knowledge of Canada, the United States, Europe, Australia, the Philippines, Singapore, Malaysia, and Thailand. Her clients typically have sales between $5 and $100 million, and no in-house expertise to manage international expansion. They look to Lever for implementation advice regarding alternatives such as strategic alliances, distribution agreements, and plant construction. She helps them to obtain financing and submit proposals to foreign governments. She also coordinates teams of lawyers, accountants, and other experts to expedite expansion plans.

In her career, Lever has never consulted for a woman-controlled company. "Expansion is a big challenge for most women, but expanding internationally is a major challenge," she says. "Women in general and Canadian women in particular are more comfortable with their companies being a smaller size, a size they can control. Unfortunately, most Canadians are a bit parochial in terms of doing business internationally, or they just think of the United States. The Canadians who do look at doing business internationally either have an ethnic background, are new to the country, or they've been exposed to the international market and are comfortable with it. International expansion is still quite an intimidating prospect to a lot of people."

Lever points to the fact that women-owned businesses in Canada typically have revenues of less than $200,000. "You have to have a larger base than that before you can even consider doing business globally," she says.

Married with no children, Lever has been an entrepreneur since 1988. She started her career in the United States working in a data-processing center and then moved to England when her husband-to-be was transferred. She went to law school there and upon graduation accepted a job in corporate finance.

"I thought it was tremendously exciting, but I realized that I don't have the disposition to work in a large company and I'm not good at large corporate politics. I compare myself to my husband, who has always worked for a Fortune 100 company: he can survive because he's made of something different. He's less emotional and steers clear of all the politics. I have a big mouth. In the corporate world, I always felt like a square peg in a round hole."

When the two returned to Canada, Lever went to work for a Montreal-based consulting firm in corporate finance. She stayed there for four years and then became restless.

"I got to the point where I only wanted to work with people I liked. And the only way I had any control over that was if I worked for myself." For six months she agonized over whether to quit or not. "I was making really good money then, and I thought that if I quit this job, maybe no one would ever pay me this much money again. But I had a couple of mentors who sat me down and said, *You can do this. You're smart.* I ended up doubling my salary in my first year."

She remembers at the time of her decision to quit that a number of people said it was a "gutsy thing" to do. "That wasn't gutsy. Gutsy is when you're a single mom with a couple of kids and a mortgage and you quit a secure job to do something that you believe in. *That's* risky. I have a husband who makes a very nice income, so I don't have to worry about a mortgage payment. My walking away from a high-paying job wasn't going to affect our lifestyle at all. If I had been totally self-supported, would I have done it? Yes, but I probably would have done it differently. I would have had a plan and done it more methodically and not gone off on a wing and a prayer."

Some of Lever's clients at the consulting firm used her as soon as she set up shop. For new business, she relies entirely on referrals from clients and various export agencies in the Canadian government, as well as the leads she gains from speaking at conferences. "That's how I make contacts, meet people, and get clients," she says. "I don't even have a marketing brochure."

Lever's ambition is simple: to be happy with what she's doing, to do a good job and make a nice living doing it. "I don't want to build a large consulting company, and maybe that's why I'm not as aggressive in marketing as others are. I want to know I'm making a difference." But this doesn't mean that Lever doesn't care about money. "If your bottom line isn't number-one priority, you might as well go and work in a nonprofit organization because you just won't be successful in the long term."

Lever and her two partners in the U.K. identified a new market niche: entrepreneurial training programs targeted at women in Eastern Europe. Women in the region had been the first to lose their jobs when the state-owned companies were privatized. Existing training programs were, Lever felt, too academic.

"We had a lot we could say and do from a practical point of view. Particularly in Eastern Europe, many of the women we've worked with are well educated, but communism had limited their exposure and imagination. So it's not like working in a developing country where they don't understand some of the concepts. They understand them but don't know how to apply them. So we are helping women look at the skills they already have and transferring those skills to the workplace or to an entrepreneurial environment and teaching them how to recognize opportunities."

Andrina Lever recalls that after speaking at a conference in Australia, she was asked by a woman in the audience for some general advice on expanding one's business. "My answer was that I think women have to learn to start thinking like men. I don't think you have to think like a man all of the time, but I think sometimes we get sidetracked on issues like visualization and self-actualization, and it doesn't do us any good."

As an example, Lever points to a workshop at the same conference, where a very successful businesswoman led the session. "Her company's a hell of a lot larger than mine, but she talked the whole session on visualizing where you want to be in five years. I burst out laughing. I said I know where I want to be: in a big wicker chair with a glass of champagne. I guess different things work for different people."

LOOKING AND ACTING THE PART

The Physical Part

If you leave the room and someone says, I wish I had the nerve to wear something like that, *you've made a mistake.*

— Roz Usheroff

Dress is important because when people don't know you, what else have they got to go by? They don't know your personality or what you're capable of.

— Shelley Fisher

I used to be into big hair and miniskirts. I had a very sexy presentation. Then I went through a phase where I cut off all my hair and wore pantsuits because I wanted to get rid of anything that was associated with being feminine. I was trying to build my confidence. Now I enjoy being female. We have all these tools — the way we can do our hair, makeup, all these things. It's such a great advantage.

— Giselle Briden

I learned the importance of a uniform in the corporate world. You have to wear the uniform and assimilate. Always dress in a suit. Avoid feminine clothing and sexy clothing. Your dress is like a police officer's uniform; it's the uniform of a businessperson.

— Marnie Walker

I have a navy suit that I wear to the bank because I know they like navy.

— Tracey De Leeuw

It's absolutely about self-respect, and it's tactical in the sense that it makes an impression. Of course, it's also about living your day to the full.

— Wanda Dorosz

Let's face it, we human beings are a superficial lot. We think attractive people are smarter and better than the rest of us. Shoplifters understand this. They dress well because they know that a good presentation prompts others to make all sorts of positive and generous assumptions about them.

Tracey De Leeuw is beautiful, and she finds that it is not always an asset. "It's distracting to men. They assume I'm not smart," she says. "They look at me, and they don't think about business. So I start fast out of the gate and make them understand that I have a brain early in the conversation."

When Brenda Schiedel was twenty-six years old, she learned about the importance of dress the hard way. "I wore something in the summer that was too summery — too sheer and flowery. The customer just didn't take me seriously, and I lost a big order because of it. I knew it was the way I was dressed because my price was better and my service was better. I saw the competition. The only difference was that they were professionally dressed."

Schiedel's rule is to look the way her customers look. If she's calling on a bank or an insurance company, she wears a black or navy blue suit. If she's calling on a golf course — a significant market in her awards and recognition business — she wears a high-quality sweater. "I dress for my customers, absolutely."

A concern with image is not simply vanity. It is a strategic opportunity to affect how others perceive and relate to you. Dressing well shows a sense of pride and reflects how you run your business — smartly or sloppily. "It's not about being pretty or handsome. It's about polish," says Usheroff.

A complete look requires a current hairstyle, classic clothes tailored to your body shape and the right colors for your complexion and hair, well-applied makeup, and polished shoes with no scrapes or signs of wear. Classic clothes endure more fashion cycles, and it's harder for others to figure out how much you spent or didn't spend. Makeup that emphasizes your eyes and mouth strengthens your communication power. And these days, when it comes to jewelry, less is more.

With a spectrum of makeup, hairstyles, footwear, dresses, skirts, and pants, women have more opportunities to express their individuality — and more opportunities to make mistakes than men have. Because of the variety of dress choices, women do not have the benefits of anonymity offered by a man's blue suit, white shirt, and black shoes. Each choice a woman makes about her lipstick, jewelry, colors, and styles says something about who she is.

Dorosz often travels overseas, and consequently can be sitting in the same clothes for twenty hours. She always dresses impeccably, despite a fleeting envy for fellow travelers clad in soft sweatsuits and running shoes, and she has never been stopped and questioned at the border.

"Others may say, *I don't give a damn what people think,* but the truth is your appearance makes an immediate impression. If your dress affects how you're perceived by a customs officer, how many times in a day does it also communicate something about yourself to others? So tactically I think it's very important."

And she adds, "It is also absolutely about self-respect." When Dorosz was a girl, she noticed that her aunt wore the faintest, barely discernible suggestion of eye shadow. One day she asked her why she bothered to wear something that no one could see. Her aunt replied, because *I know it's there.*

She finds that many women under the age of thirty-five are terrified of looking sensual and feminine. "You'll see low-heeled shoes, long skirts, monochromatic colors, and no makeup or jewelry because they don't want to invite a come-on. From a mile away, I can tell that person has no confidence. We are physiologically who we are. Pretending otherwise is a mistake."

As a personal consultant with Holt Renfrew, Martha Fruchet works to match clothing to women's preferences, budgets, and body types. She offers the following advice based on her experiences:

- Think of what you'll be doing in the clothes you buy. "When customers are being fitted, they often say they want the skirt shorter. I tell them to sit down. When they do, they realize how short the skirt really is. If you're standing in front of the mirror, the length looks great. But you're also going to be sitting in business meetings, and if the skirt's too short, it's going to give the wrong message. I make them move around in the jackets to make sure it fits. Can you drive? Can you use the computer? You don't want to get into a straitjacket. They don't think of these things when they're standing in front of the mirror. You have to be comfortable."
- There are often economical shortcuts you can take in clothes. For example, instead of a silk blouse or a $150 T-shirt, you can buy a cotton T-shirt for $8. You show a tiny bit of white under your suit, and no one's going to know you don't have a silk blouse on.
- The way you carry yourself can make an expensive suit look like firesale fodder. Keep your shoulders back and your chin up. Not only will your clothes look better, but your voice will project farther.

Fruchet is aghast at how otherwise well-dressed women wear unpolished shoes or shoes with heels in need of repair. "They look at themselves from their heads down to their knees and then they stop. It's extraordinary." She recommends a basic shoe wardrobe in black, brown, and navy. "And if you find a pair of shoes that you really like, buy two or three pairs and put the extras away. The styles don't change that much. Most women want basics that last. They don't want to be too way-out fashion wise, which is clever."

But what concerns Fruchet more than shoes is women's underwear. "It's just awful. They haven't bought a bra in twenty years and then they wonder why something doesn't look good on them. You have to start on the inside and work out. Go and get fitted with the proper bra. Your size changes, and many women don't realize it. They could be wearing a bra that fit them when they were twenty-five but now they're forty. When you have the right bra on, it changes everything."

She recommends the use of a girdle when necessary. "One client wanted a dress but thought she looked too fat in it. I said, *Fine, I'll get you a panty girdle for support.* She said, *You're kidding.* I told her if she didn't want to do a hundred sit-ups a night, then this was a good option."

The two other problems that Fruchet often sees are poor posture and thinking that one is older than one actually is. Fruchet finds that women become more conservative as they age, sometimes too conservative. "I have women say to me, *I can't wear that, I'm too old.* Just because you're fifty doesn't mean you're over the hill and should dress in black. There are women today at fifty who are gorgeous. Women are much more fit and do much more than they used to. When women my mother's age turned fifty and sixty, life was over; today fifty-year-olds are just starting. Everyone should look good. It doesn't matter what size they are, what budget they're on, or how old they are."

Ellie Rubin, president of Bulldog, believes in dressing with a visual twist. She will wear a conservative blue banker's suit but with a really short skirt. Or she'll wear a suit with a more modest length to the skirt, but the color will be wild. Or she'll wear her long hair in a unique way.

"You should always wear one thing that makes you smile when you look at yourself in the mirror — whether it's stockings with a little design at the ankle or a piece of jewelry that's just a bit wacky. I absolutely think that everything you do, from the things you put on your desk to the way you dress and the jewelry you wear is critical because it's what people remember. And they remember details much more than people think they do."

Fruchet is somewhat more reserved about making a unique statement through dress. "I don't suggest it because people aren't focused on what you're saying. They're focused on what you have on," she says. "You don't want your clothes to wear you. You want to wear the clothes. Of course, if you are working in the media or are a starlet, you can wear whatever you want."

THE SPIRITUAL PART

Take the word think *out of your vocabulary.* Believe *is better. And stop apologizing. Stop asking for permission.*

— Roz Usheroff

Men are naturally accepted as having authority and knowledge. Women have to prove it.

— Marnie Walker

Every man I meet wants to protect me. Can't figure out from whom.

— Mae West

When a woman chooses to be independent and entrepreneurial, the way she represents herself to others must shift. A woman's personal mythology shifts away from the endangered damsel in the dragon's clutches to that knight with the sharp sword and fast horse.

Getting rid of female attitudes and behaviors that suggest low self-esteem and vulnerability is the first step toward feeling powerful and confident. Shyness, fear of failure, and the need to seek approval are the three big image crushers.

A 1993 study of male and female attitudes to risktaking found that women tend to have less confidence in their abilities and lower expectations for success.[5] They are, the study says, more critical of their own performance, take less credit for their accomplishments, and blame their failures on their lack of ability.

As an entrepreneur, there is no room in your life for self-doubt and timidity. Shy doesn't get you more clients or new orders, doesn't help you raise the visibility of your company in the marketplace, doesn't motivate your employees or impress your bank manager. Show courage. Recognize that the buck stops with you, and instead of dreading it, enjoy it. Here are some strategies for building and demonstrating confidence:

- Roz Usheroff suggests that you hold an image in your mind of people you admire and then let them inspire you. When she's nervous, she pretends she's Audrey Hepburn.
- Although it might not be a natural instinct to dominate a meeting, Marnie Walker believes women have to if they want to be seen as winners. "Unless I assert myself, I will not be seen as dominant. So I pump myself up, rehearse the points I want to make, and get my adrenaline going before a meeting. It's almost a performance. You have to deliver what they want you to deliver."
- Learn "firm." Elizabeth Hunt, a presentation and communications specialist, was told by a client: "I grew up in a family which stressed the importance of being polite and kind, and that you could expect to be treated in the same way. I'm not a pushover, but I will let things go for quite a while before I step in. Then I become the iron woman. It's hard for me to find the gray area between being soft and being hard." Knowing how to act firmly and being comfortable with that is a lesson women learn later rather than early in life, says Hunt. One of her associates tends to offer one piece of criticism to clients draped in fifteen compliments. "I told her she has to learn to communicate the problem and not to cover it all up like a mother would do. We have to learn to give feedback and provide information, to not apologize for it, to be comfortable with it."

- Confidence has to be part of your spirit, and projecting confidence has to be the only way you communicate, regardless of how you truly feel. People assume that you know what you're talking about if you *sound* like you know what you're talking about.

- "I've learned not to take things personally," says Marnie Walker. She says she's been tossed out of a lot of places, including a bank that refused her a mortgage because her age was "pregnancy prone." Walker didn't get angry. She simply went to another bank. She applies the same objectivity to those she works with. "You can't just work with people you like. If you happen to relate well to someone, well, that's a bonus."

- The need to seek approval is communicated in the way one talks. Speaking in question marks is a female behavior, in which each sentence ends in an upward inflection. It sounds childish and tentative.

- Wrapping a *mea culpa* around an otherwise declarative sentence is another error made most frequently by women. Examples of this include: "You probably have already thought of this, but ..." or "This might not work, but ..." or "This might be a stupid idea, but ..."

- No one in business should ask permission to speak, which is what these common phrases do: "I don't know if this is the right time to ..." or "You might want to consider ..." As Usheroff points out, nothing beats a simple, assertive "I recommend ..."

THE TACTICAL PART

I'm not the kind of entrepreneur who will go for the jugular, and sometimes you have to for your own benefit.

— Dianna Rhodes

We judge men and women differently in the public arena.
Women have to be aware of that and decide how they're
going to play it.

— Elizabeth Hunt

Self-esteem isn't everything; it's just that there's nothing
without it.

— Gloria Steinem

Women entrepreneurs spend a great deal of their time with people —
with employees, suppliers, bankers, customers, and competitors. How
well they interact with these people has direct impact on the bottom line.

Roz Usheroff, who coaches executives and managers on projecting
confidence through their physical presentation and voice, finds that
entrepreneurs are aware of the bottom-line value of their image,
whereas employees tend to look at her service as a way of fireproofing
their careers.

Here are some of the tactics women use to make their dealings with
others as productive as possible.

Make it better for your audience than it is for yourself

Tracey De Leeuw believes that in order to sell anything, it has to be
better for the customer than it is for herself. In any meeting or presentation, she focuses on the benefits for her audience.

Listen for the truth

For Dianna Rhodes, the most difficult thing about being an entrepreneur is
learning not to be defensive in the face of criticism. Rhodes loves her
company and her product line; they are a part of who she is. "It's a hard
lesson to learn, not to be defensive but to openly take the criticism and deal
with it as if you're dealing with someone else's product or service," she says.

Convey supreme self-confidence

Basically, all tactical advice about the way you move and where you choose to sit and behave concerns self-confidence — magnifying it and communicating it. If you don't project confidence, your audience won't have confidence in what you're saying.

The cardinal rule is to act in a manner that highlights your certainty. Unfortunately, women are often less effective at getting recognized because they don't talk enough about their accomplishments; when they do, they don't sound assertive or confident enough.

Be aware of the impact of your voice

Hunt finds that women face unique problems in their presentation and interaction with men.

People tend to describe an attractive voice as low, rich, and powerful. "Because of the bias toward *low* being better, women start out with a disadvantage. And a voice that goes up when it's tense is called shrill, which we associate with women."

Second, women use a rising inflection more often then men, which is perceived as uncertain. They also use more tag phrases such as "Do you see?" or "Do you know what I mean?" which ask for assurance or feedback.

Third, Hunt notices that women say things such as "I hope you'll agree with me" instead of "I know you'll agree with me," and that they tend to use the plural: "We feel this way" instead of "I feel this way." Hunt says, "We should take much more ownership and be much more present in our language. What's needed is assertiveness in the vocal tone, the language that's used, and the body language — without coming across like a stern person. Margaret Thatcher had to learn a friendlier approach to things: smiling and using anecdotes to reveal her human side."

Hunt's advice is for women to be aware of these kinds of prevailing perceptions and then to devise a strategy of how to communicate. Behaving like men is not the answer. In Hunt's experience, this solution is judged negatively. "If you want to be very firm and strong, you must physically and vocally appear strong. Work on lowering a high-pitched voice or projecting a soft-pitched voice. Make sure your voice is strong and your manner forthright." Here are some ideas on how to increase the impact of your voice:

- Keep your voice as low as is comfortable.
- Most women speak faster than men do, so slow down.
- Don't be afraid of pausing. Practice pausing at a place in your communication that discourages interruption. For example, you are less likely to be interrupted if you say, "I think the critical issue here is [pause]" rather than if you say, "I think the critical issue here is investor relations because [pause]."
- Most women use "um" more frequently then men do. Don't say "um."
- Reduce the use of emotional verbs such as "I hope," "I feel," and "I'm thrilled." Use more action verbs such as "I want" and "I need."
- Don't use ambiguous qualifiers such as "kind of" or "a bit." Use absolute qualifiers — "very," "significantly," "never" — or don't use any.

Assess your body language

Many of the lessons women received as a child about how to sit and gesture are the antithesis of an image of authority and confidence. When Hunt works with women on their body language, her first task is to get them standing up straight and using large body gestures to compensate for their smaller size. This means not holding your hands tightly at your side or clasped in front of your stomach.

She also discourages women from a very female gesture — touching the chest. "You don't see men putting a hand up to the chest to show how sincere they are. But when women say, *I feel,* they do exactly that. I would like them to use a broader, open gesture. I tell women to watch Jay Leno. He uses his hands out in front of him, which makes him seem even larger than he is."

Here are a few more body language pointers:

- Women nod too much. Cut it out. Men view it as a sign of agreement. Women use it as a sign of understanding and empathy, but only other women know this.
- Sitting like a perfect lady makes you look small and powerless. Taking up physical space is aggressive body language that men use and understand. Angle your chair (if you face front directly, you look stiff), sit on its edge and push it back from the table. Spread out your papers on the table in front of you and keep your hands on the table, clasped if possible. When speaking, gesture assertively and keep your shoulders square. Ellie Rubin, who is a small woman, compensates for her size by employing big movements — walking heavily, knocking on doors assertively. She tries to avoid situations that make her feel really little, like standing at cocktail parties where her line of vision is level with most men's chests.
- Keep your hands empty except when using communications tools like pens and pointers. Playing with jewelry or a strand of hair, picking lint off your clothes, clicking a ballpoint pen, fiddling with eyeglasses are all distracting and self-conscious behaviors.

Focus on winning your goals

Hunt advises that before you walk into any meeting, you know the following:

- who your audience is;
- their expectations;
- the context in which you are presenting your information or argument; and
- your desired outcome.

When Hunt sits in on meetings, she often observes people desperately waiting to blurt out their piece of information. "They don't find the right opportunity; they don't position it; they don't listen really carefully to what's going on and then use it to sell what they're saying. It's not enough to simply state the facts. You have to tell people what you want them to believe."

Women tend to be more indirect than direct, she finds. "With men, you can be indirect to a point and then you need to be direct to ensure they understand what you want and what the outcome should be."

"If you listen to the person who spoke before you and say, *You know, John, that was a very interesting point,* then you have related to what he just said. If you add, *It really reflects the same problem that I'm having,* all of a sudden that person and everyone else who accepts John's point will be engaged in what you say next."

Women also interrupt less often and let men control the situation. It's a frequent pattern for a woman to bring up a topic only to have a man introduce a new subject. She's found that men interrupt, not because they don't want to talk about her point, but because they think their point is more important. "Women need to be aware of this pattern," says Hunt. "And it's in their best interest to make sure that their point is covered, and *not* be polite and let it go."

While Hunt doesn't suggest that women should try and change men, she says it's important to be aware of the dynamics in a meeting and intervene when the message gets thwarted. "I would maintain the polite female form, which is not to act aggressively as a man would or to do what he did," she says. "I would let the conversation move to John's point and then say, *We need to come back to the point that I brought up initially.* If I just said, *John, you interrupted me,* then he's going to see me as a bitch. It's just unfemale behavior to do that. And I wouldn't say, *Perhaps I didn't make myself clear,* because this is taking the blame for it."

Other tactics that can help in achieving your goals include:

- Pause when entering a room and after saying something significant.
- Develop small talk skills so that you can survive a dinner with a business client whom you hardly know. Small talk should be about neutral subjects with which you are familiar. Hunt counsels people to walk in with a few subjects that they feel they

could talk about, for example, the front-page news. Sports is not the most popular small talk conversation, she finds, and also believes that family is an inappropriate topic. "Many people don't feel comfortable disclosing their family situation, especially young women or women who have children. I certainly don't want males relating me to their wife or their mother."

- Always have your business cards and hand them out at the beginning of the meeting.
- Sit in a strong place — at the short sides of the table and near the meeting leader. Don't hang around the fringes.
- At the beginning of a meeting with unfamiliar people, draw a map of the table and write everyone's name down.
- Take any opportunity to stand up while saying what you want to say. The physical act, be it standing or moving around the room, or at a minimum, leaning forward into the group, also acts as a form of engagement.
- If the meeting is concerned with something negative, don't sit directly across from the client — Marnie Walker finds that this can be the most adversarial spot in the room. Get out of his or her direct line of vision because you don't want the client identifying you with the negative issue. And if you want to be seen as competing, sit across from your adversary.
- If you're late to a meeting, don't just slip in quietly and sit down. Doing so appears timid and sacrifices an opportunity to make a more positive first impression. Rubin says, "I'd rather upset someone because I have to interrupt and say, *I'm really sorry I'm late, but I'd like to introduce myself. And could anyone give me a quick summary of where we are?*"
- If you're seated at a table and introduced to someone across the table from you, stand up and shake the person's hand.
- Avoid the female tendency to hold one's fingertips together in a steeple — it looks supplicating — and avoid hugging yourself, crossing your arms, clutching books to your chest, nodding your head excessively or cocking it to one side. Keep your

hands at your sides with your chest open and confident, and don't look down when you walk.

- When speaking, use your audience's vocabulary and mirror their body language and the pace and volume of their words. If you do this well, your audience will feel intrinsically aligned to you, even if your goals or views are different.
- Smile more. It shows confidence and makes others feel liked.
- Make eye contact frequently. If you're speaking to a large group, make regular eye contact with all parts of the audience. Make eye contact when you're shaking hands, which means extending a flat palm with the thumb north, a firm grasp, and please — no fingertip handshakes.
- When you're getting stared down, switch your gaze from one eye to the other.
- To avoid being interrupted, use your fingers to tick off the points you want to make.
- When standing, use broader sweeping gestures.
- Know your audience. Get informal support for your idea before you walk into a room to make a presentation.
- When faced with a question from the audience during a formal presentation, step back to draw the whole room into your answer, repeat the question, and then answer it while looking at the audience.

NETWORKS AND MENTORS

Women's networks are valuable at different stages of your life. You can outgrow them.

— Dianna Rhodes

I believe that we are always attracted to what we need most,
an instinct leading us toward the persons who are to open
new vistas in our lives and fill them with new knowledge.

— Helen Iswolsky, *Light Before Dusk* (1942)

According to the *Random House Dictionary,* a mentor is defined as a wise and trusted counselor and teacher. Who could deny the value of a mentor, except someone who also shuns fresh vegetables, safe sex, and exercise?

Yet many healthy, fit, and successful women entrepreneurs reject the notion of a mentor. Isabel Hoffmann has never had a mentor in the sense of someone to look up to and follow. "Literally, I get goosebumps and my whole body shivers when I'm asked to be a role model to someone. I say, *No way.*"

When it comes to women entrepreneurs, a mentor is better defined *without* the adjectives *wise* and *trusted.* Hoffmann learned about running a business — in her view, the *wrong* way — from her father. She neither trusted his business judgment nor found it wise, but he was a teacher, nonetheless, and a wise person. Marnie Walker also views her father with distrust, but she absorbed his business acumen.

Entrepreneurs and mentors are oil and water. Entrepreneurs are loners, protective of their independence and distrustful of authority. They see their learning as internally driven. Their mentors, if any, tend to grow spontaneously out of naturally founded, deeply rooted relationships, such as an entrepreneurial father or a past boss.

When entrepreneurs do talk about mentors, they are wrongly naming friends or short-term sources of expertise. Friends are invaluable, but they are not mentors. Says Andrina Lever, "My mentors are people who say, *Of course you can do it,* when I'm losing my confidence. They give me ideas and emotional support." Nora Forsey depends on her parents to bring her back to earth when she gets her head in the clouds.

Or the entrepreneur will identify as a mentor someone who gives them the knowledge they need. But these relationships are typically short-lived. Says Tracey De Leeuw, "Business mentors come and go. Someone might stick around for six months or a year, but my work is heady stuff, and it's hard to keep on track. My dad is my ultimate mentor."

Entrepreneurs subscribe to networking only insofar as it has a direct, bottom-line impact on business. Women's networks are places they speak at, not join. Elizabeth Stewart, past-president of the Canadian Association of Women Executives and Entrepreneurs (CAWEE), doesn't belong to any women's networks. "At CAWEE we saw the membership stay pretty well flat after a certain growth period. Our drop-off rate was balanced by new memberships. We asked ourselves why people don't stay, and the answer was pretty simple. There comes a point when your own focus on your business requires you to network with different people. You keep your contacts, but you keep them personally. It's a case of *Fish where the fish are*. If you do a lot of business with automotive dealers, you have to connect with whatever associations automotive dealers are involved with. It becomes an issue of balancing your time."

Isabel Hoffmann not only doesn't network, she just doesn't get it. She recalls an hour-long networking visit from another female CEO of a technology firm. "At the end of the meeting, I still didn't have a clue what she wanted," she says. Networking is too oblique for her style. Why waste time casting about when you can cut out the fluff by picking up the phone and getting to the point?

Winner of the 1995 Entrepreneur of the Year Award, Hoffmann also doesn't "get" the Women Entrepreneur of the Year Award. "I believe that the reason women have problems is that they have not really believed that they are equal. They are still differentiating themselves."

Giselle Briden doesn't belong to a women's network. "I'm really apprehensive about putting myself in an environment where people are talking about our limitations or how we're being held back. I believe we create our own opportunities." She acknowledges that such networks have value "in the sense that women need support to get past the self-confidence issue, and women need to know what is possible. We don't have enough successful women as reference points."

Sarah Band has no desire to join a women's network. "How is it going to benefit me? I don't know the answer, but I'm not certain it provides anything more than a social outing." When Band gets together regularly with a group of women, "the topic is not business, but life."

Tracey De Leeuw travels internationally to give speeches and attend conferences, and is continually building a customized network of information systems. She has learned to maximize her business development opportunities through the course of her business day.

Effective, targeted networking can raise a business's profile in the community and provide knowledge about new customers, suppliers, and people who *know* new customers and suppliers. Unlike some forms of media advertising, which is akin to fishing with no certainty that there's fish anywhere near your boat, networking is like fishing with a net directly over a school of fish. To work, it requires two things: good intelligence beforehand that the trade shows, associations, and other events you've targeted contain your target market, and an ability to schmooze — combining interpersonal skills with knowledge in a way that inspires others to learn more about your business.

MELODIE AND KIM'S STORY

Two young women in Halifax, Melodie Stewart and Kim Doherty, have made a business out of the universal desire to network. Pro-Net Business Connections helps organizations in the Halifax area network with other companies, deriving its revenues from membership fees and networking workshops.

The idea of helping entrepreneurs network had been percolating in Stewart's mind for some time. She found that companies, large and small, knew they should be networking, but they didn't know how. Nor did they have the time to find out. So when she lost her job as director of sales with the now defunct magazine, *Atlantic Women,* she became, at age twenty-seven, the president of her own business.

Pro-Net offers networking information and seminars in networking skills throughout the Halifax and Dartmouth areas. A Pro-Net newsletter lists the time, date, place, speaker, and cost of every networking event in the city. Stewart or Doherty will make suggestions to clients about the best networking event to fit their needs.

"We're 40,000 feet up looking down at other people's businesses," says Stewart. "Most people are so focused on what they do that they don't see the obvious. Kim and I can see the obvious, bring it to their attention, and let them go with it. So that's really been the key to our success."

The price of membership is low because the two women want to build their database. Students and nonprofit organizations pay Pro-Net $150 a year for membership; small businesses pay $300; and corporations and government agencies, $600. The bulk of their clientele is small business. Each member's company profile, target market, and networking goals are recorded and cross-tabulated with the entire database four times a year.

The company's long-range goal is to become national and then global via an Intranet. But before they reach beyond their current market, the two women want to perfect what they sell and service now. Their report card is their annual renewal rate — in other words, how many first-time subscribers decide to renew. With a hoped-for renewal rate of 80 percent or more, they will be able to expand through branch offices or sell franchises with a healthy price tag.

The idea first came to Stewart when she worked for *Atlantic Women.* Her sales job and her capacity as president of Business Network International in Halifax meant that her days were filled with a flurry of breakfast meetings, lunch functions, committees, and boards. "I was driving home one night and realized that this networking was turning into a business. It all came to me that I could make money at this."

Stewart moved to Halifax from Toronto when she was nineteen years old, older and wiser than her years. Her mother had been diagnosed with cancer when Melodie was twelve. "I became Mom. I cooked and cleaned and, when she got better, thank God, I couldn't go back to being twelve years old anymore. I couldn't follow the rules that were laid down for me, so I left." Stewart has been living on her own since the age of fifteen. Today her parents are her best friends, and her mother is in complete remission.

Without completing high school, she took a five-month sales and marketing course at a community college and began working in sales and advertising. Most of her sales skills and work ethic were learned in the field or are innate: her uncles, now retired, were the number one and two salespeople in Canada for Snap On Tools, twenty-five years running.

Stewart's partner, Kim Doherty, moved to the Maritimes from Montreal with her mother, who had remarried. "Her new husband and I didn't get along very well," she recalls. "I moved out when I was eighteen. It wasn't a happy time."

On graduating with her bachelor of commerce in marketing from St. Mary's University, Doherty plowed through a stream of short-term market and research jobs, most of them government contracts. One day, while she was waiting to be interviewed at a corporation, she decided she couldn't deal with the bureaucracy and politics of a large organization and walked out.

Doherty met Stewart — where else? — at a networking event. Doherty's last employer was Stewart's first customer: "Kimberley put a sticky note on the cheque with a happy face and the words: *This is invoice #0001*," Melodie recalls. Later, Doherty offered to provide support in the office while Stewart was out selling. The offer was for a week, and she's still there, as a 49 percent equity partner.

Pro-Net was created in early May of 1996, and Doherty joined at the end of the month. Their partnership works because each woman brings different yet complementary skills to the table. "Kim's very logical and analytical and business minded," says Stewart. "I'm more the visionary, dreamer type."

For example, Stewart does not write cheques. "I don't understand accounting, and I don't have any interest in it. I always think that when I'm sitting in front of a computer or balancing a chequebook, I could be out there in front of a client."

By nature an intuitive decision maker, Stewart is starting to look at opportunities and decisions through her partner's eyes. "I make a decision very quickly. It's not always the right decision, mind you, but I'll do it pretty quick. That comes from being in sales and being on the road for so long, where I had to make a decision then and there. But I know her well enough now that I can predict what she's going to say. It's like when you've been married to someone for long enough, you just know that they're going to be mad at something you do. By the same token, she's starting to have a little more confidence out there with her social skills because of me."

The company is situated in the Technology Innovation Centre in Dartmouth, where all administrative support is provided to tenants, including answering the phone, typing, and faxes. Doherty manages the company's finances and networking database, publishes a monthly newsletter, and does some marketing and sales.

The speed and aplomb with which Stewart created her company was dazzling. She watched the doors lock forever at *Atlantic Women* on a Thursday, and called all of her clients to explain that their advertising dollars had fallen into a black hole. "I had sold them the advertising. I took their money, so they remembered me."

That weekend she developed a business plan. By Tuesday she was selling subscriptions and issuing invoices, not to mention winning support from her bank and prospective landlord. The concept that had been jelling in her mind for the past year was put into fast-forward action, despite some significant roadblocks.

Her last paycheque bounced. What was even worse was that Stewart's employer had left her with a $12,000 debt. Stewart had generously charged some of the magazine's costs, such as a printer's bill, to her personal credit card.

"I was in big trouble financially," she says. "The bank called me and told me to forget about the pre-approved mortgage I had recently obtained to buy a house, so things were really very bad." Stewart dealt with her weak financial situation by owning up to it. "I didn't hide from anyone I owed money to," she says. "The first thing I did was pick up the phone and call everyone, regardless of whether a bill was owed or not. I said, *Look, this is what's happened.* I'm playing ball with them, and they're not giving me too hard a time. I do make payments here and there, but I'm not current."

Her attitude toward her former employer, who left the province after the magazine closed, is magnanimous: "She must think everyone in town hates her because she left me and the business community holding a pretty big bag. I'd like her to know that I realize she didn't set out to hurt me. In fact, if it wasn't for what happened, I wouldn't be where I'm at now."

Stewart and the other employees were called together and told that the magazine was going to close. Then the creditors came and removed the physical assets and locked the doors. In the next days, Stewart wouldn't leave her boss. "I stayed with her because I was afraid she was going to take her life. I helped her pack. The bank was foreclosing on her house. We sold her golf clubs and found her a hundred bucks. I hadn't yet realized how *my* own life was turning upside down. The next day I called her, and she said she was okay. When I called again, she was gone."

Untrustworthy employers is a theme in Stewart's history. In her previous job, where she worked from age eighteen to twenty-three, she had a difficult relationship with a male boss twice her age. "He was totally manipulative. I couldn't sneeze if he was in the room. I dealt with it. I learned how to use my knowledge of him to my advantage when I needed to. Then I decided it wasn't right and I quit. He owed me $3,000. It was my first time down that road."

Her boss at *Atlantic Women* introduced Stewart to networking by taking her to the Halifax Women's Network. "I was very nervous. We walked in together to a sit-down dinner for about eighty people and she said, *You go sit over there.* I couldn't believe it. I said, *You're going to leave me?* and she said, *Yes, we're not going to meet anyone if we sit beside each other.* That was one of the best things she ever taught me. Now I'm on this network's board for the second year in a row as the public relations chair, and networking is what I do for a living now. I'm sure sooner or later I would have gotten into it, but Gail helped me get there."

Stewart took her business plan for Pro-Net to a banker, who said he would like to help her. "He thought it was a great idea but that there was no history on this type of business, so he couldn't justify a loan. However, he said, *If you can do something to really wow me, I will.*"

Stewart contacted some friends and associates and learned about the Technology Innovation Centre, a business incubator facility for information-technology businesses. "I came over here with my business plan and sat down with the director," she says. "By the time I left the building, I had negotiated an office with a phone and furniture. The director gave me the break of my life. All the while, the fax machine at Kim's office was rolling out support letters from my clients saying, *Don't worry about the money we paid to* Atlantic Women. *We support you. We think Pro-Net is a great idea.*

She returned to her banker and showed him her lease and her letters of support from clients. "I said, all I need is enough money to print some frigging business cards and invoices and go to work. What could he do? He gave me a $1,500 loan overdraft, and that's how we got started."

To help her out, her parents wrote her four postdated, biweekly cheques for $200, and her significant other, a firefighter, pays for much of the household expenses. Stewart lives 45 minutes from Halifax; the money from her parents helped her buy gas to get to networking functions. To save money, she avoided the toll bridge and drove the long way around. "Whether I had to drive the long way and drink water at a networking function, it didn't matter, I had to be there," she says. "If I hid or didn't show my face, it would have been hard for me to establish myself."

Pro-Net also obtained $10,000 from the Canadian Youth Business Foundation (CYFB) to pay for the cost of incorporation, trademarks and copyrights, the partnership agreement, and computer training. With CIBC and the Royal Bank of Canada as the founding sponsors, CYFB provides mentoring, business support, and microlending to young Canadian entrepreneurs. Pro-Net's repayment and interest rates are attractive: in the first year of the loan, Pro-Net pays interest only at prime plus two; in the second year, the interest rate is prime plus one, and repayment includes the principal amount; in the third year, the interest rate reduces further to prime.

While there are companies that do pieces of what Pro-Net offers, there is no direct competition. For example, advertising and direct marketing companies sell lists to other companies for the purposes of lead generation rather than networking, and organizations such as the International Network Business and the chamber of commerce — traditional networking venues — have turned out to be Pro-Net clients, not competitors.

Initially, these organizations were skeptical about joining. "They said, *Why in the hell would we want to put ourselves in the newsletter with all these other organizations? We're all chasing the same membership dollars,*" says Stewart.

Stewart and Doherty needed a way to quickly establish themselves as offering a credible, value-added service. They approached the chamber of commerce with the argument that the prime reason the chamber attracted members was for networking opportunities. "We convinced them that, rather than reinvent the wheel, we could do their networking workshops. It's a win-win situation because the chamber is giving value-added to the members, we're getting exposure to forty businesspeople every month who may not have known about Pro-Net, and the members are getting networking skills."

Stewart is a tenacious woman, a characteristic she sees as crucial to any entrepreneur's success. "A lot of people say, *Don't give up. If you want to do it, do it.* And I believe that. But there's a lot more to it."

She finds it ironic that she, a high school dropout is lecturing to university students all over Nova Scotia. When she spoke to a class of occupational health therapists and physiotherapists at Dalhousie, she asked, "How many of you started out in this program thinking that you're going to have your own practice and make a good living?" Three-quarters of the class raised their hands. Then she asked, "How many of you are just going to try and get a job at a hospital?" and the same number of people raised their hands.

"So four years ago, these students had visions of being entrepreneurs, but now they've given it up because of the economic situation. I said to them, *Look, you're going to hear people say you should do it, live your dream. I'm going to tell you how hard it is to do it. But I had the balls to do it, and if you do, then nothing can stop you. It won't be easy, but it's certainly worth it.*"

GETTING UP AGAIN AFTER A FALL

Not tonight dear, I'm bankrupt.

— Bonnie Bickel

Failure is simply an evaluation. Nobody can deem you to be a failure unless you decide to believe that is the case.

— Giselle Briden

Failure is just another way to learn how to do something right.

— Marian Wright Edelman, *Families in Peril* (1987)

If you have to make mistakes, make them good and big, don't be middling in anything if you can help it.

— Hildegard Knef, *The Verdict* (1975)

More businesses than not fail in the first few years, and the causes of failure are both common and obvious: the wrong business at the wrong place and the wrong time, lack of skills and commitment by the owner.

But what about businesses that have succeeded and grown for years and then abruptly perish? When did the owners stop knowing what they were doing?

Just as you don't manage your two-year-old daughter in the same manner when she is sixteen, the skills and focus required to manage companies at different stages of their growth are different. And so, behind the growth and evolution of any successful company is an entrepreneur who has learned to grow and evolve as well.

Delegation and good administration are key. A successful owner manager who can't let go will have nothing left to let go of if she insists on expanding her kingdom within her clenched fist. And while a small business can be successful with a shoot-from-the hip approach to administration, a growing company without systems and controls will leech focus away from the marketplace to the chaos within. In this environment, all it takes is one blip in market demand or one production error to bring a company to its knees.

Also key is market knowledge, which must continually expand in depth as the company grows. Knowing that chocolate-chip muffins are a bestseller in Lethbridge, Alberta, is not justification for judging the preferences of a national market.

And then there's fortune's roll of the dice to contend with: recessions, the arrival of a larger competitor directly across the street, the sudden departure of your most important client, a supplier who decides to compete with you, and changes in consumer moods and styles. Companies that grow with no margin for error will be knocked off their feet at the first blow.

Bankruptcy is the ultimate credential for counseling others on the meaning of failure and steps to recovery. Bonnie Bickel has lived through two bankruptcies, due to aggressive expansion out of sync with market demand. She has this advice:

- Surround yourself with your friends. Bickel thought that people would think less of her, "but it's not true. My friends are proud of me and how I got through it all."

- Nothing really changes. "I'm not as special to my New York suppliers as I used to be. They don't take me out to dinner as much, but I can live with that. And suppliers still need you, especially in Canada. There are so few retailers out there. We're open with our financial situation, and they've responded with tremendous backing."

- Don't go to a large CA firm to handle your bankruptcy. In her first bankruptcy, she did and it cost her $450,000. In her second, Bickel was the receiver, and the cost was $20,000.

- Get out before you've lost it all. "You are *not* your business. It's *not* a living, breathing thing; it's just a business. Let it go."

- Keep your sense of humor. When she received telephone solicitations for charities, she would say, *Sorry, I've just gone bankrupt.*

- Next time, go in small and make small mistakes until you understand your business. Then go big.

GISELLE'S STORY

Failure, and now success, are as familiar to Giselle Briden as toothpaste and alarm clocks. Thirty years old now, she grew up poor. Today she is president of the Magellan Group, which promotes business and personal development seminars. In 1997, Magellan was the promoter behind the race between Donovan Bailey and Michael Johnson. Annual revenues exceed $6 million, and *Profit* magazine listed Magellan as Canada's ninth fastest-growing company in 1996.

Briden is planning to have children within the next three to four years. "My goal is to work like a bandit and put all my money back into the company so that I can create a lifestyle with more cash flow." Not that she's doing badly now. "I take what I need to live a very nice life. I even have my dream car — a Porsche 911."

Briden is candid about her difficult childhood. Her father, an alcoholic apartment janitor, died when she was twenty-one. He was abusive to his wife and children with the exception of Briden, the baby in the family.

"My siblings' memories of our father include a shotgun held to their heads — he was going to blow them all away and make my mother watch. My memories were bouncing on his knee because he had mellowed by the time I came along. But there was still a lot of nasty stuff that shaped the way I see things."

Mitigating a desperate situation was Briden's mother, who could be counted on to say, *You'd be great at that, dear,* when Briden announced her plans to be a rock star or police officer. "She always told me I could do it, and she still does."

With high school complete and no money for college, Briden faced an uncertain future. So she did what she knew best, having grown up around builders and contractors: renovations. With painting and plastering skills absorbed over the years, Briden began her career as an entrepreneur. "I didn't know at age eighteen that I was becoming an entrepreneur. For me, it was simply a way to make money."

She was never lacking for work because she was willing to work for less than anyone else. But her perfectionism hampered her success. It was hard for her to let other people do the work. One morning when she was twenty-one, as she awoke to another day of manual labor, she was struck with a realization: as long as she was the one slogging through the jobs, she was never going to create wealth.

"So I got up, blew the sawdust out of my nose, and said, *I've had enough. I'm never going to get wealthy this way, and I'm tired of being dirty.* That was it. I was done."

Briden called the only wealthy person she knew, a self-made millionaire she had met at a restaurant opening several years earlier. She asked him for a job. "I said, *You need to hire an executive assistant, and I'm that person.* He said, *No, I don't,* and I said, *Yes, you do.* I called him up every day for two months and finally he said okay. I worked for dirt for a year and a half; I got married to an actor; and I learned about business."

When she had learned as much as she could, she quit and she and her husband started a business. They sold training materials for multi-level marketing organizations in which products like cosmetics are sold through networks of people. The business failed when she purchased a large volume of training materials for a product whose creator was jailed soon after for promoting a pyramid sales scheme.

With the product now taboo, Briden was in trouble. "I didn't know how to deal with the situation and ended up letting the whole business fall apart. If I had been the person I am today, I would have been able to deal with it. It wouldn't have been such a big issue. But I lost everything."

Briden and her husband ended up living in a basement storage room of an apartment building while they tried to get together enough money to reboot their lives. "When you look back at truly horrible experiences in life, you realize that they are often what pushed you to make new decisions."

Briden set out to learn why some people were successful and others weren't, even with similar ambitions and intelligence. Her search led her to personal development seminars. She not only embraced the messages these seminars delivered but also bet that others would too. She and a partner built Magellan by promoting Anthony Robbins, a personal development speaker, and then expanded their list to similar kinds of speakers.

Magellan has experienced one serious financial difficulty, in which Briden was literally days away from losing her company. This time, Briden sailed hard through it. A couple of speaking events had been failures, and she and her partner had to come up with $400,000 fast.

"We gathered together the entire staff and told them exactly what had happened. Then we all went out and sold anything we could to our clients. It was an awesome four or five days with the whole team connecting and pushing the extra mile."

Briden found that she had been more stressed during her storage-room days than when she was trying to raise the $400,000. "I knew that if I fell back and said, *Oh my God, this is awful. There's no way out,* I would be absolutely accurate. So I didn't. I decided that failure wasn't an option."

The moral of this story is that failure is not the universe-crushing nightmare we've come to dread and avoid at all costs. Briden was inspired when she read that successful people have more failures than people who are failures, because failures fail once and never try again. Successful people brush themselves off and try again.

OTHER CONTRIBUTORS

BONNIE BICKEL is president of B. B. Bargoons, a chain of off-the-shelf interior design stores.

ELLIE RUBIN is president of a high-tech media asset management company, Bulldog Group Inc.

HELEN SINCLAIR is president of Bankworks Trading Inc., which sells Canadian banking products, services, and technology abroad.

ENDNOTES

Chapter 1: Burying the White Knight

1 Statistics Canada Labour Force Survey.

2 *Eight Steps to Self-Employment: A Practical Guide for Women,* EduService and the Women's Centre of Halton, Oakville, Ontario, 1996.

3 Federal Business Development Bank, *Women in Business: A Collective Profile,* 1992.

4 *Myths & Realities, The Economic Power of Women-led Firms in Canada,* sponsored by the Bank of Montreal, 1996.

5 Lois Stevenson, "Some Methodological Problems Associated with Researching Women Entrepreneurs," *Journal of Business Ethics* 9 (1990): 439-446.

6 *Small and Medium-Sized Businesses in Canada: Their Perspective of Financial Institutions and Access to Financing.* Prepared for Canadian Bankers Association by Thompson Lightstone & Company Limited, April 24, 1996.

7 Ibid.

8 Ibid.

9 Ibid.

10 S. Birley, "Female Entrepreneurs: Are They Really Any Different?" *Journal of Small Business Management* (January 1989): 32-37.

11 Lois Stevenson, "An Investigation of the Entrepreneurial Experience of Women: Implications for Small Business Policy in Canada," 1983,

as summarized by the Federal Business Development Bank in *Women in Business: A Collective Profile,* 1992.

12 Rena Blatt.

13 H. Lee-Gosselin and J. Grise, "Are Women Owner-Managers Challenging Our Definitions of Entrepreneurship? An In-Depth Survey," *Journal of Business Ethics* 9 (1990): 423-433.

Chapter 2: Having What It Takes

1 Chow-Hou Wee, Wei-Shi Lim, and Roger Lee, "Entrepreneurship: A Review with Implications for Further Research," *Journal of Business Ethics* 2: 4 (July-Sept. 1994).

2 M. Kets de Vries, "The Dark Side of Entrepreneurship," *Harvard Business Review* (Nov.-Dec. 1985).

3 K. Pugsley, "Buyer Tips for Buyers or Investors Seeking to Identify an Investment Opportunity," Ontario Ministry of Economic Development, Trade and Tourism, October 4, 1996.

Chapter 3: The Agony ...

1 H. Lee-Gosselin and J. Grise, "Are Women Owner-Managers Challenging Our Definitions of Entrepreneurship? An In-Depth Survey," *Journal of Business Ethics* 9 (1990): 423-433.

2 R. Cuba, D. Decenzo, and A. Anish, "Management Practices of Successful Female Business Owners," *American Journal of Small Business* 8:2 (Oct.-Dec. 1983).

3 *Small And Medium-Sized Businesses in Canada: Their Perspective of Financial Institutions and Access to Financing.* Prepared for Canadian Bankers Association by Thompson Lightstone & Company Limited, April 24, 1996.

4 The Canadian Youth Business Foundation was co-founded by the Royal Bank of Canada and CIBC to help youth create their own businesses.

5 E. C. Arch, "Risk-Taking: A Motivational Basis for Sex Differences," *Psychological Reports* (1993): 3-11.

6 R. Cuba, D. Decenzo, and A. Anish, "Management Practices of

Successful Female Business Owners," *American Journal of Small Business* 8:2 (Oct.-Dec. 1983).

Chapter 4: ... And the Ecstasy

1 Federal Business Development Bank, *Women in Business: A Collective Profile* (1992): 111.

2 S. Cromie, "Motivations of Aspiring Male and Female Entrepreneurs," *Journal of Occupational Behaviour* 8 (1987): 251-261.

3 *Myths & Realities: The Economic Power of Women-Led Firms in Canada,* sponsored by Bank of Montreal, 1996.

4 M. Belcourt, R. Burke, and H. Lee-Gosselin, *The Glass Box: Women Business Owners in Canada,* Canadian Advisory Council on the Status of Women, 1991.

Chapter 5: Starting Up a Business

1 M. Belcourt, "The Family Incubator Model of Female Entrepreneurship" and W. Y. Kao, "Readings in Entrepreneurship and Small Business Development," *Journal of Small Business and Entrepreneurship* and The Ryerson Centre of Entrepreneurship.

2 S. Cromie, University of Ulster, 1987.

3 J. White, *The Rise of Female Capitalism: Women as Entrepreneurs,* 1984, as summarized by the Federal Business Development Bank in *Women In Business: A Collective Profile,* 1992.

Chapter 6: Success

1 K. A. Loscocco, J. Robinson, R. H. Hall, and J. K. Allen, "Gender and Small Business Success: An Inquiry into Women's Relative Disadvantage," *Social Forces* 70: 1 (September 1991).

2 H. Lee-Gosselin and J. Grise, "Are Women Owner-Managers Challenging Our Definitions of Entrepreneurship? An In-Depth Survey," *Journal of Business Ethics* 9 (1990): 423-433.

3 A 1996 study commissioned by Canadian Bankers Association and conducted by Thompson Lightstone & Company to determine the root causes of loan approvals and turndowns, and to determine what

made small and medium-sized businesses happy with their financial institution.

4 In part because the investment in people rather than materials and equipment is not reflected in the balance sheet and keeps the capital base lower.

5 E. C. Arch, "Risk-Taking: A Motivational Basis for Sex Differences," *Psychological Reports* (1993): 3-11.

Resource Directory

The following is a listing of some of the associations, services, and learning opportunities of potential use to Canadian women entrepreneurs.

NATIONAL PROGRAMS AND SERVICES

Association of Canadian Venture Capital Companies

This association promotes the development of Canadian business enterprises through the use of venture capital and supports those involved in venture capital investments in Canada. A directory of venture capital funds is available.

Tel (416) 487-0519

Banks

Canadian banks provide free literature on how to develop a business plan and offer business planning software. They also have Web sites on the Internet.

Business Centurions Centres Inc.

Business Centurions, a company located in Toronto but with aspirations for offices in Montreal and Vancouver, helps individuals find equity or employment opportunities in small to medium-sized enterprises. Initially directed toward senior executives displaced through corporate restructurings or facing retirement, Business Centurions is now increasingly used by more junior employees and would-be entrepreneurs looking for the right business opportunity.

Tel (416) 969-1155

Business Development Bank of Canada (BDC)

The BDC is a commercial Crown corporation that supports Canadian small and medium-sized businesses. A range of products and services are made available through more than eighty branches across Canada. Their Micro-Business Program combines personalized management training and counseling with term financing of up to $25,000 for new businesses and up to $50,000 for existing businesses.

BDC holds workshops and conferences for women and produces a booklet, *Financing a Small Business: A Guide for Women Entrepreneurs,* as well as a study, *Women in Business: A Collective Profile.*

For general information about the BDC, call 1-888-INFO-BDC.

BDC programs for women include Step In, a training and mentoring program designed specifically for women who want to start — or have recently launched — a small business. Step In combines group workshops, round-table discussions, and individual mentoring to give participants the tools they need to successfully establish their businesses. Step Up is another training and mentoring program, designed for women who want to expand their businesses.

Tel 1-888-463-6232

Calmeadow

Calmeadow helps self-employed people in Canada and in the developing world who cannot access traditional sources of business loans. The organization offers access to credit from $500 to $5,000 and savings services.

Tel (416) 362-9670

Canadian Association of Family Enterprise (CAFE)

This is an organization dedicated to the well-being of family businesses by providing educational, networking, and mentoring opportunities to its members. There are fifteen chapters across Canada.

Tel (403) 220-5101

Canadian Association of Women Executives and Entrepreneurs (CAWEE)

CAWEE provides informational and networking opportunities to senior women employees and women entrepreneurs.

Tel (416) 482-2933

Canada Business Service Centres

These centres provide business access to a wide range of information on government services, programs, and regulations. Services include:

- toll-free information and referral service;
- Business Information System (BIS): a comprehensive database containing information on the services and programs of participating departments and organizations;
- Faxables: condensed versions of the BIS products accessed through the automated FaxBack system;
- Pathfinders: multiple-page documents that list brief descriptions of services and programs available on a topical basis (e.g., exporting); and
- leading-edge business products, including interactive videos, publications, business directories, how-to manuals, CD-ROM products, and external database access.

Alberta 1-800-272-9675 or (403) 422-7722
British Columbia 1-800-667-2272 or (604) 775-5525
Manitoba 1-800-665-2019 or (204) 984-2272
New Brunswick 1-800-668-1010 or (506) 444-6140
Newfoundland 1-800-668-1010 or (709) 772-6022
Nova Scotia 1-800-668-1010 or (902) 426-8604
Northwest Territories 1-800-661-0786 or (403) 873-7958
Ontario 1-800-567-2345 or (416) 954-4636

Prince Edward Island 1-800-668-1010 or (902) 368-0771
Quebec 1-800-322-4636 or (514) 496-4010
Saskatchewan 1-800-667-4374 or (306) 956-2323

Canadian Council for Aboriginal Business

With regional offices across Canada, the Council improves access to business financing and enhances the business climate for aboriginal entrepreneurs.

Tel (613) 954-4065

The Canadian Women's Foundation (CWF)

CWF offers grants to women's organizations for projects designed to help women achieve greater self-reliance and economic independence. Past recipients include the Fort Garry Women's Resource Centre in Winnipeg for their Women's Home-Based Business Training Program and British Columbia's Fort Nelson Women's Resource Society for a mentoring program to support low-income women entrepreneurs.

Tel (416) 484-8268

Canadian Youth Business Foundation (CYBF)

The CYBF is an organization designed to provide mentoring, business support, and microlending to young Canadian entrepreneurs ages eighteen to twenty-nine. It is an initiative of the Canadian Youth Foundation and corporate donors to help address Canada's youth unemployment problem.

Enterprise Centres

The YMCA-YWCA Enterprise Centre is a community-based business development agency whose primary purpose is to help all people create employment through small business development. Centres are located in eleven Canadian cities: St. John's, Newfoundland; Glace Bay, Nova Scotia; Yarmouth, Nova Scotia; St. John, New Brunswick; Moncton, New Brunswick; Montreal, Quebec; Toronto, Ontario; Ottawa, Ontario; Winnipeg, Manitoba; Edmonton, Alberta; and Vancouver, British Columbia.

Self-Employment Assistance (SEA)

The SEA program provides income support, training, and technical assistance to enable individuals to become self-employed. To be considered, you must be a qualified Employment Insurance claimant or an eligible Social Assistance recipient who has not previously participated in a self-employment assistance program funded by Human Resources Development Canada (HRDC).

This federal program has an excellent track record. Over the past three years, approximately 85 percent of all clients entering the program started their own businesses, with most of the rest finding employment. In a survey of SEA graduates two years after they had completed the course, 85 percent were still self-employed on a full-time or part-time basis. Contact your local Canada Employment Centre for information.

University Entrepreneurial Programs

Virtually all Canadian universities and colleges offer degree or certificate programs in small business. Some universities, including Mount Saint Vincent University in Halifax, Nova Scotia, and the University of Toronto, offer entrepreneurial programs specifically for women. Call the university registrar for more information.

Women and Economic Development Consortium

This consortium is a new philanthropic organization launched in 1996. It will commit $2.3 million over five years to support women's organizations across Canada that help low-income women start their own businesses. Grants of $15,000 to $50,000 a year for two to five years are available. The consortium has also brought on board the Canadian Alternative Investment Co-operative, a charity-funded organization to provide capital to low-income women and other groups that have difficulty getting conventional business loans.

Women Entrepreneurs of Canada (WEC)

WEC focusses on the communication and advocacy needs of established women business owners. It represents the Canadian chapter of the worldwide organization, Les femmes chefs d'entreprises mondiales. To be eligible, you must have four years of business ownership or a business with at least $250,000 in annual sales.

Tel (416) 361-7036

Women Inventors Project (WIP)

Women Inventors Project is committed to increasing the number of successful women inventors and entrepreneurs in Canada. WIP provides educational resources, advice, and encouragement by promoting the role of women in science and technology careers.

Tel (416) 243-0668

ATLANTIC REGION

Association of Atlantic Women Business Owners (AAWBO)

AAWBO's goal is to advance the profile and interests of women entrepreneurs in Atlantic Canada.

Tel (902) 422-2828

Atlantic Canada Opportunities Agency (ACOA)

Through the network of Canada Business Service Centres, ACOA provides a single point of contact for federal small business programs and services in Atlantic Canada. ACOA's Business Development Program provides assistance in the form of interest-free, unsecured, repayable contributions for start-ups, expansions and modernizations, innovation, marketing, training, quality assurance, public bid tender preparation, and business studies. ACOA offices are located in Moncton, St. John's, Charlottetown, Halifax, Fredericton, and Sydney.

Newfoundland and Labrador

Business Development Centres

Business Development Centres are nonprofit corporations comprised of businesspeople in various communities who provide advice and assistance in the preparation of business plans, market studies, and financial analysis to help new entrepreneurs. Loans of up to $75,000 are also available.

Tel (709) 729-2797

Enterprise Newfoundland and Labrador (ENL)

Enterprise Newfoundland and Labrador (ENL) promotes entrepreneurship, self-reliance, and economic development through a decentralized system of technical, research, and information services and business support.

Tel (709) 729-7020

Labrador Community Development Corporation

The corporation's mandate is to encourage employment and entrepreneurial activity throughout Labrador by providing loans and advisory services. Services include Small Business Consulting Services to assist clients with preparation of a business plan and refer them to appropriate agencies.

Tel (709) 896-8514

Women's Enterprise Bureau

The bureau facilitates the start-up of home-based business ventures by women owner-managers throughout the province by providing assistance with the business planning process, access to information, networking, and mentoring. Services include: Small Business Home Study Program for Women, Entrepreneurial Training Program for Young Women, Pilot Microlending Program for Women (available in St. John's, Mount Pearl, and Central Newfoundland), and Entrepreneurial Studies for Women. A video series on women and small business is available for rent or sale.

Tel (709) 754-5555

Nova Scotia

Nova Scotia Business Development Centres

Nova Scotia provides a multifaceted Community Business Loan Program and operates Business Development Centres throughout the province.

Tel (902) 426-8604

Prince Edward Island

Department of Economic Development and Tourism

This department provides information regarding relevant programs and services operating in the province.

Tel (902) 368-4799

QUEBEC

Association des femmes d'affaires du Québec (AFAQ)

AFAQ offers networking opportunities, publications, workshops, seminars, and conferences through twenty-two chapters throughout Quebec.

Tel (514) 845-4281

ONTARIO

Canadian Industrial Innovation Centre

This Waterloo centre helps individuals commercialize technological innovations that create economic benefits. The centre offers a range of services: education and entrepreneurship seminars, publications, idea and product development, and individual assistance with new ideas.

Tel (519) 885-5870

Step Ahead

Toronto-based Step Ahead was formed by the alumni of the first Step Up mentoring program run by the Ontario government and the Federal Business Development Bank. Step Ahead's goal is to assist women entrepreneurs through relevant business information, networking, mentoring, and protégée opportunities.

Membership is open to all women entrepreneurs for a fee; participation as a protégée or mentor is subject to meeting certain qualifications.

Tel (905) 940-3282

Women and Rural Economic Development (WRED)

WRED was established in Stratford, Ontario, in 1993 as a source for financial and business planning services that self-employed women in rural areas could not easily access. Services include training in business basics and assertiveness training, a forty-two-week course on planning a small business, and a program called Farm Ventures that helps rural families build their businesses.

Tel (519) 273-5017

Women's Entrepreneurship Unit and Family Business Management Unit, University of Toronto

The Women's Entrepreneurship Unit and Family Business Management Unit at the University of Toronto provide courses for women entrepreneurs and family business officers. The Women's Entrepreneurship Unit is also the initiator of the Canadian Woman Entrepreneur of the Year Awards and Conference.

Tel (416) 978-3831

WESTERN REGION

Western Economic Diversification Canada (WEDC)

WEDC sponsors a variety of women's enterprise initiatives across British Columbia, Alberta, Saskatchewan, and Manitoba. These initiatives provide business counseling; help access training, networking, and mentoring opportunities; and administer a loan fund for women entrepreneurs. Assistance is also available on issues such as working with banks and balancing family needs with running a business.

Calgary (403) 220-0221
Edmonton (403) 413-0793
Toll-free 1-800-713-3558

British Columbia

British Columbia Institute of Technology Venture Program

This program takes entrepreneurs through the steps required to prepare a business plan. A twelve-week full-time day program is followed by an eighteen-month period during which alumni continue to access the center for assistance as required. There is a tuition fee; entry is determined on the basis of a personal interview.

Tel (604) 432-8767

Businesswomen's Advocate and Women in Business Program

Through workshops and skills training, this program assists both women wishing to start up their own businesses and established women business owners. Women in Business publications are available from your local Chamber of Commerce or directly from the program.

Tel (604) 356-5118

Ministry of Small Business, Tourism and Culture

This ministry provides information, a resource library, and free individual counseling for business start-ups.

Tel (604) 660-3900

Women Business Owners Association

This association offers networking and information sessions on business management skills and market trends.

Tel (604) 878-6699

Women's Enterprise Society of British Columbia

This society helps women to establish and grow their own businesses through a federal loan program, business counseling, and information referral.

Tel (205) 868-3454

Alberta

Alberta Economic Development and Tourism

This provincial service offers a wide variety of information to entrepreneurs and businesses, including publications, information sessions, business databases, electronic information systems, entrepreneurship development initiatives, and community economic development initiatives.

Tel (403) 427-6638

Alberta Opportunity Company

Alberta Opportunity Company is a lender of last resort for the start-up and or expansion of businesses. It offers consulting services and an export loan guarantee program. There are branch offices in Brooks, Calgary, Edmonton, Edson, Grande Prairie, Lethbridge, Medicine Hat, Peace River, Ponoka, Red Deer, and St. Paul.

Tel (403) 297-6437

Alberta Women's Enterprise Initiative Association

This nonprofit company helps women start and build businesses through advice, advocacy, and a loan program.

Calgary (403)777-4250
Edmonton (403) 422-7784
Toll-free 1-800-713-3558

Venture Development Unit, University of Calgary

The Venture Development Unit of the Department of Management at the University of Calgary offers legal and business clinics for small business owners and entrepreneurs. It also operates the Calgary Business Assistance Centre, geared toward the needs of new business development.

Tel (403) 220-7149

Saskatchewan

The Northern Development Fund (Northern Saskatchewan)

This fund provides Northerners with term financing and cost-sharing for small and medium-sized business ventures that meet certain required criteria. Another initiative under the fund is skills development, which allows Northerners to access a wide variety of training seminars.

Tel (306) 425-4278

Saskatchewan Economic Development (SED)

With eight regional offices, SED's services include planning, business development, marketing, and strategic human resource assistance.

Tel (306) 787-8710

Small Business Loans Association Program

This program provides business development opportunities for the nontraditional or beginning entrepreneur, and extends financing beyond the scope of traditional lenders.

Tel (306) 787-7207/-7935/-7154

Women Entrepreneurs of Saskatchewan (WE)

Women Entrepreneurs of Saskatchewan (WE) is an organization that works with women who are considering starting a business or are operating an existing business.

Programs and services offered by WE include business advisory and lending services; business workshops and seminars that focus on entrepreneurial skill development; quarterly and bimonthly business publications; and access to computers for client use.

Regina (306) 359-9732
Saskatoon (306) 477-7173

Manitoba

Business Development Centres

These nonprofit centres are comprised of businesspeople in various communities who provide advice and assistance in the preparation of business plans, market studies, and financial analysis to help new entrepreneurs. Loans of up to $75,000 are available.

For the location of the Business Development Centre nearest you, contact your local Canada Employment Centre.

Business Resource Centre

The centre houses information on topics such as management, economics, marketing, trade, tourism, and public policy. A number of self-help publications are available free of charge, as well as database services for a small fee.

Tel (204) 945-2036 or (204) 945-2057
Toll-free 1-800-282-8069

Business Start Program

This is a loan program administered by Manitoba Industry, Trade and Tourism aimed at Manitobans who are either ready to launch a new business or who have been in business less than three months. Approved applicants attend a free two-day seminar, which covers book-keeping practices, financial and business management, sales, and marketing.

Tel (204) 945-7721
Toll-free 1-800-282-8069

Manitoba Women's Enterprise Centre, Inc.

This is one of the women's enterprise initiatives sponsored by Western Economic Diversification Canada.

Brandon 1-800-221-5819 or (204) 726-4245
The Pas (204) 627-8717
Thompson (204) 778-7811
Winnipeg 1-800-203-2343 or (204) 988-1860

MBA Consulting Program, University of Manitoba

This program in the Faculty of Management at the University of Manitoba caters specifically to the needs of small and medium-sized organizations. It offers consulting services in the areas of marketing, financial, production, and information management, as well as feasi-bility studies for new business start-ups. Consulting is done by second-year MBA students with supervision by faculty and by industry professionals.

Tel (204) 474-6671

Rural Economic Development Initiative (REDI)

REDI consists of the following programs that promote economic development and employment opportunities in rural Manitoba: Rural Entrepreneur Assistance, which helps new and existing rural busi-nesses obtain equity or financing from financial institutions; Development Support, which provides up to 15 percent of eligible project costs for innovative and unique business ventures; and Feasibility Studies, which provides up to 50 percent of costs incurred by businesses who commission independent consultants to prepare financial, market, or engineering studies associated with a business start-up or expansion.

Tel (204) 945-2150
Toll-free 1-800-567-REDI

Women Business Owners of Manitoba (WBOM)

WBOM is a nonprofit independent organization that addresses the unique needs of the woman entrepreneur by providing support, networking, assistance in business and personal skills, and advocacy. There are chapters in Dauphin, Brandon, Pembina Valley, Portage, and Winnipeg.

Tel (204) 775-7981

INTERNET RESOURCES

Atlantic Canada Opportunities Agency (ACOA)

http://www.acoa.ca

This agency of the federal government strives to help businesses get started and grow, especially small enterprises. ACOA also works to market the products and services of Atlantic Canada worldwide.

Banks

Although all banks have Web sites, the Toronto Dominion Bank of Canada's Web site stands out in terms of offering helpful information and advice (rather than bank products and services) to entrepreneurs.

BizWomen

http://www.bizwomen.com

BizWomen provides an online interactive community for women in business.

Business Development Bank of Canada

http://www.bdc.ca

Canada Business Service Centres (CBSC)

http://reliant.ic.gc.ca

The CBSCs were created to improve business access to a wide range of information on government services, programs, and regulations.

Canadian Women's Internet Association (CWIA)

http://www.women.ca

Although not specifically for entrepreneurs, this site contains a useful menu of information and services for women.

Canadian Women's Online Business Network

This excellent site offers information regarding networking, business development, global connections, and financial resources.

Export Development Corporation (EDC)

http://www.edc.ca/english/index.html

EDC is a financial services corporation dedicated to helping Canadian business succeed in the global marketplace. EDC provides a wide range of risk management services, including insurance, financing, and guarantees, to Canadian exporters and their customers around the world.

Federal Office of Regional Development — Quebec (FORD(Q))

http://canada.gc.ca/depts/agencies/frqind_e.html

FORD(Q) focuses on small and medium-sized businesses and the development and enhancement of entrepreneurship.

Franchise Handbook: Online

http://www.franchise1.com/franchise.html

This site offers articles, directories, and upcoming events regarding franchising.

National Association for Female Executives (NAFE)

http://www.nafe.com

This U.S. site is a networking and information forum for female executives and entrepreneurs.

Open Government

http://www.ffa.ucalgary.ca/opengov

This is a pilot project on the Internet undertaken by Industry Canada to provide greater access to government through information networks.

Partnership of Women Entrepreneurs Inc.

http://www.newdirection.com/thepartnership

The main goal of this organization is to support the success and growth of women business owners. The site offers an interactive business forum and numerous other sites of interest to women in business.

Strategis

http://strategis.ic.gc.ca

This Industry Canada site is a comprehensive reference tool.

Statistics Canada

http://www.statcan.ca/start.html

Statistics Canada is the country's national statistical agency, with programs organized into three broad subject matter areas: demographic and social, socioeconomic, and economic.

Western Economic Diversification Canada (WD)

http://www.wd.gc.ca

WD's mandate is to promote the development and diversification of the economy, particularly small businesses of Western Canada, and to advance the interests of Western Canada in national economic policy.

WomenBiz

http://www.frsa.com/womenbiz

This site for women business owners and entrepreneurs includes a discussion forum; business, tax, and investment tips; humor; and technology.

Women's Business Resource Site

http://www.athenet.net/~ccain

This site provides a place for women to share information about the victories and trials of doing business.

Women's Connection Online

http://www.womenconnect.com/wco/index.html

Here, women have access to current news affecting women; a library of articles related to women and issues affecting women; a directory of women's organizations; a calendar of events; and soon, a directory of women business owners. There are also links to nearly three hundred women's sites on the Internet.

Women's Wire Home Page

http://www.women.com/index.html

This site offers upbeat information across a range of topics, with links to other Web sites for businesswomen.

Acknowledgments

The strength of this book lies in the strength of the women who offered up their life stories and expertise: Marcella Abugov, Nancy Adamo, Marcia Ball, Sarah Band, Mona Bandeen, Wendy Banting, Monica Belcourt, Bonnie Bickel, Giselle Briden, Judy Byle-Jones, Barbara Caldwell, Claire Cobourn, Mary Connolly, Carol Denman, Tracey De Leeuw, Angela de Montigny, Julie DiLorenzo, Kimberly Doherty, Wanda Dorosz, Shelley Fisher, Nora Forsey, Mary Fote, Sherry Fotheringham, Karen Fraser, Martha Fruchet, Trish Haddad, Marina Heidman, Isabel Hoffmann, Elizabeth Hunt, Eva Klein, Lisa Jacobson, Paula Jubinville, Dolores Lawrence, Suzanne Leclair, Andrina Lever, Dorothy Millman, Barbara Mowat, Ingrid Mueller, Louisa Nedkoff, Dianna Rhodes, Natalie Rostad-Desjarlais, Ellie Rubin, Brenda Schiedel, Elizabeth Scott, Helen Sinclair, Elizabeth Stewart, Melodie Stewart, Babs Sullivan, Roz Usheroff, Joanne Thomas Yacatto, Audrey Vrooman, and Marnie Walker.

I would like to thank Beverley Slopen, my agent; Don Loney, my editor at HarperCollins; and Meg Taylor, my copy editor, for their respective skills and enormous tact. And above all, my thanks to Warren Walker and our two children, David and Lee, who know my secrets and love me anyway.